A Snake in My Shoe!

A Snake in My Shoe!

An Autobiography

Audrey Roth Bennett

The Book Guild Ltd

First published in Great Britain in 2017 by
The Book Guild Ltd
9 Priory Business Park
Wistow Road, Kibworth
Leicestershire, LE8 0RX
Freephone: 0800 999 2982
www.bookguild.co.uk
Email: info@bookguild.co.uk
Twitter: @bookguild

Typeset in Minion Pro

Printed and bound in Great Britain by CPI Group (UK) Ltd, Croydon, CR0 4YY

ISBN 978 1912083 572

British Library Cataloguing in Publication Data.
A catalogue record for this book is available from the British Library.

I dedicate this book to my parents, Alma and Vincent, for making me what I am and to my husband, Michael, for tolerating me with all my numerous pets.

List of Maps

Contents

Introduction

This is the story of my life. In it, I reflect on the places where we lived, as a result of my husband's work, the people we met and events that have strongly influenced my views of the world at large. It derives from an oral account of our experiences over the years and has been documented primarily for our family.

Any royalties received from the publication of this book will go to benefit the wildlife and domesticated animals in Guyana, South America, and to be managed by the animal activist Syeada Manbodh.

I am grateful for all the help given by my family, especially my husband, Michael, for his comments, contributions, suggestions etc. in writing this book. Over the years, I have discovered that there is a lot more to civil engineering than just bricks and concrete!

1

British Guiana – The Good Old Days

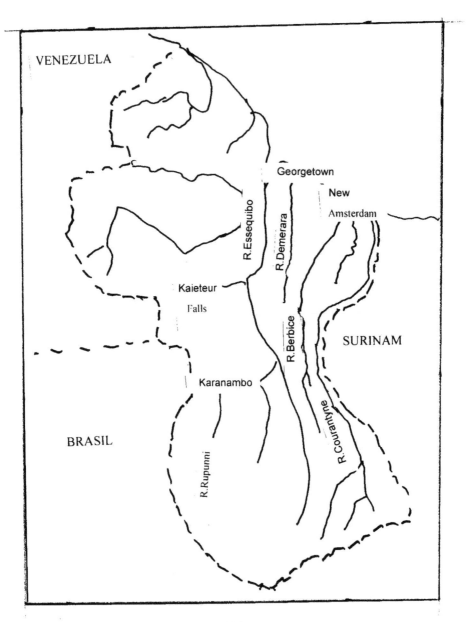

MAP 1
GUYANA (FORMERLY BRITISH GUIANA)

'Audrey, Audrey!' I was just getting ready to go to school when I heard my name being shouted by my friend, Jean Ince, next door, and wondering what she could want at this time of day I went to the porch by the front door.

'Audrey, Jacko's over here again. He's in the rafters now having just thrown an egg at my dad. Please come over and collect him.'

I'm a great lover of animals but they got me into all sorts of trouble. Jacko was a sakiwinki monkey, and at one time I had two of them, but more about them later.

I was told I was a breech birth and a very sick baby, and when an old friend of the family, Aunt Amy Messervy, came to see me, she said to my mother that I was an angel already, which upset my mother greatly, as did the thought of losing me so early in life. Because of my health issues I was christened very soon after birth.

I was born shortly before the outbreak of World War II on Regent Road, Georgetown, British Guiana. We lived in one of a row of similar single-storey houses on the road leading from the city centre to the cricket ground and Botanic Gardens. My father was born in Australia where my grandfather, Walter Roth, was a doctor/surgeon and Protector of the Aborigines. Sadly, my grandmother died when my father was just ten months old, which resulted in him having a rather unsettled young life.

My grandfather moved to British Guiana (after independence, known as Guyana) to take up a post as a doctor, magistrate and Protector of the Amerindians, the indigenous natives of the colony. My father was eighteen years old when he arrived with his father. His stepmother stayed behind in England until the family got settled. Dad spent all his working life as a surveyor and warden magistrate for the government. He married and had two sons. His first wife died at an early age. He then married my mother, Alma, someone whom both he and his wife had known for several years.

I remember Dad telling Betty (my older sister) and me about our family name – Roth. He said a journalist had once remarked that all the people he had known with the name Roth were Jews. Dad told him that Roth was not a Hebraic name but was from the German word *rot*, meaning red. Many Central European Jews changed their Hebraic names, or their family or personal description if they lacked a name, to the European equivalent. Our great-grandfather came from Poland and his original surname had been Vöresch.

Mathias and Anna Vöresch were driven out of southern Poland by a Russian pogrom and made their way into what became Hungary and settled in Kosice, now the second city of Slovakia. They had four sons, David, Felix, Emerich and Mathias. Sadly, Mathias Senior died before his last son was born, and the baby was named after his father. Anna was allowed to run a kosher restaurant in the city and through her hard labours was able to give all her sons a good education.

Mathias, after qualifying as a doctor in Italy, went to Vienna to see his brother Felix, who had become a successful stockbroker, and meet his nieces and nephews. On returning to Kosice he found fierce fighting going on between Austrian and Hungarian armies. Louis Kossuth (a Hungarian patriot) had set up a provisional government in Debrecen and was fighting for an independent Hungary. Mathias was soon helping the injured soldiers and after a while he was sent to Debrecen to get further medical supplies. While there he was approached by a senior member of the provisional government asking if he knew anyone who spoke several languages and would be prepared to go to England to seek help for the cause from their agents over there. Mathias said he would go.

First, he was smuggled over the border hidden in a hay cart, then imprisoned when he could not produce his passport, which he had been told to leave behind. In Paris he eventually reached his brother, David, who had a very successful practice there. He had invented a calculating machine which was in use by the French government, and had even been over to England to discuss mutual projects with Charles Babbage (inventor

4

of the calculating machine which was the forerunner to the computer). By the time Mathias reached London the cause was over; Russia had intervened on the side of Austria and Kossuth and his government had fled into Turkey. Mathias could not return home, so he set up a practice in London, married Anna Maria Collins, my great-grandmother, and raised nine children.

Dad said there was always a question as to how 'Roth' should be pronounced; should the 'o' be as in 'broth', or as in 'both'? Dad's Uncle Felix once had a hip flask with the following inscription:

> *To Felix Roth,*
> *though rather loathe,*
> *came two little grouse,*
> *he shot them both.*

My mother was born in Surinam, as were her siblings, but when she was two or three she went to live with her Aunt Isabel. My Great-Aunt Isabel – we called her 'Auntie' – played a great part in our lives even though I was not her favourite. My sister Elizabeth (Betty) shone in her eyes no matter what she did.

Our next-door neighbours were the Ince family, and the family next to Auntie was the Salamalay family. They were an Indian couple who owned a shoe shop in Regent Street. They sold the house to the Too Chungs, a Chinese family. One daughter was a teacher and the other a nurse, who lived with their father and a sister, Sybil. They also had two sons, Victor and Hector. Both families were very friendly, having long chats with my aunt through the window.

I remember one night when we heard a very loud crash coming from the direction of the Too Chungs'. When we looked out it transpired that a thief had got into their house and had been disturbed by one of the brothers. The thief, in desperation, jumped through a closed glass window, cutting himself very badly, which enabled the police to apprehend him by following the trail of blood.

I was very young when the Second World War started, but Dad told me about it when I was much older. He was made a warden, and had to go out every evening to make sure everyone had closed their shutters, and that they were not showing any lights that might indicate to any German planes flying over the city where the houses were. It was said that German submarines were known to be on patrol just off the coast. Later Dad was sent to the North-West District to look after the Aruka estate and I remember Mum taking Betty and me on a big boat to visit him. Nanny Muriel came along too.

When the war ended, Dad hired a jackass cart (dray cart) and we all jumped aboard, together with friends and neighbours, for a drive around the town to celebrate the occasion. Dad still dressed in his pyjamas!

My father was one of the first nominated members to the Legislative Council by King George VI, and because of this my parents were often invited to Government House and various functions. Unknown to us, a young maid called Dora, who 'lived in', would call her boyfriend whenever my parents went out. Late one night my parents came back from a party at Government House, bringing with them Magistrate Togo Low, a good friend of my father's. He and his wife were from Malta and lived in a large house in the Queenstown district. I often visited them there, and their gardener, who was always busy tending the plants and always had a smile for me, would present me with a flower from the garden when we came to leave.

As my parents got out of the car that evening our neighbour opposite, Mrs Pinkerton, came running over to say there was a man in our house and another one outside. Mum and Dad managed to hold the man downstairs while Togo went upstairs to phone the police. My mother then followed him to see if he had managed to get through. What she found was Togo, in his befuddled state, talking into the earpiece with the mouthpiece against his ear! I should explain that our phone was the old 'daffodil' type with the mouthpiece at the top of the stem and the earpiece on an extended cord. When the culprit appeared in court, Dad asked the judge to show leniency.

One of my close friends was Jean Ince next door. We can still remember the many instances of thieves trying to break into our houses. Jean's father kept beautiful orchids and canaries in his house, which were always on display and a target for thieves. Dad made a watercolour painting of the flowers and signed it *VR – Vincent Roth*. We were always nervous when it got dark around six o'clock as that was the time when thieves tended to strike at some poor unfortunate household.

Apart from these encounters we lived a very sheltered life. We both had nannies to take us for walks to the Botanic Gardens in our prams with our dollies. As I grew older I can recall having three different nannies at different times.

My favourite nanny was Muriel Northe, and later her sister Sheila. Muriel is now ninety years old and living in New York. She came from a very religious family and my parents would allow them to take me to their home in a village called Kitty. Their mother was one of the gentlest and kindest ladies I have ever met. Her children called her 'Mama' and so did I.

Most afternoons our nannies would take us in our prams to the Botanic Gardens at the top of the road to play with our friends while the nannies would chat amongst themselves, probably about how they were treated by their employers. On certain days, the band would perform in the bandstand under their conductor, Sidney Henwood, and his deputy, Harry Mares.

There was a large manatee pond in the gardens and our nannies had to watch that we did not go too close to the edge of the pond, as we liked to feed the animals with grass. I remember one occasion when Betty took off her panties and threw them in the pond! There was also a cherry tree fence around an area where we were not allowed to go. Over part of the pond was a beautiful bridge, known as the Kissing Bridge, which we were not allowed to cross for some reason until we were much older.

Some years ago, I went back to Guyana, as it now is, with my children and we were staying at the Hotel Tower. When I heard that Muriel was in town I invited her to dinner to meet my family. When we no longer had a need for a nanny Dad gave Muriel a job at the museum of which he was the director, and when he opened the zoo in the Botanic Gardens he moved her up there.

We were brought up to respect everybody regardless of his or her colour, class or creed. We always had to smile and say, 'good morning' or 'good afternoon'. When our fathers came home, if we were playing jacks on the front porch at the top of the stairs, we had to tone down our voices. The houses were constructed to sit on top of brick piers as the city, in places, was below sea level and liable to flood. The entrance steps rose across the facade to a small porch at the top. Jean, Betty and I liked to play and read here as we could see the passers-by and enjoy the cool breeze that was always blowing. Betty and Jean would spend hours here reading their books. The roofs were of corrugated iron so it was quite noisy inside when the heavy rains came.

Mr Ince, who was from a very old Guyanese family, worked for Bookers. Bookers was one of the largest employers in the colony. They owned many of the big sugar estates, a large department store in town and a shipping line, amongst other things. Mr Ince was very tall and always went to work in a white tropical suit complete with a white cork hat. He rode to work on his bicycle and, being tall, really stood out in the crowd.

Dad too used to cycle to the museum with his dog, Bonzo, running alongside him. He was really upset when Bonzo was run over by a car. He even took the dog into the council chambers on some occasions. Later, when he was too old to cycle to and from work, he had a contract with Bookers' taxis to take him to and fro. He worked long hours, going to work at seven in the morning and returning at dusk. After dinner, he would settle in his Berbice chair with a rum and Coke (or two) and read from the four or five library books he had beside him.

As dawn was breaking on Easter Sunday we were woken by the distant booming of a drum. *Boom. Boom*, it went as it got louder coming up the road, and we could hear people singing, '*Jesus Christ is risen today, hallelujah…*' It was the Salvation Army with a large crowd following behind, singing loudly at the top of their voices. Good Friday was a contrast: the shops were all closed, and we were told to be quiet and not play any noisy games. We only had fish to eat, no meat, and were woken up very early to go to the service at St. George's Cathedral. Occasionally we would also attend the service at St Sidwells.

When I was somewhat older and had been confirmed, Mummy would get us up to go to communion at St. George's, said to be the largest timber structure in the world. As we entered the church we handed in our communion card. We were brought up in constant fear of God.

Bats lived under the eaves of our house and as a young child they always intrigued me, and I am almost sure they used to drop what looked like almonds to the ground. Also, under the house was the old family car, used as a home for the chickens. Along one side of the house were two banana trees and I remember the cook telling me that on Valentine's Day if you pushed a knife into the heart of the tree, when you pulled it out the name of the person you were going to marry would be on the blade! I am afraid that as a youngster I always believed everything that older people told me. Near the old car, there was an aviary full of budgies and I would always have a word with them when I came back from school.

As my great passion was the animals that I took under my wing, my first encounter with death was my little white cat that I found lying at the door, dead. I cried so much no one could console me. I think I was about five years old at the time. Then there was Percy the peccary! I'm not sure where he came from. He would root about under the house eating leftovers. When I got home from school I would give him a pat on the head and he would give me a friendly grunt. Then one day I came home, and Percy had vanished. There were several people in the house who I knew wanted him gone.

I had many more stray cats after that, and I remember Darling, a lovely tabby cat. I remember sitting and watching her give birth to a litter of kittens. I also had numerous rescue dogs including Friend, Bonzo, and later Sally and Susie, who I took with me when I got married and went to live in the district engineer's house in Triumph, East Coast Demerara.

I was often asked to take food down to the Carnegie Buildings on Sundays, the temporary home for the museum following the disastrous fire there. I would go in to feed the harpy eagle that lived there, as there was no one to do it except for my father. My mother would ring down to say I was on my way and Dad would then look out for me.

On one particular Sunday, an old man on a bike rode up to me and asked where I was going. He said, 'Come, I'll give you a lift.' Luckily, I had the good sense not to get up on his bike.

I would spend almost every day at the zoo in the Botanic Gardens. I loved all the animals, especially the monkeys. There was a certain spider monkey called Sally. When she was called, she would come over and put her arms around me. At home I had two kinkajous as pets that would sit on my shoulders as I walked about, and I understand my mother often had to take them off my bed when I had fallen asleep.

I well remember my first kindergarten school nearby in Light Street, run by two sisters by the name of Hart. On leaving our house we would turn left and head towards town, and the second street we came to was Light Street, named after Henry Light, governor of the colony from 1840 to 1847. On the corner of Regent Road and Albert Street was Mr Gordon's shop, where we would spend our pocket money, one shilling a week. Dad gave us each a notebook in which we were to record how we had spent our money!

After this I moved on to Miss Coelho's school, which was also not far from home. She was a strange lady, tall with dark hair. By this time, I must have been about six years old and several of my friends also went to school there. In fact, the other day my friend Jean Ince reminded me of what a funny person Miss Coelho was. While sat at one long desk learning our times tables, on another one the children would be learning their alphabet – A is for apple, B is for bat etc. On another long desk the pupils were busy reciting the Lord's Prayer like parrots. Miss Coelho had a little wooden spoon she called a 'pat-a-cake', and if anyone misbehaved they soon felt the power of the little 'pat-a-cake' on their wrist. Under her house was a cabinetmaker, and this was the first time I set eyes on a coffin. We were always taken to school and collected by our parents or nannies with umbrellas to protect us from the sun.

We had many people coming to visit us at home. I remember especially an elderly nun who ran a mission in the interior, and whenever she was in town she would come to see us. On one such visit she gave Betty and me a beautiful picture of Jesus, and I still have it today. I also have a crucifix above my bed that was given to Dad by a priest. I can remember him arriving on his bike with cycle clips securing the ankles of his trousers. He had a big, heavy beard. When the bishop called, he held out his hand, on which I noticed a large ring, for me to shake. I was not a Catholic at the time and so did not realise that I was supposed to kiss the ring, not shake his hand!

We had many Catholic friends. My father had become a Catholic shortly after he arrived in the colony, saying he could not find solace in the Church of England. Nearly every Saturday morning a group of his friends – they called themselves the BBC, or Bad Boys Club – would meet in Dad's office at the museum to try his home-made liqueurs and other alcoholic beverages. One of the group was Horace Lopes; he liked to be called 'the colonel', and had served in the British West Indies Regiment in the First World War, but I am not sure whether he ever held such a high rank. He had a shed at the bottom of his garden where he would entertain his friends such as Father Crimp, Phyllis Woolford and others. Father Crimp often imbibed more than he should and fell off his bike on the way back to the presbytery to say Mass!

One day the colonel's wife said to him, 'Horace, you never go to church.'

He replied, 'I don't need to; the church comes to me!'

Another close friend of the family is Sister Noel Menezes. After leaving school she decided she wanted to become a nun. The day she was to enter the convent for the first time she came around to the house to say goodbye. Dad presented her with a camera to mark the occasion.

'Thank you very much, but I'm sorry, Uncle Vincent, we're not allowed to take anything like that with us.'

In her later years, she ran a boys' orphanage at Plaisance, which is still thriving. Sister Noel, as we call her, visits us whenever she comes over to England.

When I got married at Christ Church the Catholic priest did not attend the ceremony but did come to the reception afterwards. In those days, we had a great respect for doctors and priests and never heard of the latter molesting children as we do today, although I am sure it must have happened. Many years later I heard that Father Crimp left the church and married his housekeeper!

We were constantly reminded about having respect for the elderly. I was always being told to go and see Granny Martin, who was old and very ill. She lived around the corner in Light Street with her daughters. They were an old colonial family who wore long dresses and never went out without a hat and stockings, like my aunts and great-aunts.

We young people always wore stockings for celebrations such as weddings, and the wretched things were held up by garters and were forever falling down so that we had to keep rushing into the cloakrooms to pull them up.

The local dressmakers were extremely clever; they cut the material without patterns just by taking measurements of the person in question. We nearly always had a new dress for special occasions. I remember the can-can slips we wore underneath the dresses.

As a child, I suffered a lot from filaria (a mosquito borne illness), which meant I missed quite a lot of my early schooling and I was always falling behind the others. After my first school in Light Street run by Miss Hart, then Miss Coelho's school, my parents hired a Miss Small to tutor us at home before we went to Bishops High School, for which we had to sit an entrance exam. It was an all-girls school and some of the teachers came from England. We wore green uniforms with white shirts and a tie, and a large panama hat to protect us from the sun. Most of the pupils had bicycles. Woe betide us if we were seen on the road not wearing our hats or ties properly – we were reported to our form mistress and given a detention, and if you clocked up three detentions you had to either go to see the headmistress, who in my time was Mrs Alleyn, or stay behind and do extra work.

Mrs Alleyn lived in a house at the far end of the school grounds with her husband and two large dogs. I remember I had to go to her house once to collect an animal, I can't remember what sort it was, but I did notice how relaxed she was compared to when she was in school. Another teacher, Mrs Nobbs, came from England with her husband, who was a teacher at the prestigious boys' school, Queens College. My favourite teacher was Miss Peterkin, a tall Guyanese lady who was always so pleasant and gentle in her manner – a perfect lady. Miss Dewar was a local teacher who was also very gentle, but she had only to give you one of her looks to call you to task; I believe she became headmistress after I left. Then there was Mrs Stevenson, who was very strict.

In our English class we had to learn William Wordsworth's poem:

I wandered lonely as a cloud
That floats on high o'er vales and hills,
When all at once I saw a crowd,
A host, of golden daffodils;
Beside the lake, beneath the trees,
Fluttering and dancing in the breeze.

What did we Guyanese know about daffodils? It was all right for the expatriate girls in the class who had come from a land where such flowers grew.

When Dad asked me what I had done at school that day I told him about the poem. He explained that, being a colony, we were supposed to learn about the mother country, its monarchs, customs etc.

I said, 'Surely there must be Guyanese poets whose work we could learn about as well.' Dad was on the school's Board of Governors and I think I was a great cause of embarrassment to him as I was always getting into trouble.

Several classmates came to me and said, 'Audrey, why don't you bring your pet monkeys to school one day? We would love to see them and we are sure that the teachers would be interested too.' I went away and gave it some thought and, a little later, decided to do as they had asked. So, I packed the two kinkajous in a box and took them along to school with me. This made me a little late so I had to hurry into class and put the box down beside my chair.

It was Miss Francis' class. As soon as she entered the room one of the girls jumped up and said, 'Miss, Audrey Roth has brought her two pet monkeys into the class for us to see.'

Miss Francis turned to look at me. 'Audrey Roth, is what I'm hearing true?'

'Yes, Miss Francis, it is.'

'This is impossible,' she said, and stormed out of the room.

We all started to talk about what would happen and after a few moments Miss Peterkin came into the room and over to my desk and looked down at the box holding the two monkeys.

'I gather from Miss Francis that you have brought two monkeys into the class in this box. You should have known this is not allowed – please take them home right away.' With this she left the room and I followed her with my box.

When I mentioned this incident to another of my favourite teachers, Miss Graham, who loved animals, she said, 'Silly woman.' Miss Graham's sister, Mrs Wilson, also taught at the school and I got on very well with her as well.

I remember one time when my friend Jeanette and I were at the school nativity play in which my sister Elizabeth (Betty) was the Angel Gabriel, Miss Stevenson happened to be sitting behind us and because we fidgeted a lot she gave us both a big pinch! Then we had Miss Holroyd, who tended to be a little flighty in her manner. Mrs Beattie and Mrs Batty also taught us – the latter's husband was, I believe, the Reverend Batty. What names they had to our childish minds! There was also a Mrs Mackenzie, whose husband was from England and said to be related to Daddy.

When I left school, Mum enrolled me at the Miss Jones Typing and Shorthand School, saying, 'What you learn here will be useful in whatever you decide to do.'

My father was always in the public eye and very well known as he was a well-informed historian for the colony.

When his doctors told him that, after two bouts of blackwater fever, he could not return to work in the bush, he settled to a new life in town. He had become very friendly with Charles Delph, editor of the *Daily Chronicle*, through various articles he had written for the newspaper. They decided to produce a 'who's who' for the colony. Hundreds of leaflets were sent out asking citizens to complete the questionnaire, which included name, date and place of birth, education, names of parents, wife/husband, children, address and hobbies. Some used the stamped addressed envelope provided for another purpose! The finished book ran to four editions and is very useful, even today, for looking up old friends and acquaintances.

Dad later became curator of the new museum, built after the disastrous fire of 1945. He made models of the city before the fire and these are still exhibited in the museum today. He wrote numerous books on the flora and fauna of the colony, as well as his life working in the bush. He organised for exhibits from the museum to be sent to schoolchildren living outside Georgetown, knowing that this was the only way they would be able to see them. With a grant from the government he created a zoo in the Botanic Gardens, saying, 'As the citizens of the country are unable to go to the hinterland, then we must bring the animals here for all to see.'

When we started having visitors from abroad after the war the first person they wanted to see was my father. I remember meeting Lady Baden-Powell, David Attenborough, Michael Swan, Gerald Durrell and numerous others. In fact, some years ago I met Sir David Attenborough, as he now is, once again at a book launch in Tunbridge Wells, and reminded him of his time in British Guiana some sixty years ago. When I happened to mention that we had lost a number of our books about British Guiana in our travels round the world he very kindly sent me his copies of Schomburgk's travels in the colony, which my grandfather had translated from the original German into English. I also had a very nice letter from him after I had written to him about the monkeys I had seen while on a visit to India with Tim and Fiona, two of my children.

At school I was not very academically inclined but loved art, as I still do to this day. Because of this, I always seemed to be getting into trouble for talking in class. If we were caught talking more than once we were sent to stand outside the door of Mrs Alleyn's office. However, instead I would go and sit in the cloakroom where I couldn't be seen until the bell rang for the change of class. I was quite a timid child and really did not like school.

I had several friends who would be invited to parties held at Government House. I remember being invited to a costume party organised by the governor's daughter, Anne Renison, and going dressed as a clown. My father was a friend of her father, partly due to his intimate knowledge of the country for over fifty years.

Another friend of the family was Andy Sutherland, captain of one of the Harrison Line boats that paid frequent visits to Georgetown. Whenever he was in port he would invite us all aboard for dinner. Again, when a warship called on a courtesy visit we would be among those invited aboard for drinks and canapés.

As our house was not very large, when my parents wanted to invite several friends round for cocktails they would use the home of a close friend in Kingston. As their neighbour was the archbishop of the West Indies he would be invited along too.

I remember my grandfather's companion, Edith, whom we always called Granny Roth; she was a very serious woman. At one time, after my grandfather had died, she lived at Port Mourant on the Courantyne with Uncle Ralph, a friend of Dad's (he was not related to us, by the way), and Betty and I were taken to visit her on several occasions. I did not enjoy these visits as we were made to rest in the afternoon and were given knitting needles so we could learn to knit. There was a housekeeper called Jessie and a young Indian butler called George. I remember George wearing white gloves when he served us at the table. When Granny came back to Georgetown she lived in Church Street and had to have everything done for her, as she was practically bedridden following a fall downstairs some years ago.

In those days, everybody was referred to as 'auntie,' 'uncle', 'Mr' or 'Mrs'; not like today where everybody seems to be called by his or her first name. My mother, her sisters and brothers were born in Surinam, and when Mum wanted to talk to her sisters they would speak in Dutch so that we would not be able to understand what was being said. Auntie was very good at sewing and had a machine that had to be turned by hand to operate it. She made all our dresses, but I hated it when I had to stand up while she pinned the hem up. Our clothes were always admired, but when Auntie got too old to sew I had a dressmaker to do the work for me. For nearly every party, we girls had to have a new dress. Auntie had a companion called Nene, whom I adored and really missed when she passed away.

Quite often at the weekends a group of us would go to the Tower Hotel or Carib on the seafront to the dances they put on there. The band was always very good, especially when they had a steel band and the limbo dance.

I can remember going to Roden Rust in West Coast Demerara on a holiday. As the house was almost on the beach I could see the boats passing up and down the Essequibo River; to me they appeared to be very close to us in the water.

Nanny Muriel was always in the water with us and I can remember very well one of the house dogs running into the water behind us with her towel, which poor Muriel had left her teeth wrapped in! We searched and searched but we knew of course that it would be impossible to find them. I reminded Muriel about this incident during one of my recent weekly phone calls to her in New York.

I remember Muriel telling us how she had named her daughter Audrey after me, and how she had turned out to be as mischievous as I was.

One of our neighbours was Sybil, a sister of the Too Chungs who lived next door to Auntie. She was much older than me but very childlike, and would come to see us always clutching her doll. She never had much to say for herself but obviously liked the company. She loved to make golden apple jam and we could hear her, two doors away, banging the spoon on the pot after she had tasted it.

Opposite us in a large two-storey house was the D'Ornellas family. They were Portuguese and, or so it appeared to me, always having babies. When they moved, they sold the house to a Dr Carto and his family. He had retired from the psychiatric hospital in New Amsterdam. His daughter and son-in-law lived with him and his wife, and their grandchildren, Hazel and Ronald Dummett. I became very friendly with Hazel until she moved away from Georgetown.

There was a Portuguese Aunt Adele who was quite old and would come over to visit Auntie and her elderly companion, Nene Roomes. Nene had beautiful long hair, which she always kept in a bun. I can remember her going to have a cataract removed at a Chinese doctor's private clinic in Kingston. After the operation, she had to lie on her back for days without moving. I was often told to go to her house and read to her because her sight was failing. Once when I was with her a priest came to give her communion, a white cloth being laid on the table for the service. When she died, her funeral was announced on the nine o'clock news. In those days, there was no television so everyone turned on their radios to hear the death announcements. I can still see the huge procession of cars following the hearse on its way to the cemetery. In those days children did not normally go to funerals.

Around June we had the Dorcas Club fair. Dad was the patron and the fair was held every year to raise money for the poorer families in the community. There was always a queen and her attendants, and a fancy-dress competition. I once dressed as a piano, Dad having painstakingly made a keyboard to go with the costume. On another occasion, I went as an Amerindian, and another time as an East Indian bride and Betty as the bridegroom. I can't say I really enjoyed having to get dressed up for these various events.

A May Day fair was held each year at Kitty, where girls danced around the maypole with colourful ribbons, wearing beautifully starched dresses. Easter was the great time for flying kites on the sea wall, where there was always a steady breeze. Sometimes our kites were bought for us, or we used homemade ones – they all had wonderful long tails. People who were keen, like the Zitman family, would go as early as half past seven with their children, June Ann and Nancy. The Zitmans were also keen racegoers at the D'Urban Park racecourse, which they went to with the Cox family, who owned a garage if I am not mistaken.

Attending Miss Coelho's school with us was Andrew Zitman. Miss Coelho apparently liked to drink, and in the class was her niece, who was always being told off for no good reason. My friend, Jean Ince, reminded me that Miss Coelho liked her rum and Coke and when she ran out she would send her poor niece to replenish her supplies. We did not remain there very long once our parents found out what was going on. In those days, we had slates to write on with a hole in the middle for the pencil.

In our younger days when we had birthday parties our nannies would always be present to watch their charges. The big attraction at these parties was the ice cream. This was made in the old-fashioned way, usually under the house in a small barrel. Ice and salt would be packed around the container holding the mixture and a handle was turned to turn it into ice cream. It was a lengthy process and many hands were used in the making. Mum was very generous with her ice cream, always sending a little to each of the neighbours.

Mum had a good heart; when Marion, the maid, came to work for us she was pregnant, and when Clive was born she had nowhere to leave him so we kept him in the house. As he grew he developed into a very pleasant boy who endeared himself to the family, and as he started to talk he called my mother 'Mummy Roth' and Dad 'Daddy Roth'. I believe they managed to get him a place at St. George's School not far from where we lived.

Mum also helped another little child called Elaine. When Mum was visiting my sister Betty, who had moved to Trinidad after marrying, a friend came to visit who had adopted a little girl from a very poor Trinidadian family. The father, who had only one leg, and mother, kept on producing children and they all lived in one room in a very run-down area of the town. With the father not working the children did not have a lot to eat and often went hungry.

'Why don't you adopt one of the children?' the visitor asked my mother. Mummy thought about it for a while, then asked my father, who was not too keen on the idea as he was not well at the time and getting on in years.

The girl's parents did not want the child adopted as they considered her part of their future. In the end, Dad relented (as did her parents), and Elaine came to stay with us. She only had the clothes she was standing up in and when she was taken to have a shower she screamed and screamed, as she had never experienced a modern shower, only bathing from water coming out of a stand pipe. All she wanted to do when she arrived was eat and then eat some more. When she was taken to the doctor he advised that she was to be given only very small portions at a time until her stomach got used to the rich food she was being given to eat.

She really was a lovely girl with long hair and blue eyes. As Mum was not a Catholic like Elaine, she asked Mrs Da Silva, mother of Maureen and Phillipa, and the sister of Dr Rosa, to take her to Our Lady of Fatima Church, which was not far from our home. This she did gladly every Sunday morning. When it was time for Elaine to be confirmed I had a most beautiful dress made for her out of voile material I bought from Bookers, and a lovely pair of shoes to match.

By the time she was six or seven she could still hardly read or write, so Mum wrote out a lot of simple words and stuck them round the house, and would take Elaine to them and get her to say what was printed on each card. Clive was still living with us and going to the local school.

One day Mum received a letter from Trinidad saying the family wanted Elaine back as her mother was expecting another child and she wanted Elaine to help look after the infant when it arrived. Mum asked the priest to write a letter to say how well she had been doing attending school and church regularly, and that it was in her interests to stay on with us, but to no avail.

By this time, I was married and had just had my first child, Dinah. My husband Mike and I were then living out at Triumph on the East Coast, ten miles from Georgetown. I would often take Dinah, her pram, and two of my dogs, Sally and Susie, to see Mum and Dad, and when I went for a walk to the gardens Elaine was very happy to come along and help me to push the pram. I still have a photo of the two of us in the gardens. Mum made arrangements with someone she knew who was going to Trinidad and agreed to take Elaine with her. When she was told she was going back to her family she ran down the stairs crying her eyes out – it was all very sad. I heard from one of the St. Aubyns in Trinidad that later on, a relative had sent for her to go to America and, as a teenager, she was murdered by her boyfriend – a very sad tale.

Both Betty and I had music lessons. Betty was learning the violin and her teacher, Miss Meikle, came to our house while I went to Miss Bernice Waddell's for my violin lessons. For the piano, we were taught by Gloria Smith, who lived opposite Auntie. I became very friendly with Bernice. When Mike and I were to be married Bernice very kindly made a recording, with Father Heasman's blessing, of the ceremony. Another of Bernice's pupils was Felicity de Caires.

Talking of music, I have always loved hearing the bagpipes and whenever I hear them being played it reminds me of Dad. Dad, when he was feeling well, would entertain us with the sword dance having spent his early life in Scotland. When our second daughter, Fiona, got married her sister, Dinah, arranged for a piper in full ceremonial dress to be at the church and reception afterwards. It made my day.

I also had ballet lessons from Miss Bunny King, who lived on Middle Street with her parents. Dad knew her father very well as he had been superintendent of the famous Mazaruni Prison opposite Bartica on the Essequibo River. It was a great tragedy when, many years later, Bunny was murdered in her own home and the murderer was never caught. It was said nothing appeared to have been stolen.

Living next door to Bunny was my friend Wanda who lived with her parents and two sisters. Sometimes I would be invited to her house for lunch and we would play with our dolls. When I invited her in return, a car would bring her round and we would play with our dolls on the porch. Wanda eventually married John Willems, a very close family friend of ours.

I introduced Wanda to Rita and Agnes Ferraz, who lived above their shop on Main Street. They sold a popular 'punch' made from peanut butter and milk. I also introduced the Ferrazes to my friend Camille Henriques, who later married Dr Bill Murray, an eye specialist. Rita and I loved to play duets on the piano when we got the chance. Agnes was keen to meet Bill Murray as she wanted to go to England to study optics. Some years later when I returned to Georgetown to see my parents, I contacted Camille as she had a daughter, about the same age as Dinah, who had been asked to be an attendant at the forthcoming Joy Fair, and asked if Dinah could attend with her. They wore lovely white dresses with crowns on their heads and small harps in their hands.

Just before Christmas Mum would invite our friends who lived close by round to sing traditional carols, one of us playing the piano. Among those who came were Margaret Carter, whose father was a dentist; Jean Ince from next door; June Anne and Nancy Zitman and one or two others. Mum loved singing and played the mouth organ like a professional. Our singing parties were held over at Auntie's house where the piano was kept. By this time, a passageway had been formed which made it very easy for us to come and go between one house and the other.

A whole crowd of us would go carol singing with Miss Mansfield on an open lorry to raise funds for the Dorcas Club. I remember Bernice Waddell taking me with a group of carol singers from the Portuguese Club to entertain the patients of the Mahaica Leprosy Hospital with her violin. Bookers also had a choir, so there were many venues for the singing of carols at Christmas time.

My first job was at the Royal Agricultural and Cultural Society on Company Path, where I helped the librarian, Miss Martin. I really enjoyed my time there as I met many of the locals and the expatriates who were also members. From there I moved to Bookers Stores as a window dresser under Mr Mcloughlin, a small Scotsman. The stores had many windows so we were kept pretty busy arranging new displays. It was always said that 'BG' did not stand for British Guiana but for Bookers Guiana!

Then Sir Anthony Tasker, a charming gentleman, suggested I got a job at the Petroleum Marketing Agencies. I quite enjoyed working there, the office being on Main Street, almost opposite the Ferrazes' shop. When I first started, I worked with Ivor Fernandes, a very quiet, pleasant Portuguese gentleman; then a Mr Spittal, a Scotsman, who came back in the afternoon after what looked like a very liquid lunch!

There was another man there, Mr Blackwell, an Englishman. My father was forever writing to the local papers complaining about some topical issue or putting someone right about the colony's history.

Mr Blackwell and Mr Spittal would call me up almost daily – 'Miss Roth, have you seen what your father has written in today's paper?' They meant it in a very pleasant way but it used to annoy me at times. Also working in the office was Minx, a niece of Magistrate Brown; we got on well together and often had a good laugh over some trivial thing or another.

One day when I was working away on the first floor of the office I heard a loud bang and a screech of brakes. Being ever curious, I went to the window to see what was happening. I saw that a dog had been hit by a Land Rover. Without thinking I ran downstairs and into the street and spoke to the driver, who was looking down at the injured animal.

'Put him in the back and I will take you to a vet.' When I got back to the office Mr Spittal commented on my absence but commended me for the action I had taken.

When I came to leave for my forthcoming marriage they presented me with a very nice canteen of cutlery.

Jaques and Marie Willems were very good friends of the family; every evening, about six o'clock, Uncle Jaques would come to the house for a rum and Coke sundowner and discuss his problems with Dad.

When he was younger, Dad would hoist the Union Flag on the flagpole on the porch as he had done in his days as a warden and magistrate in the bush. In the evening he would lower it, saying, 'The sun should never set on the Union flag.'

Every evening when he came home from work Dad would sit in his Berbice, or planter's chair as it was also called, by the window in the gallery with his feet up on the extended armrests and read his books with his first rum and Coke of the day. He always had several library books on the table beside his chair and would read a chapter or two from each, every evening. When he was not feeling well he would go to his room and we would be told to be quiet.

Dad had had a hard life living and working in the bush. He had suffered with malaria and two bouts of blackwater fever that finally ended his working days in the field. He wore a hearing aid as he suffered some deafness as a result of sleeping in tents when out on survey work. One day when my half-brother, Walter, came around to see him I happened to refer to Dad as 'the old man'.

'What's that, what's that – who's calling me an old man?' I did not realise he had his hearing aid on! He gave me a cross look and said I had no respect.

Quite often when we were alone together he would point to each finger on his left hand in turn and say, 'Whatever happens, Daddy loves you', which I thought was rather sweet. Dad enjoyed smoking his pipe with the Rupununi tobacco he got from the interior, and the occasional cigar. He smoked in the office but not at home as far as I can remember.

In June 1951 King George VI awarded Dad an OBE (Order of the British Empire) for his services to the colony.

In later years, we would pay frequent trips to St. Joseph's Mercy Hospital to see Dad in bed hooked up to numerous wires and tubes following an operation for the removal of gall and kidney stones. When he came out the surgeon, Dr Romitti, a friend of Dad's, gave him the stones he had removed in a little jar!

What really upset his well-being was an incident one Sunday at a party at the Willems' house. Unusually for Dad, he was sitting at the edge of the pool when Jaques, for a prank, decided to give him a push. Dad fell awkwardly and needed assistance to get up. Back on the poolside he complained of back pains, so they laid him down and called a doctor. Ever after that he complained of back pains. It was not like him to sit at the edge of the pool – usually he would sit in the shade talking to another non-swimmer.

I always lived in fear that my parents would die and leave us if we were naughty. Many years later when I told my mother of my fears she was quite surprised.

Respect for people of all ages and colours was drummed into us as children. There was some prejudice directed at people who were not white, or who had dark, curly hair. We got on well with everybody regardless but occasionally we would say, 'He or she is Chinese, Portuguese, East Indian etc. by way of identifying them.' A very good friend of Dad's, Charles Broomes, a farmer, would send us boxes of oranges and grapefruits from the North-West District.

My mother always told us to say, 'good morning' and smile, a habit I still have but feel some people don't deserve.

After one Christmas I went to Surinam to stay with a Dutch friend for a short holiday. They were a lovely family who welcomed me so warmly. I remember the older daughter climbing in through my window after she had sneaked out earlier in the evening to meet her boyfriend. She had obviously been drinking as she started to throw up all over the floor; something I have never done, as I do not like alcohol apart from the odd rum punch or an occasional sherry.

On most Sundays Camille, a few friends and I would go for cycle rides along the sea wall and then back through the city. When I was in my teens I was allowed to have a Velocette, a bicycle with a motor on the front wheel. The Velocettes were imported by the Willems Timber Company, and one evening I heard Jaques Willems, whom I referred to as 'Uncle Jack', talking about them, so at the age of fifteen I became the first girl in the colony to own one. I was asked to have my photo taken for the local press. A test had to be taken in front of the chief of police, Mr Cleare. I passed as it was quite easy, though whether it was because I knew the examiner I don't know. When I was issued with a licence an error was made as it also allowed me to ride a motorbike and drive a car! In later years, I took another test that allowed me to drive in the United Kingdom with an international driving licence.

I was only allowed to use my 'putt-putt', as I called it, for short distances, and I was never to go along the sea wall or to Bel Air, and if I did it would be taken from me. One evening as the sun was going down I decided to go for a ride, and on my way, I ran into (not literally) my friend Eve. Eve lived with her grandparents and an aunt and uncle as her parents were working overseas and sent her an allowance every month. As she did not work she would ride around for most of the day on her bike, visiting friends around the town.

On this particular evening, I had not long had the bike and was still carrying L-plates and was going to break all the rules. Having met up with Eve, she climbed up on the back of the bike and off we went. We were chugging along in the breeze, Eve's hair blowing in the wind at the back. We drove up along the sea wall, then on to Bel Air and then around the town. As we were entering South Road a dog ran out from a house and started to run alongside the bike. Eve screamed and put her feet up on the handlebars, which caused me to lose control with the result that we ran into a lamp post!

An Indian woman looked out from her window and shouted, 'He nat me dag, he nat me dag.' Eve was quite badly bruised and the putt-putt suffered some damage.

Another incident I remember very well and which nearly put us in deep water was the time we went on a picnic up the East Bank with Margaret Carter and her parents. Jean and I left the party and wandered off to a nearby trench, where we found a small canoe close to the bank. We both decided to get into the boat, where we found a couple of poles. We started to push ourselves along towards a *koker (Dutch for sluice gate)*, which we did not realise was open, which meant that we were gradually drifting into the Demerara River. Fortunately, a man who was close by saw what was happening and came to our rescue.

Before our houses had piped water we all had huge vats in the back yard to store the rainwater off the roof. A man would come round and put small fish into the vats to eat the mosquito larvae that caused malaria and filaria. Mosquitoes will lay their eggs on any patch of still water. After the war, Dr Giglioli eradicated malaria by spraying everywhere with DDT. He and his wife were guests at my wedding I was very friendly with his wife as she had numerous dogs as pets.

For lunch, I would go over to the museum and join my father. My mother would send the lunch down with the maid – usually a salad. Also working in the store was Stella, with whom I became quite friendly. It so happened that my father went over to Trinidad to see my sister Betty and her husband, Hugh Tilley. As he didn't allow anyone in his office when he was away it meant that I had to make other arrangements for my lunch.

I happened to mention it to Stella just before Dad went away and she suggested that I went to the boarding house run by Bert Nunes and his wife, Sue, on Middle Street. As we approached the house I saw a little sports car parked outside.

'That's a nice-looking car,' I said.

'Yes it is, it belongs to a new lodger we have. You will probably meet him as he must have come in for lunch.'

As we were finishing our meal a tall young fellow came from the front where he had been eating.

'Hello, Stella, how are you today?

'Hi, Mike. Let me introduce you to my friend here, Audrey Roth. She's having lunch here while her dad is away in Trinidad.'

He then asked me if I would like to go out with him for a drive in the car. I said I would like to very much but first I would have to tell my mother as my father was away.

He said he would pick me up after work and take me home so he could meet my mother. When he arrived outside the office he had his boss sitting in the car; Mike had apparently told him that he was picking me up and that his boss, Adamson, would have to sit in the small seat at the back. The car, being a sports model, only had two doors.

We had a great respect for everyone. I had friends who were Muslims, Hindus, Seventh-Day Adventists and other minor religious sects. One of which was the Jordanites; they wore long white robes and would stand on street corners with a bell and a lamp in their hands. Many years later when I was married and living in the country, one of the night watchmen was a Jordanite; he always gave us a bit of a scare when we drove home after dark and waited for him to appear and open the gate to our compound.

British Guiana (BG) was known as the Land of Six Peoples: European, African, Indian, Chinese, Portuguese and Amerindian. The Spanish were the first to arrive although they did not settle in the colony, instead they moved on to what is now Venezuela. The colony consisted of three provinces, Essequibo, Demerara and Berbice. It was occupied by the Dutch, French and British. Each left their mark. Wharves were known as *stellings*, sluices as *kokers*, and words like *bateau* and *crapaud* were in common use for boats and frogs.

With this diverse population, each brought their own culture and customs with them. The most important time for the Muslims – in those days we were not aware as to whether they were Shia or Sunni sect – was Ramadan. Because Muslims base their months on phases of the moon, each Ramadan usually falls three weeks earlier than in the previous year. During their fast nothing must pass their lips between sunrise and sunset, so they have to be up early in the morning before sunrise to take their breakfast and then wait for the sun to go down before they may start their supper. Because BG is close to the equator, sunrise and sunset do not vary greatly throughout the year, unlike other parts of the world.

At the end of Ramadan when the new moon is sighted, they celebrate what is known as Eid ul-Fitr. Special food is prepared to be shared with family and friends, new clothes are worn and houses redecorated. All Muslims should try, at least once in a lifetime, to make a pilgrimage, the hajj, to Mecca, and can then call themselves 'hajji'.

One of the most picturesque festivals is the Hindu festival of Divali, the 'festival of lights'. To better understand Divali it is necessary to know something about the great Hindu hero, Rama. Ramayana, a holy book for the Hindus, sets out the story of Rama. King Dasharatha had three wives. His first bore him a son, Rama. Prince Bharata was born to his second wife, and Lakshmana to his third wife, but Rama was heir to the throne. The king's second wife, Queen Lausalaya, was jealous of Rama and wanted the throne for her own son. As a result, Prince Rama and his wife Sita were driven from the land and sent into exile. However, Prince Bharata took no part in this plot. He always kept Prince Rama's shoes on the throne and awaited his return. In exile, Rama fought many demons including Ravana, who had captured Sita and taken her to his place over the seas. After many years, Rama returned to the throne, and to celebrate, the people held Divali.

The festival is held in November; houses are cleaned, new furnishings are bought and special foods prepared. Metai, halwa and other delicacies are made and shared with family, friends and neighbours. Around each house clay cups called diyas are filled with oil and a wick, and after dark are lit with such a dramatic effect that families walk round their streets to admire the spectacle.

Another Hindu religious holiday, Phagwah, occurs in March to celebrate the triumph of good over evil. Traditionally on this day, Hindus wear a white dhoti and enjoy the day by throwing a red liquid over each other and their animals. The dye, *abeer*, symbolises the blood of the tyrannical King Kiranya, who was ordered to burn alive his son Prince Prahalad because of the suffering his people endured at his hands.

Georgetown had a selection of odd characters who wandered the streets and, in most cases, were quite harmless. One was 'Frowsie Self', who went around saying, 'Wen ar get de po'er ar gun giv' you al' a car an' fridge.' Sadly, he did not get elected so nobody got a free car and fridge as promised!

Cato was a somewhat deranged fellow who wore short pants and rags and often exposed himself to people in the street for money, saying, 'Ah want a penny tuh buy a pantie fuh me sister.' Once, in court on a charge of indecent exposure, he saw Forbes Burnham, lawyer, one-time mayor and president, and shouted out, 'Uncle Forbes, get up an' talk fuh me, man. Yuh gun leh dis coolie magistrate do this tuh me?' For once it seems Forbes was lost for words!

One day I was walking past Fogarty's thinking about nothing in particular, when a youth came up to me and said, 'Putagee, go back to your own country.'

'This is my country,' I said, 'and I'm staying here.' All fair-skinned people were considered to be Portuguese.

Many years later when Sister Noel Menezes was in England I

happened to mention this incident to her and she said the same thing had happened to her. She had seen a motorist park his car very badly so that it could cause an accident and went over to point this out to him. After a few abusive words he told her to go back to her own country.

'Sir,' she said, 'this is not your country and it is not my country, it belongs to the Amerindians.'

I loved the city in which I was born: the magnificent St. George's Cathedral, one of the largest structures constructed out of wood in the world; the elegant town hall and, close by, the law courts with the bust of Queen Victoria in front, although she did lose her head during one of the troubles that struck the colony; and lastly, the imposing Public Buildings, where my grandfather and father spent some of their time.

And what did we teenagers do with our spare time? There was the Brown Betty cafe, just behind Water Street, or Bookers' Soda Fountain, and at Christmastime Fogarty's Store was a must, and there were lots of parties to go to.

I celebrated my twenty-first birthday with a small party at home. My father had a very large key made from wood, which he presented to me as I was about to cut my cake.

Mike and I were married a week later. The ceremony was held at Christ Church at five o'clock in the evening when it is much cooler. The church was beautifully decorated with red antirrhinum lilies my sister had brought over from Trinidad. We had over three hundred guests and the reception afterwards was held at the Willems' house on Croal Street, which had been beautifully decorated by Mr Wolstenholme, the curator of the Botanic Gardens, as a wedding present to us. We had a small band and we were enjoying it so much that we forgot about the time because we had to be the first to leave.

When he left his Quaker school, Sidcot, Mike did not know what he wanted to do, but decided he wanted to get his national service over first. When he could get no information as to when his call-up might be he decided to look for a job and became an articled pupil with a small firm of consulting civil engineers, attending college part-time one day a week. He eventually did his national service in the Royal Engineers, who in their wisdom, as Mike was now on his way to qualifying as a chartered engineer, decided to make him a clerk! This was a blessing in disguise as he was taught to type, which became invaluable to him later on. He was posted to Germany where, at an army school, he learned German.

His father had died at an early age in 1952. His younger brother, Antony, was doing his national service in Egypt at the time of their father's death; Mike became head of the family while still in his mid twenties.

When our daughter, Dinah, was born eleven months after our wedding I was the happiest person in the world. She was born in a private room at the Public Hospital. My doctor, Dr Bhattacharya, was a Pakistani with an Irish wife, and a daughter Joy. He was friendly with my father as he was always in the zoo with his little daughter. Much to my regret I was told not to nurse the baby because of my reoccurring illness.

Our home was only a few minutes' walk from the sea wall, so it was great for the dogs as they loved the sea, and especially when one of the church sects had the ceremony of total immersion in the muddy Atlantic rollers.

When Mike was having a day in the office or had gone out in the Land Rover I would put our baby daughter in her carrycot in the car, and with Sally and Susie in tow I would take them into town to see my parents.

They loved the drive and were good company for me. They were really very friendly pets, in fact, too friendly. When we moved back to live in a ground-floor flat on Carmichael Street they allowed thieves into the house without giving an alarming bark whilst Mike and I were out for the evening.

When I moved up to Triumph I took my parrot Robert with me; he was a green Amazon who loved to talk. During the day, he would sit in his cage on the front porch. Mike would sometimes get tired of his repertoire and tell him to shut up. Soon Robert added this to his other string of phrases and would shout out, 'Hello, how are you? Shut up.' He was so loud that people visiting the office could hear him and complained about his noise, so he had to be moved out of general sight.

We had a very nice gardener-cum-handyman called Seram who kept the garden in order and pumped water up into the head tank every day to ensure we had sufficient water as we had no mains supply. Neither did we have any electricity except for a generator that was run in the evenings from six until ten o'clock from the adjacent government compound.

We put the tennis court back into use and Mike got Seram to create a nine-hole putting green. When our friends came up from town they would enjoy a game of tennis or a round of golf. Mike allowed Seram to bring his cow into the compound to help keep down the grass. It used to amuse me to see Mike going around the grounds in the evening with a bucket and spade to collect the cow manure for use in the kitchen garden.

Mike's mother wrote saying that as she could not come to the wedding she would definitely come out for the birth of her first grandchild. The day of her arrival soon arrived and Mike and I, together with Dad, Mum and Jaques Willems, all went down to the wharf to meet her. As the Bookers boat neared the *stelling*, Mike soon spotted his mother leaning over one of the ship's rails, eagerly looking out for us. After the introductions, we all went to Regent Road for Mike's mother to meet Auntie. Later on we went on up to Triumph to make our guest at home.

'Da', as she said she wished to be called, soon took to life in the country, going for long walks on the beach with Sally and Susie before returning home for a rum on the rocks! Da was the name Mike had given his maternal grandmother, being too young to say, 'Grandma' and so this name was used by our children to refer to their paternal grandmother.

One thing I forgot to mention was that at the time of our wedding we had to decide who should be Mike's best man. Mike did not know many people very well, except for one couple who arrived at the Park Hotel where he was staying before he moved to the guest house where I first met him. George and Helen Smith had recently married and come out to BG as George was going up to New Amsterdam to take up the post of district engineer. Mike had been to New Amsterdam to see them on one or two occasions and had also taken me to meet them. We got on well together and so Mike had said he would ask George to be his best man. However, George said he would like to make a film of the occasion for us but to do this would mean he could not function as best man, so Mike asked his friend from public works, John Webberly.

Da had not been with us very long before Mike's brother, Antony, called in to see us as he was on his way to Bogota to work with his Uncle Oscar. Da too would go on to Bogota to see her elder brother. Apparently, Oscar had sent the family food parcels after the war as rationing was still in force for some time to come. Before they left we had several barbecues in the evenings at the edge of the tennis court.

Shortly after Antony left, Helen Smith's mother, Mrs Stuart, came out to see her first grandchild, Fiona. As Helen and George had come down to meet her we decided that Da and Mrs Stuart should make a visit to Kaieteur Falls together with Mike. George said he would spend the day with me and his baby daughter. They came back full of the wonders of Kaieteur and the picnic they had had at the edge of the falls. Mike thoroughly enjoyed the trip as on the return flight he sat in the co-pilot's seat and had a first-class view of all there was to see.

Mike decided, when Dinah was about eleven months old, that we should have a holiday outside BG. We settled for a small hotel at Hastings in Barbados.

Our room was right on the front and we could hear the water flowing in and out below our room. We spent many happy hours on the beach; Dinah loved the water and Mike enjoyed his daily dip. In the room next to ours was a young Canadian woman. We became very friendly and when we hired a car to tour the island she would come along too. Some evenings, after Dinah and I had retired Mike would sit up talking to Margaret Trubiak – I am sure it was all above board!

In the summer of 1960 we knew that Mike's contract with the government was coming to an end and we were not sure what to do as I was expecting our second child in the coming December. Then one day Mike said he was going to go through his district with Steve Naraine, Deputy Director of Public Works, and Barry Manson Hing, Executive Engineer of Sea Defences. As the other two were going on to see George Smith in New Amsterdam, Mike said he would come back by train to Beterverwagting station, the estate next to Triumph.

When Mike got home late in the afternoon he said that he had some good news for me. During the day, Steve had said to Mike that Barry was going on six months' leave and they would like Mike to take over while Barry was away as he was the only qualified engineer available at the time. If he accepted he would be moved back to Georgetown and a new district engineer would be sent to take over at Triumph. This was great news as I would be able to have the baby I was expecting in Georgetown, and as Mike said, we would miss an English winter.

Timothy was born in December. The following morning Mike had to go to an important meeting at the Ministry of Works with Steve Naraine and, after the meeting, Steve told the minister that Mike had just become a father for the second time.

The minister said, 'Congratulations. You know, Mike, three quarters of your family are Guyanese. You have done some good work for us and we would like you to come back after your six months' leave.'

Not many people know that the world's rarest stamp, the British Guiana one-cent stamp of 1856, was printed in Georgetown. In the 1850s, when communication between the colony and England was slow and uncertain, it happened occasionally that the local post office ran out of supplies of stamps, with the result that the publishers of the *Royal Gazette* were called upon to produce temporary issues until fresh stocks could be received from England.

Owing to the lack of facilities at that time for the class of printing required for postage stamps, the local efforts were somewhat crude, so, to lessen the risk of counterfeiting, each stamp, before issue, was initialled either by the postmaster or one of his clerks.

In February 1856 Messrs Baum and Dallas printed a set of two stamps, a one-cent and a four-cent, in black on magenta. It is not known definitely how many of these were printed, but that the number must have been infinitesimal is evidenced by the fact that recently the 'one-cent black' was sold at auction for over four million pounds!

In 1872 a Mr Vernon Vaughan found the stamp hidden away with some old family papers in a musty Berbice attic. Young Vaughan was at the age when all schoolboy philatelists consider the gaudy pictorial stamp to be the ne plus ultra of a collection and, in order to raise some funds to buy some of these enticing specimens, he gladly sold it for six shillings to a Mr Neil McKinnon, a member of a well-known Berbice family and a popular solicitor. Mr McKinnon kept it for a few years in his collection, which he eventually sold, as a whole, to a Mr Thomas Ridpath of London for $528. From here it found its way to America where, in 1940, it was sold for almost $45,000.

The myth of El Dorado has always been associated with British Guiana and many an expedition has been mounted in the past to search in the hinterland to find the lost city of Manoa. In the early days of discovery, the whole of the north coast of South America was referred to as Guiana. Today, moving from west to east, we have Colombia, Venezuela, Guyana, Surinam (Dutch Guiana), Cayenne (French Guiana) and Brazil. Manoa was said to be located on an island in the middle of a large lake. The streets were said to be paved and the buildings roofed with gold. The King of Manoa had his oil-anointed body covered daily with gold dust. It is probable that the idea of a gilded man was conceived from certain Inca customs when, on ceremonial occasions, the Inca or the high priest did actually have powdered gold affixed to his body by means of certain resins.

According to Von Humboldt the supposed site of El Dorado was a somewhat mobile one within this vast territory, and was moved gradually from west to east, from the source of the Rio Negro right across to the isthmus between the Takutu and Rupununi Rivers in what is now Guyana. It is easy to imagine the wretched Incas of Peru, enslaved and tortured by the Spanish Conquistadores in their tireless hunt for gold, in a vain hope of ridding themselves of their tormentors, starting the story of the golden city across the mountains to the east, as far away as possible from their own country.

As early as 1739 the Dutch Commandeur of Essequibo sent one Nicholas Horstman up the Essequibo River, to find a connection with the Amazon. Accompanied by two Dutch soldiers and four able creoles to serve as guides and interpreters, Horstman left Kartabo on one of the epic journeys of Guiana.

Horstman never returned to the Essequibo. He did, however, reach Para in 1740, where he met La Condamine, to whom he handed over his journal. Extracts from this were subsequently found many years later in the National Library in Paris. From these we learn that on the 11th May 1740 the party entered the reed-covered lake known as Amucu by the Indians, to reach the two islands in the middle. From the lake they entered the River Pirara, which took them out to the Ireng River. The lake covered what is now the Rupununi ranch lands. With regard to the name Manoa, since the time of Walter Raleigh there was a settlement of Indians on a great lake occasioned by the overflowing of Lake Amucu in the rainy seasons.

Before 1831 the country consisted of three colonies; Essequibo lay to the west and was separated from Berbice by Demerara. Essequibo and Berbice were the first to be colonised by the Dutch. Demerara was developed later, and was occupied by the British, French, Dutch, and finally the British again. To this day it is only the coastal strip of Guyana that is fully developed.

The first inhabitants were the Amerindian tribes, who are thought to have migrated east from Asia, through North and Central America to South America, where they spread out over the continent. In the 18th and 19th centuries there were many tribes. But by the beginning of the 20th century there were less than a dozen remaining, the chief among which were the Akawaio, Wapishana, Macushi, Arecuna, Warao, Carib, Arawak, Patamona and, in the far south of the country, the Wai-Wai. It is said that many perished by coming into contact with Europeans, from whom they contracted diseases that were alien to them.

In the Dutch provinces slaves were imported from Africa, and when slavery was abolished in 1834 the question arose as to who would take their place. Efforts were made to import free Africans from the West Indies but this met with little success. Considerable numbers of Portuguese from Madeira were then brought in, but they found the climate and work too onerous, and those that did not fall sick and die drifted into the towns to become pedlars and small shopkeepers.

In Mauritius, it was discovered that East Indians worked well in the cane fields. So, recruitment began in Calcutta and Bombay for indentured labour. Soon boatloads of Indians began to arrive in the colony. The final influx of cheap labour was from China. They founded a settlement at Hopetown on a creek off the Demerara River, some twenty miles south of Georgetown, from where they later spread throughout the colony. Thus, British Guiana became known as the Land of Six Peoples: Amerindians, Africans, Portuguese, Indians, Chinese and Europeans. Each brought their own language and culture, mosques, temples and churches (all built along the coastal fringe). English remained the official language.

The oldest part of the city of Georgetown is Brickdam, so named as the road surface was built using bricks, instead of the usual burnt earth. The strips of land on either side were built by the French in 1782, who called them *la Novelle Ville* – the new town. When the Dutch resumed possession of the country the following year they named the infant settlement Stabroek, after Nicolas Geelvinck, Lord of Capsieum, Bakum and Stabroek, the then-President of the Dutch West India Company.

As the town grew, by the addition to it of the front lands of the adjoining plantations, Vlissingen, La Bourgade and Eve Leary to the north, and Werk-en-Rust, Le Repentir and La Penitence to the south, it was, on the 29th April 1812, named George Town, after King George III, the reigning sovereign. In 1842, the city of Georgetown was set up by royal warrant.

Water Street was so named because it ran along the river foreshore and formed the original river dam protecting the plantations from tidal water on their river frontage. At first all the building lots were on the eastern or landward side of the street, the land on the western or river side being termed 'mud lots', on which were constructed the wharves or *stellings*, with warehouses for the storage of merchandise.

High Street formed the leading thoroughfare from the East Bank to the East Coast and constituted, as it were, the Kings Highway. That portion running through Cummingsburg somehow got designated Main Street, by which name it is known today, but its proper name is certainly High Street.

Camp Street was so named because it was the leading thoroughfare to the camp or garrison at the extreme north end of the city. Kingston originally resembled a little English village with cottages set aside amidst gardens, and was built by the officers of the garrison for their private residence. Some authorities say it was named after Lieutenant Colonel Robert Kingston, who built the first British outpost here in 1781 at Fort St. George, whilst others claim it to be named after the reigning king.

Cummingsburg was formerly Plantation La Bourgade, and was laid out in streets and lots by its canny proprietor, Thomas Cumming, who called the district after his family name in 1807. A special feature of Cummingsburg was the provision of freshwater reservoirs in the centre of its wide double streets running north to south. These were stocked with small fish to keep down the mosquitoes and were later planted with Victoria Regia and lotus lilies by Mr Luke Hill, the town superintendent.

About 1897 the reservoir in Main Street was filled up and converted into a shell walk and officially named Queen Victoria Promenade, in

36

honour of Her Majesty's diamond jubilee. Despite this it is known today as Main Street Avenue. In later years all the other Cummingsburg reservoirs, except that in East Street, were filled in and converted to promenades.

A tramway system was set up in Georgetown in 1877, the tram being pulled by a horse, but a few years later the routes were electrified. There were three different routes; it was possible to travel from Peter's Hall on the East Bank to the sea wall, New Garden Street, Middle Street and Croal Street, and Main Street, Water Street, Broad Street and Camp Street. My grandfather and father used this service when it was in operation. When it was scrapped in 1930 Edward Sill, a family friend, bought most of the track to use for hauling timber on his estate up the Demerara River.

British Guiana had the first railway built on the South American continent in 1848, first to Mahaica and later extended to Rosignol, West Coast Berbice. Another line was built from Vreed-en-Hoop to Parika on the Essequibo River. In the late 1950s a line was built from Matthews Ridge to the Barima River for the export of manganese ore.

The river terminus was close to what was to become the infamous Jonestown.

One evening, on returning home we discovered we had been burgled. The thieves had forced the mesh on our bedroom window, climbed in and then lit a candle in a wardrobe to assist them in their search. When we checked our belongings, we found they had got away with a couple of Mike's shirts.

The next morning a police constable came to the house to take a statement. He took hours to write down our statements. I was very unhappy at this intrusion, and as it was not long before we were going to England on long leave we decided to move into Regent Road and stay with Mum and Dad.

The political situation was getting worse by the day. One afternoon, returning to the office after lunch, Mike set off down Regent Road as usual but was back in a very short time to say he had run into a tear gas attack in Light Street and that we should all stay indoors.

Then on Black Friday the bubble finally burst. As I was sitting in the gallery after lunch we became aware of youths running past the house carrying large radios, bundles of cloth, small cookers and stoves; then we could smell burning and columns of black smoke started to drift up the road, and black particles to settle everywhere.

'Georgetown afire, de town burnin', was being shouted all around, and as we looked out from the steps we could see a huge column of black smoke rising up from the city centre. Mike said he would not be going back to work that afternoon, and as looting was obviously rife he brought the car in under the house.

Dad came home soon after and we got the latest news from him, not that he had seen much as he was anxious to get home. From reports we got from various people the worst affected area appeared to be Water Street between the two banks and Stabroek Market. The looters continued to pass the house long after dusk and the smell of burning still hung in the air, and the sky was red from the still-burning buildings. As Dad and Mike sat in the gallery drinking their rum and Cokes we wondered what the morning would bring.

Next morning Mike took the car out from under the house and went to the office via the sea wall, considering this to be the best way to go to be well clear of the city centre. He had not been in work long before Adamson called him into his office. He asked how we all were and then said that a lot of buildings in Water Street were in a dangerous condition and he would have to go along and make sure they were safe. The workshop was rigging up a dragline with a ball hammer and Mike was to escort it down to town and use his judgement on what should stay and what should come down. The fire had destroyed an area between the banks down to the market and eastwards almost to the High Street.

Mike told us how, just as he was about to start to demolish the Bookers office, a senior executive of the firm arrived and asked him to save what he could. It had a classical facade and it was this man's wish that this should be saved and incorporated in the new building when reconstruction started.

Our extra six months soon passed and, as Mike had six months' leave owing to him, we decided to go to England and decide our future. It was soon time to pack up and leave. Our car too had to be shipped to England, and this Mike also had to arrange.

Then came the day of our departure. After some tearful farewells, we were on our way to Atkinson Field and New York. We flew by British West Indian Airways with stops at Trinidad and Antigua. It was a pleasant flight by a turboprop Viscount and I remember thinking how blue the West Atlantic below us looked. As we came into Idlewild Airport the sky appeared to be full of aircraft either holding, taking off or landing.

We were met by a relative and taken to their flat. It felt very cold after the heat of BG and the next day the first thing we did was to go out and buy some warm clothes.

The husband was our chief guide during our stay. Our shopping completed and the children taken care of, we set out on our first sightseeing tour. After crossing the Triborough Bridge into Manhattan our first port of call was the Empire State Building. We were whisked up to the top by a couple of lifts and then we had the whole of New York spread out before us: Central Park, the shipyards of New Jersey, Greenwich Village and the Hudson River. On one side a new Pan Am building was under construction.

Back at street level we walked to Times Square and Broadway; then on to the United Nations Building. After lunch at a typical American restaurant we drove round Manhattan then through Greenwich Village and Wall Street, a regular rubbernecking exercise. On the following day we drove out to look over a show house on a new estate on the north side of the city; then to an amusement park where Dinah, who was with us this time, had a ride on just about everything that moved.

The platforms of Central Station were clean and tidy but rather dark and gloomy as a result of being located below ground level. Here we boarded an express train for Washington and settled ourselves in an open carriage so that we could put Tim's carrycot on the table between us. After passing under the Hudson River we were out into the daylight of New Jersey with its huge billboards and advertising signs. The journey took about three and a half hours with one intermediate stop at Baltimore, I think it was. I remember we crossed a river more or less in the middle of the town.

On arrival at Washington we were met by Ralph Rice, an old friend of the family, who took us straight away to the hotel where he worked as a manager. Here we were installed in a huge suite with everything to hand.

As we could only manage one full day in the capital, Ralph had to take us on a whirlwind tour of the city in his car. The first place we saw was the White House and a glimpse of the Capitol Building in the distance. After passing through Georgetown district we finished up with a visit to the cathedral set on a hill amidst a small woodland. In the evening, Ralph entertained us with dinner in his apartment, which he shared with his friend John.

The next morning we caught a train back to New York. Although tired after all our travelling we had to be up early the following morning as we were off on the final stage of our journey to England.

As we drove towards the Hudson River we suddenly saw the giant superstructure of the *Queen Elizabeth* in its black-and-white colours. Once past the customs we were soon being shown to our cabin with its twin beds and two cots.

It was a lovely spring day with a nip in the air; however, the sun was shining brightly so we were soon up on the top deck to see the ship set sail, and what a send-off we had. With floating fire-tenders all around sending huge jets of water up into the air and helicopters circling overhead, it was just as one always imagined it to be. Soon we were clear of the southern tip of Manhattan and past the Statue of Liberty, and then out into the open sea.

As the crossing was quite rough we hardly went up on deck again, but then one had little reason to as the ship was like a floating city with a cinema, swimming pool, games rooms and, in one of the funnels, a children's playroom where Dinah spent many happy hours.

Poor Tim developed a septic toe and was confined to his cot after a visit from the ship's doctor. The voyage was not without incident. The man in the cabin next to ours died after the second day out. He and his wife were on their way to visit their son who was working in Europe.

As I had to look after Tim I ate several of my meals in the cabin, with the result that Mike had to dine alone. As it happened he was not completely alone as he shared a table with a British Embassy official, his wife and small son, who were returning to the UK after a tour of duty in the States.

The man became quite talkative when he heard we had come from British Guiana and asked a lot of questions about the state of the country. He was rather put out when Mike said he thought Jagan was a good man, and Mike had visions of being reported to the British government as being pro-Communist. Nevertheless, he tried to explain to the official that of the two, Jagan and Burnham, he thought Jagan was trying to do more for the country and its peoples than Burnham would should he come to power.

On the third day we woke up to find ourselves in Cherbourg. We sailed again mid-morning and later that day on a cold, wet evening we went up on deck to see that we were coming up Spithead, with Cowes on the port bow. We had arrived.

We disembarked next morning, the day being wet and miserable, and boarded a train waiting in the station alongside the quay. As we pulled out we had our last glimpse of the *Queen* as she towered over the terminal building.

Once through customs we were soon on the train bound for London. As we travelled along the engine seemed to pour smoke and steam for most of the journey, obscuring our view of the countryside through which we passed. As we neared Farnborough Mike pointed out to me Cove Barracks, where he had done part of his national service.

Mike's mother was waiting for us at Waterloo and to see her grandson for the first time. From the station, we took a taxi to a garage where Mike had arranged to pick up our new car, a Riley 1.5. The formalities completed, we got everyone in together with our luggage and with the car well down on its springs made our way to Guildford. It was not an easy journey, what with a heavily laden car and strange roads, however, we eventually reached our destination and the house Mike's mother had rented for us.

The house we stayed at was on Horseshoe Lane West between Guildford and Merrow. It was quite large, detached with a big garden which tapered towards the rear. We bought tinned milk for Tim from a little corner shop just off the main road and took both him and Dinah to the health centre in Merrow for check-ups and doses of orange juice and cod liver oil. We soon settled down to a regular pattern of living.

'Dinah Minor', as 'the colonel' used to call her, was usually downstairs to have breakfast with Mike. He would have a boiled egg and she would ask for a spoonful by saying, 'Tay Daddy aig', and always referred to water as 'lawley'. Whenever we went out in the car, on our return, she knew where she was, as she would say, 'Nairly haim.'

Shortly after our arrival Mike won £25 from a premium bond, with which he bought a portable typewriter which we used to type this original script.

Eventually our Metropolitan arrived back in the country and Mike had to go up to the London docks to collect it.

When we heard from the BG government that they were not prepared to pay us a salary in sterling as Mike had requested, it meant he had to start looking for another job. Scanning the adverts in the *Daily Telegraph* he saw that Binnie's were looking for field staff for the huge Mangla Dam Project in Pakistan. He wrote off and after a short wait was called for an interview, which was conducted by the senior partner, Geoffrey Binnie.

When he returned, Mike told me that the interview went quite well; then turning to our family situation Binnie said, 'I see from your form that your wife was born in British Guiana, which is a multiracial society and I wonder whether... I mean, is she...?'

Mike could see he was embarrassed and knew what it was he was trying to say in as polite a way as possible, so he cut him short, saying, 'No she is not – her father's Australian and her mother Dutch.'

'I'm sorry to have to ask but the authorities out there are rather sensitive about some nationalities and we don't want to cause any problems at this stage.'

After a week or so Mike got a formal offer of a post as the section engineer, which he accepted. He had to get our next-door neighbour, a retired doctor, to witness his signature. It was rather funny because while we were getting this signature the doctor asked us where we had got our gardener from and whether we thought he would be prepared to do some work for him. We had to explain that our 'gardener' was Mike's brother!

During our stay, Mike's old friend Michael Page, his wife Margaret and their two sons came to visit us on Dinah's birthday. He too is a civil engineer working in Essex, and had a hand in the design of the mini-roundabout. It was over twenty years since Mike had last seen him.

We spent about three months at Merrow; then, as our tenancy expired, we moved to a house at Three Cups Corner, halfway between Heathfield and Battle. Opposite was a small chapel with a large notice at the front with the words *'The wages of sin is death'* which caught our eyes every time we looked out of the bedroom window. For our fruit and vegetables, we found a little shop on the outskirts of Hailsham. The lady who sold them always referred to them as 'His Lordship's' as they were grown on the nearby Hailsham estate.

During our stay there we visited my Guyanese friend, Eve, who was married to Norman Brooks and had a young daughter. They were on leave from the Seychelles, where Norman was working for Cable and Wireless.

After a shopping trip to Battle I discovered I had lost my engagement ring with its blue Mazaruni diamond. I was heartbroken. However, on enquiring at the police station next day we were delighted to find that it had been found and handed in. Nice to know there were honest people about.

It was then time to part with the old Metropolitan. After having some repairs to the sills, which were starting to corrode, we sold it to a dentist in Uckfield. When we handed in the Riley for shipment to Pakistan we hired a small car to enable us to get around and about.

After six months leave we bade farewell to family and friends and set off for Pakistan excited as to what was in store for us there.

St. George's Cathedral and Museum

Public Buildings, Georgetown

My Mother

Dad working on his marquetry

Kaieteur Falls

A House like ours

Stabroek Market

Key of the door

Our wedding cake

My wedding

Da, Dinah, Dad, and my Mother at Museum

Our house at Triumph

Da, Me, Mike and my Mother at Christening

Cheddi Jagan, District Engineers and wives

Party at Regent Road
Back row: Dad, Jaques, Mike, Audrey Forbes, Me, Horace Lopes and Father Crimp
Seated: Da, Marie Willems and Mum

Our Wedding

Muriel – my Nanny

My Family

2

Mangla, Pakistan

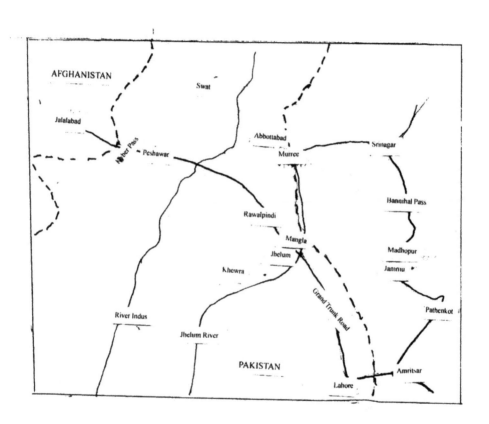

MAP 2

PAKISTAN

On the day of our flight to Pakistan in the Summer of 1962, we ordered a large taxi to take us to Heathrow as included in our luggage was Tim's pram. Mike had been rather concerned how the airline would treat such an object so one day when he was up in London he went to British Airways office and asked. On producing our tickets, he was politely informed that the ticket had been issued by Pakistan International Airlines, not British Airways.

The tickets were for first-class seats so we had a very comfortable flight in a Boeing 707. We were given the front-row seats with a cot on the floor in front of us where Tim spent most of the journey. The third seat was across the aisle next to a wealthy Pakistani businessman. He told me he owned a heavy engineering works in Lahore that we would be welcome to visit at any time.

Before we left Three Cups Corner, Mike had been told that another engineer, Vic Lawley, would be travelling out on the same plane. It was not until we were off the ground and free to move about that Mike was able to make his acquaintance. He was going out as a contracts engineer on a bachelor basis until his house was ready, when his wife would join him.

As we had no home in England and nowhere to leave our wedding presents and the children's toys, we had them all packed up including a Belling stove as we had been told that no cooker would be provided in our house when we finally moved in. This was another problem we had to solve. We knew that we would have to wait a while before our house would be finished and Mike was due to go out on a bachelor basis to start with.

Mike said, 'The best thing is for us all to go out together.'

On arrival at Karachi we had to wait several hours for our onward flight to Rawalpindi – this was not easy as the children were getting restless and very tired.

When we finally arrived at Rawalpindi we were met by a German geologist and his girlfriend from Mangla. They had some good news: we were all going to Mangla and we were going to be put up with a couple already established in a temporary home. Our hosts were John and Evelyn McKenna; she was a very devout Roman Catholic and so we started to adjust to our new lifestyle.

We had our meals together and paid for half the household bills. We had not been there very long when Tim was diagnosed as being extremely dehydrated and had to be admitted to the camp hospital. As they had no cots Mike had to get hold of a Land Rover and take our cot to the hospital where Tim was to spend the next few days. I worried all the time as to how he was getting on when I was not with him.

Mike did get some adverse comments about bringing his family out with him but when he explained our circumstances people understood. As Vic spent days away in Lahore on business we really felt we had the house to ourselves. When he was home, Vic seemed to enjoy a bit of home cooking.

Our permanent homes were being built up on a ridge overlooking Mangla and the Jhelum River known as Baral Colony. There was a main street running right through the middle of the estate. On one side were the Americans, the main contractors for the dam, and on the other side the consultant's staff of Binnie & Partners.

When our car finally arrived, we had to go down to Jhelum to collect it as all the cars had been brought up by rail from Karachi. Having the car made a big difference, as we could go up to Baral and see the house we had been allocated, and monitor the progress as it was being completed. Everybody was anxious to get settled in so that their families could come out to join them.

Mike was working on the spillway section of the dam under Bryan Cox and his deputy, Gavin McKenzie. Once their permanent office was finished life settled down to a regular pattern. One of Mike's engineers, Peter Lacey, and his wife lived in a smaller house opposite ours and they would go off to work in the morning and come home for lunch.

After a week or so, one Saturday morning, we were given the use of the section's long-wheelbase Land Rover for a trip to 'Pindi', as we called

Rawalpindi, to do some essential shopping. The driver, a tall, lean Pakistani, clad in baggy shalwar trousers, shirt and waistcoat, the traditional dress of the region, proved himself to be capable and knowledgeable even though he spoke little or no English.

The Mangla branch road joined the Grand Trunk Road four miles to the south at a village called Dina. It was some sixty miles to Pindi through undulating country and a few small villages. On the outskirts of the city were a large army camp and the residence of the president. Pindi did not strike us as being a very large town; it consisted of one- or two-storey buildings with long, straight and broad streets. The shops were not at all pretentious but quite adequate. The main hotel, Flashman's, was set in its own grounds and shaded by large trees.

Our nearest large town was Jhelum some ten miles east of Dina on the right bank of the Jhelum River. It consisted of two parts, as did most towns and cities: the town itself and the cantonment area, which housed the army. Jhelum City, to give it its full title, was a very congested place, with horse-drawn carts, rickshaws and flies. The flies were everywhere and on everything. We used to go there once a month to buy our liquor ration until the camp commissary was established. Pakistan being a Muslim country, drinking was prohibited.

There was not a lot to do in our spare time; Gavin and Arlene McKenzie started a Scottish dancing group, which we went to for a few sessions, while others started attending Urdu classes. When our permanent houses were allocated we would go up to Baral Colony to see the progress being made and tried to estimate when ours might be finished. The roads were all named after Binnie's more prestigious projects. We were to live on Dokan Avenue, named after a dam in Iraq.

Our house with three bedrooms was situated next to two larger, four-bedroom houses. There was a reasonable-sized lounge with a dining area at one end. The lounge had a large fireplace formed out of local stone with highly polished terrazzo floors. Two of the bedrooms had a common bathroom while the third had a bathroom en suite. The kitchen overlooked the back and side of the house, which was L-shaped in plan.

From the front, we had a good view over the valley to the fort at Mangla. The gardens, if you could call them that, were just open spaces with no walls or dividing fences. At the back beyond the servants' quarters was a large wall, which screened us from the cinema and swimming pool. All the rooms had air conditioners, which could be used as heaters in winter. When I say winter, the winter months were in fact warm and sunny except in the morning and evening when it was cool enough for cardigans to be worn.

Eventually our house reached a stage where it was habitable and we moved in. First, we had to see the office manager, Brigadier Meikljohn, and collect our furniture, which included a three-piece suite, dining table and chairs, beds, two cots, a cooker and a refrigerator.

Our biggest disappointment was when we came to unpack our own personal effects. They had all been handed in to a firm of packers in London who had shipped them out to Pakistan. Nearly all the china and crockery was broken. As we had no home in England we had brought all our things, mostly wedding gifts, with us and now it was all smashed to smithereens. We had been told to bring a cooker with us as none would be provided, so we had brought our Belling stove in one of our packages only to discover that a large electric cooker was to be provided. Luckily our record player and records survived the journey so we were able to fill the house with the sound of music.

Once in the house we had to engage a houseboy. In Pakistan, the old colonial system persisted. In a large house, there would be a bearer, who more or less ran the house, looking after the clothes and serving drinks and food at table; a cook, to prepare and cook the meals and a houseboy to do the washing-up and all the other odd jobs in the house. We did not want a house full of people so we looked for a young boy to do the cleaning and washing-up and a cook.

They all came, young and old, with glowing testimonials but their deeds hardly matched the words on their *chittis*, as they are called. Much later we even tried an ayah(nanny), but even she did not last more than a few days. Beside the house there was a small servants' quarters which the ayah used, and a washing line on which to dry her large baggy trousers.

We then had to get a gardener, or mali, to make something of the wilderness outside. Having cleared the area of all the builders' rubbish, he would arrive every morning with a sack of dried grass, which he proceeded to plant and then flood with water with the hope that it would grow, which in fact it did. There were no such things as lawnmowers so it all had to be cut by hand with small scythes.

Our neighbours were also busy doing much the same thing. On one side were Sheila and Keith Davies with their two children, Gareth and Marion. Keith was in charge of the design and drawing office. Our other neighbour was a Canadian family, with their four or five children. Jim, a small, well-built fellow with glasses, was a grouting specialist, and a bit of a rough diamond. His wife, Barbara, was a smallish, rather quiet woman and somewhat harassed, what with keeping Jim under control and looking after their brood of children. Their eldest, Pauline, was twelve or thirteen years old whilst the youngest, Scott, or Skat as they called him in their strong Canadian accent, was about four.

Although we had moved into our houses they were not a hundred per cent complete so we still had workmen about the place and the houses further up the road were still under construction. There was a great fuss when a painter tried to molest Pauline while Barbara was out shopping.

The main spine road in Baral divided the British homes from those of the Americans and was also the main shopping street, which included the commissary, church, petrol station, restaurant, swimming pool and bowling alley, and at the far end was the community school.

Our cars came up by rail from Karachi to Jhelum so we had to go down to the station to collect them. Although our Riley was an export model with a low compression head the petrol in Pakistan was of such an inferior grade that the engine 'pinked' like mad on the slightest incline and the only way to overcome this was to add aviation spirit to the petrol, which was available at most garages.

This was not our only problem; shortly after the car arrived we lost the petrol filler cap and stuffed a sponge into the pipe as a temporary measure. For some reason the car had been left outside the garage and on coming home for lunch in the Land Rover Mike was just in time to stop Tim topping up the tank with the hosepipe he had taken from the mali!

We almost lost our mali, who stayed with us longer than any of the houseboys. We had been out somewhere and on returning drove straight into the garage. Going in out of the strong sunlight the interior appeared to be almost pitch-black, making it almost impossible for us to see.

Suddenly Mike was aware of something directly in front of us. He braked immediately; then saw that it was the mali on his knees saying his prayers!

Talking of the garage, the driveway was constructed after we moved in. When it was set out they extended it along the front of the house to the front door so Mike asked them to continue the concrete on round and down to the entrance to form a complete loop, and so ours was one of the only houses to have such an imposing entrance. I think Mike got the idea from the house in Merrow that had the same layout.

Bryan Cox was rather surprised when our car arrived and he saw that we had the same model as his private car, which in those days was considered quite a prestigious model as far as small cars went. As a senior engineer on the project he had a company car, a Humber Snipe, for his official duties.

As the workmen finally finished their work in and around the bungalow we were able to settle down to a more regular routine. Houseboys continued to come and go but the mali stayed and persevered with the garden. To encourage him Mike found an old wheelbarrow abandoned on the site that he picked up with the duty Land Rover and gave it to some friendly workmen who welded it up, and in the end, it proved to be quite serviceable. To improve the quality of the lawn Mike had a roller made up from a length of pipe, which he had filled with concrete around a steel bar to act as an axle. A length of reinforcing rod, suitably shaped, served as a handle. The mali was delighted with his new acquisition and was much envied by his counterparts in neighbouring gardens. Much later we invested, like several others, in a lawnmower which we bought in Pindi during one of our visits.

When the drive was concreted Mike got the men to cast a slab at the side of the house on which to build a paddling pool from the bricks left lying round the garden, in which Dinah and Tim and their friends spent many happy hours. Another simple pleasure for them was going to play on the swings and roundabouts in the school playground where we often went after tea.

Rich buffalo milk was delivered to the door each day, as was a local English-language newspaper. Periodically we received a copy of the *Daily Chronicle* from our old gardener, Melville, in Beterverwagting, Guyana, with a note wishing us continued good health.

I joined an art class at the school, which got me out of the house, while Mike stayed at home with children. On Sundays Dinah attended the Sunday school run by the church.

One Sunday at the beginning of February we had our first long outing in the car. We decided to go to Murree, the old British hill station above Pindi. It turned out to be a day of mishaps and adventure. To accommodate the children, we put one of the cot mattresses on the back seat on which they could play or sleep as they wished.

We had not gone very far along the Grand Trunk Road before Dinah was sick, which meant we had to stop and clean her and the car before we could continue our journey.

After leaving Pindi, as we made for the foothills we passed round the site of the new capital, Islamabad, that was under construction. As we began the long ascent up to Murree the scenery changed as we entered large forests of deciduous trees, which as we reached the higher altitudes changed to mainly conifers. We were beginning to enjoy the dramatic views of the plain below when the engine began to splutter and then finally died on us. Mike soon diagnosed the problem – we had run out of petrol! We were stuck in what appeared to be the middle of nowhere and there was little or no traffic on the road. Whatever were we going to do? The children began to get fretful and I blamed Mike, quite rightly, for his oversight. Fortunately, a bus came growling up the hill and when the driver saw we were in some kind of trouble he pulled in to the side and asked if he could help.

Mike explained our predicament and at once he offered to bring us a can of petrol on his return journey. During our enforced stop we ate our lunch, which, fortunately, we had brought with us.

Before long our bus driver friend was back with the petrol as promised, and after paying and thanking him for his kindness we were soon on our way again. We discovered we had stopped just short of Murree so we had not lost much time.

The township appeared to consist of one long main street dominated by a very English-looking church. Just beyond the town we found, to everyone's delight, that the ground was covered with snow. This was the first snow I had ever seen and it seemed odd that I should have travelled some nine thousand miles to see this phenomenon. While the children and I were revelling in this new plaything, Mike discovered some horse chestnuts, which we took back to Mangla and managed to get one of them to germinate, so we planted it in the garden.

Although working in a Muslim country we observed Saturday afternoon and Sunday as our weekend. Sundays were usually spent at home but were not always as quiet as one might expect. One Sunday I was sitting reading the paper when suddenly I had a jolt as though someone had bumped into my chair, but I knew that Mike and the children were at the other end of the room. On hearing a cry from one of the children and turning around, I noticed that the ceiling light was swinging to and fro although no one had been near it. We then realised that we had just experienced our first earth tremor.

As our houses were all electric, should the power go off we were without all essential services. The power did occasionally go off for short periods and we learned to live with it, however one Sunday it went off early in the morning and by lunchtime was still off. What were we going to do about lunch? Sitting in the lounge pondering over the problem Mike suddenly hit on the idea of using the large ornamental fireplace. Collecting a few bricks and some wood, we soon had a fire going and so we could have a hot meal as usual.

Shortly after our visit to Murree, Mike was laid up in bed with a bug he must have picked up and even had a visit from Dr Dhody, one of the project's medical team. We also had a visit from Doris Cox when she heard that one of Bryan's 'boys' was off work. When Mike recovered and Bryan was away from Mangla for a day or so, we invited Doris over to dinner.

As was usual on such occasions, small talk generally turned to people working on the site. Doris was someone who was rather conscious of her social position in the Binnie hierarchy.

'You know that young geologist, Peter Fookes? Well, I had to get Bryan to speak to him when I discovered that he was calling Bryan by his first name in the office.'

The Muslim month of fasting, Ramadan, started in the last week of January 1963. At the end of Ramadan there was the festival of Eid ul-

Fitr, which lasted several days, so we took the opportunity to see a little more of the country. The sighting of the new moon signals the end of Ramadan.

For this break we drove west to beyond Pindi towards Peshawar; then turned off northwards to the town of Abbottabad, which was a garrison town. Again, we put a mattress in the back of the car for Dinah and Tim. On the floor at the back of the car we carried tins of food for them as we had learned that children were very susceptible to stomach upsets when they ate local food.

We found it quite cold as we climbed into the foothills of the mountain range on which Murree stands, and as a result we had to have the stove in our room lit during the evening. The following day we drove northwards up the lower part of the Kagan Pass that was quite impressive with the mountainsides rising steeply on either side of the narrow valley. After our midday lunch, we made our way back to Mangla.

It was about this time that Bryan Cox told Mike that he was to stop his routine duties and take charge of the drilling and grouting operation that would be supervised by our neighbour, Jim. Mike explained to me that where the main dam joined the west side of the valley and where the main spillway was located, they had to ensure that the ground was completely impervious and to make sure this was so they had to drill a series of holes and check the permeability of the ground by means of water tests.

This was something quite new to Mike and he was glad of the opportunity to have something new to deal with, but he had not allowed for the unpredictable Jim. He was like several we have met since. He was a very practical fellow, liked to call a spade a spade, but had a great lack of tact. He was at war with the establishment. He said he had been promised 'this and that' when interviewed for the job but to date none of them had been fulfilled, with the result that he was always on the point of resigning. He would produce a letter he said he was going to send to the Chief Resident Engineer(CRE), but when Mike read it he found it was full of expletives and pointed out to him that sending such a letter would not help him and offered to rewrite the letter with more suitable phrases.

The drilling and water testing of the embankment was quite a long and laborious job and involved a lot of work outside normal hours, but it was very pleasant in the cool of the evening, Mike told me, to sit up there watching the stars and hearing the howl of the hyenas in the hills further up the valley.

From the test results, it became apparent that they would have to do some grouting to reduce the permeability, so Jim had to set to and come up with some grouts that might be used. He was particularly keen to use something he called 'One-Shot MonoSol' but try as he did, he could not get it to work. From what Mike had seen and read he was sure it was something to do with temperature, but he could not get Jim to agree so in the end, one afternoon, on his return to the laboratory after lunch Mike took some ice with him in a flask and got Jim to do the experiment once again, but this time with the materials suitably cooled and, as Mike predicted, it worked.

The workmen who were assigned to the drilling and grouting operations, on hearing Jim's eternal cry of being about to resign, with an eye to the future, had typed out the most glowing reference letters saying, *to whom it may concern*, that they had carried out the work almost single-handed under the expert guidance of Mr Jim, which they had the temerity to ask Jim to sign, and in his present mood he was quite happy to do.

Because of the large volumes of concrete, over one million cubic metres, to be placed in the spillway, Cox managed to get approval for two of his inspectors from his previous job, the Val-d'Isère Dam on Jersey, to come to Mangla, and so we were joined by Arthur Martin and Ted Payne and their wives. Arthur was a quiet, methodical fellow while Ted was more outgoing, but then he was much younger than Arthur. I became quite friendly with Arthur's wife, whom we always knew as Mrs Martin. We would go to the cinema and other social events while Mike stayed at home with Dinah and Tim.

In March, Mike was chosen to go with Chris Bartlett, the deputy resident engineer on the tunnels section, to Lahore to attend a talk given by the President of Pakistan, Ayub Khan. They had to leave at dawn to arrive in time for the meeting, however the journey was very pleasant as they were chauffeur-driven in one of the Humbers. When the meeting was over they went to Chezans Restaurant on the Mall for lunch. Before setting off for home they visited a nursery where they bought some roses for our two gardens.

To celebrate Dinah's third birthday, we had a large party, and to protect our guests from the heat of the sun we hired some awnings to erect over the table and chairs. We also arranged for a donkey to be on hand to give all the children rides, which proved to be very popular, and thus a great success.

In July we had another break. Cox had given Mike a few days off to make up for all the extra hours he had worked on the drilling and grouting operation. We spent the time in the mountains above Murree at a small hotel in Nathia Gali that stood at a height of over eight thousand feet. To get there we had to drive over a pass of some ten thousand feet and only just made it with the engine 'pinking' away like mad. The hotel was constructed of timber and consisted of a series of terrace-like chalets. There were some glorious views all round and still quite a bit of snow could be seen, but was not close enough for the children to play in it.

I was not long in making friends with a Mrs Waheed, a well-educated Pakistani, also on holiday at the hotel with her beautiful granddaughters. She came with us in the car when we went to a village, Kala Bagh, somewhere north of Nathia Gali, and introduced us to some excellent curry and other local delicacies.

When we came to return home, Mike saw from the map that if we continued beyond Kala Bagh we could cross to Abbottabad where we had been earlier in the year and return that way. What the map did not indicate was the state of the road – it was after Kala Bagh that the surface deteriorated to that of a cart track and we had to reduce our speed to almost a crawl. It was as we were descending rapidly to a river crossing that we almost skidded over the edge of a precipice when Mike slammed on the brake and the wheels locked.

Once across the river the road improved, then, just as we were approaching Abbottabad, we were stopped by a line of traffic that had formed ahead of us due to a tree that had fallen across the road. By this time, it was mid-afternoon and we still had a long way to go, and it was impossible to return by the way we had just come. Fortunately, a route was made round the obstruction and we were able to continue our journey.

In September we had another break, this time going up the Swat Valley. To get there we had quite a long drive of some 230 miles, first through Pindi; then on along the Grand Trunk Road to Nowshera where we turned off to the north to cross over the Pass of Malakand and then into Swat, where we stayed at the Swat Hotel.

Although it was bright and sunny the air felt much fresher and cleaner than in Mangla. The principal town, Saidu Sharif, was not large and consisted of mainly single- or two-storey buildings. It was in some ways partially autonomous, the day-to-day administration being under the control of the Wāli of Swat. We paid a visit to his summer residence outside the township where he had some wonderful garden furniture carved out of what looked like white marble.

Most of the men in the valley wore woollen hats that were typical for the district. Then there was another type that was in effect a brimless hat, decorated with flower motifs. We bought several of each as souvenirs.

In the nearby village of Mingora there were some ancient ruins dating back two thousand years, I believe, which we visited, passing on the way an open tent where young girls were weaving a long, narrow carpet.

On our second day there we took a packed lunch from the hotel and drove up the valley for some sixty miles. The scenery was fantastic; a rushing mountain river of ice-cold water dominated the valley, growing narrower as we drove northwards. At the lower end the fields were under cultivation and buffalo roamed at will over road and field alike, but as the day passed the scenery became more barren as the valley sides closed in, and rising so steeply and to such heights that it was difficult to see their peaks, which were covered with snow. There was a scattering of habitation along the road but conditions must have been very harsh in winter. We turned around where the road crossed a very rickety timber suspension bridge that I was rather fearful of, and was glad when we were back on terra firma again.

At the Swat Hotel, we met another British couple, Doug and Joyce Cammack, and their three children. He worked for ICI (Imperial Chemical Industries) in England, but was currently in Pakistan at a place called Khewra, south-east of Pindi where the company operated a salt mine. During our stay, we became well acquainted and they invited us to visit them a couple of weeks later, which we accepted.

To get to Khewra we drove as though going to Pindi, but after some thirty miles from Dina we turned off to the south, driving a further sixty-five miles through desolate hill country until we came to Khewra, which was like an oasis in the desert. The factory complex dominated the town that was served by a branch railway line over which the trains were hauled by steam locomotives.

The Cammacks occupied a very nice house built in the old colonial style with a large swimming pool in the grounds, which they shared with Doug's young assistant, Armstrong, and his wife.

A week after our return from Khewra the Bhattacharyas arrived on our doorstep. Since leaving BG we had kept in touch with them, and when they heard we were in Pakistan, wrote saying they were planning to visit some relatives there and would like to look us up if it was convenient. We rather liked them so had no hesitation in inviting them.

After a day showing them the site and the surrounding area we all went off to Pindi in our car – quite how we all got in I am not sure. On our arrival there, we took a room at Flashman's where I stayed with Dinah, Tim and the Bhattacharyas' daughter while Mike took our guests up to Murree. On our return, we all went for a ride round the town in a tonga (a horse and trap) before setting off back to Mangla. The following day we bid farewell to our guests at an airstrip that we had previously been unaware of, just outside Mangla.

In early November a Dostian Fair was held in the shopping area car park. There were stalls selling fruit, home-made cakes, camel seats and all the other usual fare. The main attraction, however, was the donkey and camel rides. After much persuasion, Mike tried a ride on the latter, a not very friendly-looking beast. Once in the seat the painful operation of getting up began.

First the animal rises onto its front knees, which throws one back in the seat and sets one grasping for the pommel at the front; the next minute one is being hurled forward as the beast rises onto its hind legs; then one comes to an even keel as he finally straightens himself up.

The plod around the car park was not very comfortable as one sways from side to side, but glad that there are other forms of transportation in the world. Coming down to earth again was as horrendous as the take-off. The day was rounded off with a fireworks display that was quite spectacular.

Then came what was, I think, the highlight of our stay in Pakistan. For the past year, our friends and neighbours had been going off to Kashmir for their ten days' local leave, and with the tales they brought back of the beautiful scenery and wonderful food we realised that for us too, this was a 'must'.

Due to the pressure of work Mike was unable to get away during the summer months, and also, we felt it would be too much travelling in the heat, especially for the children, so we decided to wait until the 'fall', as the Americans on site called it, when we knew the weather would be better for travelling and Mike was sure his leave would be approved.

To look at the map one would think that to go from Mangla to Srinagar would be a fairly simple matter, as it is only ninety-five miles as the crow flies, but since the dispute with India over the state of Kashmir, the direct route from Pindi to Srinagar is blocked by the United Nations troops manning the ceasefire line some sixty miles beyond Pindi. So the only way to reach Kashmir was to drive to Amritsar in India and then travel northwards from there, making the journey twice as long as it really needed to be.

But for this dispute, the journey would have been very simple: one would simply put the luggage in the car and drive off, but after a few enquiries from various friends who had already made the trip, we discovered there was a two-month 'red tape' battle to be fought first to get the necessary documents to get the car and ourselves out of Pakistan and into India.

A visit to the Muslim Commercial Bank in Mangla to purchase travellers' cheques was the next priority. This was quite a straight forward operation, the only peculiarity being that one had to pay for them with a cheque from a British bank.

About a week before we were due to leave we sat down one evening and drew up a list of all the things we would need to take with us, and from the size of the list we produced it looked as though we would need a bus rather than a small four-seater car. We also got three suitcases out which we put in the spare room so we could pack them as we collected the various items together.

So, on Tuesday 12th November Mike left work and hurried home to tackle the hundred and one jobs there were to do before the morning. After a quick cup of tea, it was out into the garage to check the car over, top up the battery, radiator, master cylinders, etc. and then a trip to the petrol station to fill up with some good, rich petrol.

Having checked the car over and had supper, the children were put to bed so we could do the final packing. The dining table was covered with our travel documents so Mike could check them in detail to ensure none would be left behind. We finally got to bed just before midnight. Considering the excitement, we all slept well but it was a short rest as we had said we would get up no later than half past five as there was still a lot to be done before we could leave.

The biggest job of all was to load up the car. On the floor at the back was a holdall full of tinned food, our basic rations for the children and our midday meal if there was nowhere suitable en route. On top of this we put a cot mattress as we had done on previous trips. On the roof rack were two cases and a collapsible cot for Tim. The boot was filled to capacity with two more cases, drinking water, petrol cans, rope and anything else we had left out of the cases. And so, at nine o'clock, after a final check round the house, the 'house boy' was paid with a promise of 'holiday with pay' if he was back at the bungalow on the 24th November and stayed with us to the end of the month.

It was an ideal day for travelling, bright and sunny, but not too hot. Dinah was quite excited as she realised that today was something special, and kept saying, 'We're going on our holidays, we're going on our holidays', which to her meant spending at least one night away from home.

At Jhelum we crossed the river, which at this point is about a mile wide but at this time of year was almost dry. The only disadvantage with the bridge over it was that it was only wide enough for one-way single-line traffic, and of course as luck would have it we had to wait a quarter of an hour before we had the right of way. Once across the river the road was almost dead straight across the plains to Lahore, except for a low range just after the river crossing. The road is tree-lined all the way and the countryside is devoted to the cultivation of wheat and sugar cane.

Between Gujarat and Wazirabad we crossed over the Chenab River that we were to see later on our travels. Gujranwala was the only large town we passed through and fortunately there was little traffic about, so we passed through fairly quickly and were in Lahore just after midday.

After crossing the River Ravi, in which we noticed a lot of dead turtles on the sandbanks, we were soon in the city, which as one approaches is dominated by the huge Badshahi Mosque, said to be one of the largest in the world. We drove up the Mall, past Kim's Gun (featured in Rudyard Kipling's story) outside the Punjab University, and then we were in the heart of the city. The Mall is found in most cities of Pakistan, and is the equivalent of the High Street in British towns, a wide road flanked with tall, well-built structures, studded with traffic lights, double-decker buses and all the trimmings of a modern city.

Here we stopped to eat at Chezans, as we had no idea when we would get another meal. After a satisfying lunch, we filled up with petrol and moved on. From now on it was all new ground, which meant frequent stops to ask the way until finally at a quarter to three we reached the Customs House at Wagah, a palatial building on the right-hand side of the road. The great moment was before us: would they ask for our income tax clearance form or not? All we could do was to keep our fingers crossed and trust to luck. I stayed in the car while Mike went into the office. The customs officer sat at a table at the far end of the room, the walls of which were lined with easy chairs. It seemed we were the only customers.

He carefully went through all the car papers, entered all the details in a large ledger and then wrote a few words on a scrap of paper, which he handed to Mike together with the other papers, saying, 'Give this to the man at the gate.' Mike must have hesitated, because he added, 'That's all, you may proceed.' So, out Mike dashed before he thought to ask for the income tax clearance form. We drove off and back onto the road and had only gone a short distance when we were stopped and told to report to a police officer sitting at a table under a tree. Apparently, all he wished to do was to stamp our passports and copy out all their details into a large ledger.

This formality completed, we were ready to leave Pakistan. Back in the car we drove some fifty yards to the actual frontier, guarded by a Sutlej

Ranger of Pakistan and a bearded, turbaned Sikh soldier of India. They both scanned our passports, handed them back and waved us on. We drove on and into the courtyard of the Indian Customs House, more or less a replica of the one we had just left.

Here the procedure was almost a repeat performance, although here they asked to see our camera, for which they gave us a receipt which we had to present on our return. Both sides were interested to know what currency we had and were satisfied when Mike said that we had only travellers' cheques. The customs officer, on completing the documentation on the car, said he would like to see the engine number on the vehicle. When we got outside he was so fascinated with the car (as apparently, he had never seen a Riley before) that he forgot all about his earlier request to see the engine number.

We were now through with officialdom and ready for the road and India. The first thing we had to do was to advance our watches by half an hour, which made it just after four o'clock. We had eighteen miles to cover to reach Amritsar. The countryside looked much the same as before; the most noticeable thing was the number of cycle rickshaws, something not seen in Pakistan.

Our immediate task was to cash some travellers' cheques as we were without Indian rupees and without money we could do very little. Mike had been told it was possible to do an exchange at Amritsar railway station so that was our first port of call.

With money in our pockets we set off for the Government Rest House at Madhopur, sixty miles further along the road towards Srinagar. It was a long sixty miles driven mostly in the dark and we finally reached our destination at half past seven, having driven 238 miles since leaving Mangla.

The Rest House was very comfortable, clean and modern. After a supper of omelettes we all tumbled into bed for a well-earned rest. We all slept well considering our strange surroundings. Dinah and Tim were awake at their usual time of seven o'clock. I was up even before them as I was anxious to see what sort of place we were in, having arrived in the dark.

The building, which was typical of its kind, was a single-storey structure, surrounded by a wide verandah, broken by large brick columns on the perimeter that supported the flat roof. This particular Rest House was set back from the road in well-laid-out gardens, which contained a badminton court and some large relief models of the area indicating irrigation projects.

After breakfast, we loaded up the car and made arrangements to stay here again on our return. The day was dull but fine and by nine o'clock we were on our way.

First, we crossed the river by an old multi-span steel bridge, the new one still being under construction. Just beyond this we came to a checkpoint where we had to produce our passports and pay a road toll to enter Jammu and Kashmir. Leaving this place, we drove along a good, straight road over undulating country for sixty miles to Jammu. The road undulated as watercourses were crossed by fords; luckily it was the dry season, as on one such ford a notice stated that once the water reached a certain level the road was unusable.

Arriving in Jammu we filled up with petrol and then started climbing into the foothills, the road becoming a series of hairpin bends that reduced our speed considerably. After about ten miles we were stopped at another toll gate, and immediately after this we drove into a 150-yard-long unlined tunnel, the happy hunting ground for hundreds of bats. As might be imagined the windows were soon tightly shut. We emerged into another valley where the road was just as tortuous. We kept the car topped up with petrol at almost every pump we came to as from then on they would be few and far between.

Just as we were finishing lunch it started to drizzle, which it continued to do for the next six hours. We were now climbing quite rapidly and soon reached the pine forests. At an altitude of 7,500 feet we started the long descent into the Chenab Valley, and after about an hour and a half we reached the river itself, which we crossed by means of a long and narrow suspension bridge. The road here was studded with small hamlets and the hillsides formed terraces on which some form of cultivation was attempted. What hindered our progress greatly was the fact that the Public Works Department was constructing about fifty new culverts under the road, and to do this they tore up the road and constructed a temporary diversion that was usually very rough and if one was not careful could damage the sump of the car.

Shortly after leaving Ramba, where we had crossed a river, we had a narrow escape. After a particularly rough stretch of road, which was mostly underwater, we heard a crash and then the next thing we knew was that the roof rack, complete with contents, was sliding off the roof onto the bonnet and then down onto the road. How it missed the windscreen I don't know; the only damage was a small scratch on the bonnet. We were sure the rain and rough road had worked the fixings loose. After about a quarter of an hour we were on our way again, climbing out of the Chenab Valley. The rain was now falling quite heavily and daylight was failing. The road in places was overhung by the cliff face of the mountainside, and several waterfalls disgorged onto the road together with any stones or rocks that had become dislodged on the hillside above, so from now on Mike had to keep his eyes glued to the road.

The bulk of the traffic on this stretch of the road consisted of army trucks, buses and heavy goods lorries, the latter being the most common. They were usually open trays with high, close-boarded sides mounted on a Bedford or Mercedes-Benz chassis and, invariably, on the tailboard were the words *horn please* or *use dipper at night*, an almost courteous instruction in the best manner to overtake. These instructions need not always be adhered to but usually had to be resorted to in the end.

On the back of nearly every truck there was a man, or perhaps he should be referred to as a porter, and his comfort was dictated by the nature of the goods being carried. He may be sharing the back with a load of blankets or a herd of buffalo. One of his duties appeared to be assisting cars and other road users to overtake his truck. Once he had woken up, sometimes quite literally, to the fact that you wished to pass, he made his way to the tail of the truck where he pushed a button that rang a bell in the driver's cab. One was then at the mercy of the driver, who on this stretch was usually a bearded Sikh. He would take a look in his mirror to see who it was that wished to overtake him, and if he liked the look of you would make a genuine effort to give you room to pass.

After another hour's driving we came to our last check post. These posts, as well as being toll houses, were also checkpoints as one was not to exceed a given speed and over the first stretch we were actually half an hour ahead of schedule, but our roof rack incident balanced things out for us.

Just before this last checkpoint we saw a petrol pump and decided to stop and fill up as we did not want to run out on a nasty wet night such as we were experiencing. Anyway, after sitting by the pump for ten minutes and endless blowing on the horn, all of which was to no avail, we decided that the rain was too much for the pump attendant and we were forced to move on, hoping there would be another pump shortly.

Another hour's driving brought us to the summit and we entered the mile-long Bannihal Tunnel, which was one-way, single-line working. Fortunately, the traffic control signal was showing green so we were able to drive straight on. The tunnel was well lit and in places lined with brick and concrete; otherwise we were driving through natural rock. As we emerged we entered the Vale of Kashmir.

Far below us on the right-hand side were the lights of a village, and snaking down to them we could see the pinpricks of light from the headlights of trucks on the road. By now, the rain was confined to a fine drizzle, but we appeared to have caught up with the tail end of a large convoy of lorries, and the road was too narrow and tortuous to do any 'dipper by night' overtaking. Fortunately, the convoy was moving fairly fast and we soon reached the village of Qasi Gund. Here the road on either side was lined with lorries and traffic was reduced to moving at a snail's pace until it stopped altogether. Despite repeated blasts on the horn nothing moved, and neither way could we move as we were hemmed in on all sides. Finally, Mike got out and walked ahead to see the cause of the hold-up. There appeared to be an endless line of trucks ahead of us and most of the drivers had deserted their cabs for a hot cup of chai from the teashops in the village.

After half an hour, the truck in front of us started to move and then we were off ourselves. From what we could see, due to the trucks parking on both sides of the road, the road had been reduced to the width of a single line of traffic with the result that two trucks had met head on and neither would give way to the other. It was now eight o'clock and we still had some thirty miles to cover to reach Srinagar. However, the road was clear and the rain had stopped so we were able to make up some of the time lost. The road, from what we could see by the car headlights, was fairly straight and lined on either side with tall poplars, very similar to the roads in Northern France. On reaching the brow of a low hill we saw the lights of Srinagar reflected in the lake.

Most of our friends who had visited Kashmir had stayed on houseboats on the various lakes around Srinagar, however with the cooler weather and two small children, we felt something on terra firma would be more appropriate for us. As we would be here for only a few days we decided to stay at the Oberoi Palace, so as we entered the outskirts of the town we stopped and asked a cyclist standing by the roadside for directions to the hotel. His directions were quite simple and we felt that in a very short while we should be eating a good meal at the best hotel in Kashmir.

The road took us along the lakeside, which had numerous houseboats moored to its bank, while on the pavement were several characters who started to wave to us as we passed, obviously proprietors seeking our custom. At last we saw a notice saying, *Oberoi Palace fifty yards ahead*, so we slowed down and then saw the entrance on the right-hand side of the road. However, as we swung into the entrance there was a large notice on one of the gateposts saying, *Closed for the winter*. What a blow. Fortunately, Mike knew there was another hotel in the town that was supposed to be 'second best', so we decided to turn back and try our luck there.

We turned around and headed back to town. As we reached the promenade along the lakeside we saw a tonga ahead with a man waving to us. As the tonga's path was rather erratic Mike had to slow down, and before we knew what was happening the man jumped down from the tonga and came running to the side of the car. Then other characters started to come over from the pavement. All we could do was to stop, as we were afraid we might run someone over.

It transpired we had about half a dozen owners of houseboats and their minions around us, all trying to win our custom. It was almost impossible to convince them that we wanted to stay at a hotel as they went on to extol the virtues of their houseboats. The children were now waking up in the back of the car and starting to cry, as they, like us, were tired and hungry. Finally, one man, who must have realised we were adamant, said he would take us to a hotel if we followed his tonga, so feeling this was the best way to resolve the matter, we agreed and shortly afterwards we arrived at the hotel Mike had intended to go to once he saw the Oberoi

Palace was closed, and that's how we came to spend three days at Nedou's Hotel.

The main building of the hotel was a long, rectangular two-storey structure standing well back from the road. Between the road and the main block was a large lawn shaded with huge trees. Two two-storey blocks that contained the private suites occupied the other two sides. Our rooms were on the ground floor of one of these blocks. From the driveway one climbed four or five steps onto a long verandah. Each suite led directly off this verandah. The door opened onto a living room, behind which was a large bedroom with en suite bathroom.

So, we had finally arrived in Srinagar, having driven a total distance of 470 miles from Mangla. As we were feeling cold we had a fire lit in both the lounge and bedroom and before long we were tucking into a large meal before the fire. During the night we were glad of the blankets on the bed, as it was quite cold.

We were somewhat disappointed when we woke up next morning as it was a cold, dull day and was just starting to drizzle.

As we went over to the dining room for breakfast we were besieged by a horde of men who wanted to act as guides, sell us shawls, show us houseboats, clean the car etc. In fact, the one thing that marred our visit were these people who pestered us in this way everywhere we went.

The dining room was a huge, bleak room and the only other occupants beside ourselves were an Australian on holiday from New Delhi and a couple of very English-looking widows. The manager of the hotel, we discovered, was an Englishman born in Lahore, who hoped shortly to visit the city of his birth.

On returning to our room we were again accosted by a horde of people, the principal characters we came to know as Samad Shah, Wali Mohamed, Salarma Doona and the car cleaner. Samad Shah wished to sell us some shawls and show us his houseboat while Wali Mohamed wanted us to visit his wood-carving factory and houseboat. Salarma Doona had come, we think, to protect his good name as nearly everybody who had come to Srinagar from Mangla had stayed on one of his houseboats and he probably felt that there must be something radically wrong that we should wish to stay in a hotel. We were sure that the cyclist whom we had asked the way the previous night had done some fast riding round after we had driven off, in the hope of earning himself some commission, knowing full well that the hotel he had just directed us to was closed, hence all our visitors.

Srinagar is some five thousand feet above sea level and lies at the southern end of Dal Lake, nestling at the foot of the mountains. A large fort built on the top of a rocky outcrop dominates the town, straddling the River Jhelum and various waterways. The main street is wide and bright and full of activity. One thing that really impressed us was the clean-looking meat hanging in the butchers' windows; perhaps it was the 'off-fly' season that did it. As most of the inhabitants are Muslims one was again conscious of the predominance of men and the women in purdah.

As the day was dull and wet we stayed in our room for most of the day and rested after our travels and tried to dry our laundry in front of the fire. Luckily Saturday dawned bright and clear and we were able to see the Vale of Kashmir in its true glory. Wali Mohamed and Samad Shah were still hanging around hoping for a sale so we arranged to meet the former at ten o'clock and the latter at half past two.

First, we drove along the lakeside to see if we could take a few photographs while the weather was fine. The warm sun appeared to have had the desired effect of instilling some life into the populace, as there was renewed activity on the houseboats and the odd punt, or shikara, as they are called, made its way across the lake. We went past the Oberoi Palace and up the hillside to what is called Milk Colony, where some very attractive tourist bungalows were under construction. We then returned to the hotel where Wali Mohamed was waiting to take us to his factory. He wanted us to go in his car but we preferred to follow in our own car, so we were quite free to leave when we wished.

The factory was an old stone-built warehouse on the banks of the Jhelum. We entered through a narrow doorway and then up an equally narrow, winding wooden staircase onto the second floor where he had a remarkable display of woodwork. It was a bit of a nightmare with two small children who wanted to touch everything but it was a place one could not leave without purchasing a few souvenirs. On the first floor, shawls and carpets were on display and we couldn't resist a carpet with animals of the jungle woven into the design.

Promptly at half past two Samad Shah was knocking at the door.

As this was our last afternoon we asked him to show us the sights of Srinagar. So once again we set off along the lakeside to see the Shalimar and Nisbet Gardens that were really at their best in their autumnal hues. As we left, each of the children was given a posy of chrysanthemums by the chowkidar (keeper) of the gardens.

Mr Shah was dying to show us his houseboat, so we agreed to go provided it was not too much out of the way. One entered by means of a narrow gangplank into a small hallway. Leading left was a passage to the two bedrooms, each with two single beds and a bathroom with shower and WC. Directly to the right of the hallway was the dining room, and beyond that a well-furnished lounge with large French windows. At the time we were there the sun had already set and it was beginning to grow cold, so the view and surroundings were not as attractive as they would be in summer. On leaving we noticed a large boiler perched on the stern, obviously the provider of hot water for the bathroom. As it was now getting late we hurried on to Mr Shah's shop in town to see his selection of Kashmiri silks.

As luck would have it both Mr Shah and Mr Mohamed arrived together whilst we were having dinner with their respective wares we had purchased from them during the day. We had hoped to avoid this clash because, as they both sold the same merchandise, they were probably jealous of each other. Wali Mohamed, once he had shown us the various items we had bought from him, got his assistant to wrap each carefully in paper and then sew them up in one compact canvas bag.

Now that we had all our purchases we could start to pack for an early start in the morning. As in all hotels the staff always know when the guests are leaving so that they can be on hand to collect whatever baksheesh is being offered. We decided that to help us with an early start we would pay the bill the previous evening and order breakfast to be brought to our room.

Sunday dawned bright and clear. Breakfast came promptly and the remainder of the packing was soon done and we were ready for the road by nine o'clock. The manager himself brought the packed lunches over together with a bar of chocolate each for Dinah and Tim and wished us 'bon voyage'. Although we avoided most of the hotel staff, our room-bearer still managed to have a sweeper, chowkidar and foreman lined up by the car when we finally came to leave. Mike was, however, prepared for this and had sufficient small change ready.

As we drove out of Srinagar we appeared to be surrounded by snow-capped mountains, a most beautiful sight. The road along which we were driving was, as we had thought it to be on the night of our arrival, lined with some of the tallest poplar trees we had yet seen. The entrance to the Bannihal Tunnel was just above the snow line, and needless to say we had to stop and let the children get out and sample it. After a final look back at the Vale of Kashmir, we got back into the car and drove off into the gloom of the tunnel.

Shortly after crossing the Chenab River we stopped for lunch. It would seem from the amount of lumber in the river that it was used as a means of transporting timber to the sawmills. Having finished lunch, we began the ascent over the watershed. Once we reached the altitude of the conifers, we stopped to collect some pine cones, some of the largest we had yet come across, to use as decorations at Christmas.

The rest of the journey to the Rest House at Madhopur was uneventful and even though the weather was fine we did not arrive until eight o'clock. We were aware when we booked for our return visit that we would be in another building as the previous one was fully booked for that date, so knowing this we drove straight to the other building as we arrived. The staff in charge who greeted us spoke very little English and seemed unaware that we were to stay there that night. Mike took the man who had more knowledge of English to the Rest House of our previous visit to find out what arrangements had been made.

When we got there, we found the place in complete turmoil as it was being redecorated from top to bottom. We gathered the governor of the province was to make a tour of inspection and was going to use the Rest House as his base. It was fairly obvious that they did not really want us, but here we intended to stay. We finally managed to get some beds made up but the only sustenance they could raise was a pot of tea so we had to fall back on what we were carrying with us.

Despite the problems we spent a comfortable night and were packed up and ready to leave by eight o'clock next morning, except for breakfast. The previous night we were told breakfast would be served in the Rest House amidst the painting and decorating, but when we got over there they had changed their minds and suggested we went to the railway station at Pathankot.

Once again fortune favoured us with a bright and sunny day, so the thought of a delayed breakfast did not worry us unduly. Pathankot was only twenty miles away and we were there by nine o'clock. After a good breakfast of boiled eggs, toast, marmalade and coffee at the station we were soon off on the road to Delhi.

Just after leaving the station we had a moment of panic when Mike stopped for petrol and thought he had lost the travellers' cheques, but after a quick search he found he had put them in a different case. Except for the large towns of Jullundur, Ludhiana and Ambala, through which we literally crawled at a snail's pace amidst buffalo carts, buffaloes, rickshaws, tongas, bicycles and the general populace, we could maintain an average speed of fifty-five miles an hour. The tree-lined road was generally straight and in good condition, and on the whole, fairly free of traffic.

We covered the last seventy miles to Delhi in the dark, not that the flat countryside had been very interesting apart from the towns and the odd river we crossed. The Grand Trunk Road brings one into Delhi and not New Delhi. And had we known this earlier we should probably not have had the experience we did.

Unfortunately, we had no street guide and drove on assuming that one passed from the outskirts to the suburbs and so to the city centre. Well, we reached the outskirts and what we thought were the suburbs, then reached some huge gate structure which we took to be the threshold of the city because beyond were brightly lit shops and a general hive of activity.

The only hotels we knew of by name were the Asoka, which was considered one of the best, and the Airlines, in which a bachelor from Mangla had stayed and which therefore was a possibility. It was now getting late and we were very hungry so we stopped to ask where we were and how to get to one of 'our hotels'. The Asoka, we were told, was six miles away but the Airlines was quite close and comfortable, so the Airlines it would have to be.

We soon found it because it had its name on the facade of the building in neon lights. It stood directly on the road opposite a main line marshalling yard. A shop on the corner was blaring forth Indian music.

It was hardly a district for an airlines hotel, if indeed it did have anything to do with air travel. Railway Hotel would have been more appropriate. Mike parked the car and inspected the place before committing himself.

He came back to tell me he had been shown a long, narrow bedsitter, air-conditioned with a bathroom en suite. It was passable and we really felt too tired to set off and look for something else that might be five or six miles away. On enquiring about a garage, they said there was none but the car would be all right on the road as they had a night watchman. I was not too happy with the place, and the children too sensed that it did not give them the freedom to which they were accustomed 'on holiday'.

The dining room was just across the courtyard; however, Tim and I were too tired to face a formal meal and would have something sent to the room, so Dinah and Mike went for supper on their own. The dining room was deserted except for an Indian Army officer and his wife and one or two other nondescript gentlemen. The room was decorated for Christmas and a radio was churning out music, which to Western ears was very harsh. Mike said afterwards that he decided on the European menu and afterwards wished he hadn't. The potatoes were cold, the carrots out of a tin and the lamb out of the fridge, where it was probably kept until it was all used up. During the meal, two men came in and sat down at an adjacent table. They ordered curry that was quickly served. At the sight of the rice, Dinah decided she too would like some rice, which, when served, she tucked into with great gusto.

We went to sleep with the firm intention of moving out first thing in the morning. Between the road and the railway was a builder's yard, in which we spotted some monkeys playing. Dinah and Tim were fascinated and we had the greatest difficulty to get them to leave the window.

The receptionist was rather surprised that we were leaving so soon. We said we had changed our plans and had decided to go straight on to Agra. When we discovered we were very close to Delhi railway station Mike went over there in the hope of picking up a street map of the city. The bookstall there had no such map, but he learned the way to New Delhi, as by now he was a little disappointed with Old Delhi.

We soon found ourselves in Connaught Circus, the very hub of New Delhi, and there before us was the BOAC (British Overseas Airways Corporation) office. They were supposed 'to take good care of you' when flying, so perhaps they could help us earthbound travellers now, even though we were not even potential customers. A short while later Mike came back with a gaily-coloured street plan on which were marked all the principal buildings and landmarks and the names of one or two hotels we might try. We now knew where we were and had a good idea how to find our way around.

The blow came after we had tried the second hotel given to us by the girl at the BOAC – they were both fully booked. As we sat studying the street plan and discovered where we were, we noticed that there was a hotel indicated quite close by, so, without further ado, we went round to have a look. We found it, The Ambassador, standing back off the road in its own grounds. This looked more in our line: pageboys to open the doors, carpeted foyer etc. Yes, they had a double room vacant and were a little taken aback when I asked to see it, muttering something to the effect that it was 'very comfortable, I can assure you, Madam'. A quick look at the room was enough to satisfy me. A sharp command from the reception desk soon had us, baggage, cot and cases safely installed in the room.

We had no sooner sat down to relax for a few minutes before unpacking, when a bearer arrived with a plate of fruit marked *with the compliments of the manager*. The first real comfort of our holiday. The room contained two single, very comfortable beds, a three-piece suite, a writing desk with phone, and a cocktail cabinet, not filled with the 'compliments of the manager', unfortunately. The room was fully air-conditioned and the French windows led out onto a small balcony, overlooking the lawn and road. After a short rest and a sample of the manager's fruit, we all had a hot bath, and, when dressed again, felt ready to 'do' Delhi.

The hotel was built in the shape of a triangle, with the dining room in the centre, a large octagonal room with a high vaulted ceiling. Meals in the dining room with the children were a problem. Breakfast was the most successful as they were usually hungry and looked forward to their fruit juice, cornflakes and eggs. Lunch and dinner were more difficult, and after the first evening we had the remainder of our evening meals served in our room.

The trouble was that the children never seemed hungry, and as a result would not remain seated at the table. Tim would crawl off on his hands and knees pretending he was a dog, which resulted in two or three waiters hunting under the tables for 'our doggie'. Dinah's main attraction was the three-piece band that played spasmodically during the lunch hour. She would rush off and play her piece at the base end of the piano, irrespective of whether the artistes were performing or not. It seemed, that the management, far from being annoyed, seemed to encourage them; it no doubt caused a pleasant diversion from their normal routine.

On the Tuesday afternoon, we decided we would drive towards the fort and Jama Masjid Mosque, which are on the border of Old and New Delhi. As we approached the mosque we noticed a performing baby monkey. We stopped to let the children watch its antics. The owner, by rattling a small drum at different tempos, was able to get the monkey to give his version of the Dance of the Seven Veils. I must say I hate to see animals being exploited in this way.

We found ourselves entering the Chandni Chowk area of Old Delhi, narrow streets crowded with tongas, cycle rickshaws, bullock carts, cyclists and the odd cow nosing about in the rubbish. This part reminded us very much of Pakistan. The street appeared to get narrower and narrower, until we found we were in a cul-de-sac. The street was far too narrow to turn around in, so we had to reverse to the nearest crossroads, a most hair-raising experience, especially when it comes to trying to explain to a bullock that what is normally the back of a car is, in this case, being used as the front. On busy, narrow roads such as these, one tends to follow the crowd, but after a while we found we were on the same stretch of road that we had been on earlier – we were obviously lost. A passer-by must have realised our predicament, because he came over and asked if he could help. It appeared we were heading out of the city in the wrong direction. Following our helper's directions, we were soon on the right road and shortly afterwards we found ourselves passing the Hotel Airlines.

As we had not yet decided when we should leave for home, we thought it best to visit Agra on the Wednesday so as to have a day's break from driving. So, Wednesday morning saw us off with a packed lunch for Agra and the Taj Mahal. A very good road, which in places is in the process of being widened to form a dual carriageway, serves the 125 miles between Delhi and Agra and the only large town en route had a bypass. The road passes across the flat plains of Northern India, which appear to either lie fallow or be devoted to the growing of wheat. On quieter sections of the road we would come across a troop of monkeys playing, but they soon scampered up into the trees at the sight of our approach.

As the milestones dropped to single figures, we saw minarets rising above the treetops – could this be the famous Taj? Our hopes rose, only to be dashed shortly afterwards when we discovered they belonged to Akbar's Tomb at Secunda. Soon afterwards, however, we were in the City of Agra, or I should say, on the outskirts, because as we entered we saw the turn-off to Fatehpur Sikri, which Mike had decided we should visit first, as it was another twenty-five miles beyond Agra, and he wished to do as much of the driving as possible before we stopped.

Fatehpur Sikri, Akbar's Capital, was built in 1569 and with amazing speed too, and it is said that most of the sandstone used in its construction was brought to the site already prepared. Akbar, so the story runs, although well provided for with wives, longed for a son and heir. Children that had been born had not lived long, and so on hearing of the great spiritual powers of a Muslim saint, Sheikh Salim Chishti, who was said to live in a cave near Sikri, he went and consulted him. The saint foretold of the birth of a son in due course, and Akbar, on finding one of his wives pregnant, sent her to live in the vicinity of the saint. And it so happened that Akbar was blessed with a son and heir and so decided to make his capital there, which he called Fatehpur, City of Victory, after the conquest of Gujarat.

The extent of the palace was hard to believe, having everything that could be desired, even to the extent of central heating. A separate palace for each wife, a large tank or pond, with an island reached by bridges, gardens, pavilions, a columned hall, a folly in the form of a pyramid of terraces, a little temple for a guru, a court in which to play puncheesee, chess, with human chessmen, a court for the administration of justice, and every other kind of court. Then after fifteen years this great city that had become a focal point in the trade routes of the east was deserted. Various reasons have been given: that the water supply gave out, that the saint complained of too much noise, and that political necessity required Akbar's presence in the northern part of his empire.

And so, it was to this spectacle that we drove. It stands on an area of high ground, rising above the plain. The palace and village are surrounded by a substantial wall, some seven miles in length and thirty feet in height. As usual we were besieged by a guide, who at first we ignored, but due to his persistence, we decided in the end to take him under our wing. His English was not very precise, and therefore we learned most from the guidebook on our return to Delhi. Invariably his answer to every question was yes, and we were sure that he could not have been right every time.

After an extensive tour of the palace, we went on to the mosque and the Tomb of the Saint, and the Buland Darwaza, one of the largest and highest gateways in Asia and perhaps the world. These buildings stand in a huge courtyard of their own, which to enter one must either remove one's shoes, or put on 'oversize mitts' supplied by the establishment. The Tomb of the Saint, Sheik Salim Chishti, immediately draws one's attention as it is built out of white marble and stands in a sea of red sandstone. It stands on a marble plinth some fifty feet square. The dome is supported by columns, which are connected by a screen of marble lacework. A canopy of precious wood, covered with mother-of-pearl, covers the tombstone. To me, it was a most impressive memorial, small though it is, compared with others of a similar standing. As we moved away, the guide informed me that he was a descendant of the 'Holy One' as he too was called Chishti, and to try and prove his point showed us the tombstones of his forebears in the courtyard.

The Buland Darwaza is truly a magnificent gateway. As one leaves the courtyard and passes through the arch, one sees the village of Sikri spread out below, which is connected by an impressive flight of stairs, which fall in three different directions in the form of a cascade.

Feeling somewhat tired, we returned to the car where we had our picnic lunch and then drove back to Agra.

The Taj Mahal is situated on the outskirts of the city, and the signposted route took us down the Mall, through a park, to an outer gatehouse which led into the grounds containing the Taj. As we drove through the gates, on either side were formal gardens and lawns with curio shops and cafes behind. The road then opened out into a large car park, containing private cars and large, modern air-conditioned buses.

To reach the Taj, one first passes through an impressive gateway, with a massive sandstone portal inlaid with marble, some 150 feet wide and 100 feet high, with two storeyed wings on either side crowned with white marble cupolas and at the corners by open domed kiosks. As one passes up the stairs one catches the first glimpse of the Taj, framed in the gateway, and then as one moves on, one has the full majestic vista, set like a stage.

Two long, rectangular pools occupy the centre stage with fountains studded down the centre, and separated by a large, elevated pool, encased in marble. The wings are made up of a screen of cypress trees and the remainder of the stage is filled with lawns and beds of flowers. The roses being particularly eye catching. The backcloth is the Taj Mahal itself, sitting on its marble plinth, with the four minarets standing at each corner, the whole scene being reflected in the shimmering pools.

Standing at the gateway, the first thought that comes to mind is, *so this is the fabulous Taj Mahal, and it looks just like it does in any picture book*. We descended the broad stairs from the gatehouse into the gardens, and walked alongside the various pools until we reached the base of the massive plinth on which the Taj stands. Here we removed our shoes and socks and mounted the cold marble steps feeling very devout. From the head of the stairs we crossed a vast marble terrace to the entrance of the pavilion itself.

The pavilion is octagonal in shape, the centre chamber being surrounded by four outer chambers, each connected by a communicating passage. The two headstones of Mumtaz Mahal and Shah Jahan lie side by side in the central chamber, whilst the tombs themselves lie in the dark, camphor-smelling crypt below.

And so we had come to see this great memorial, built by Shah Jahan for his beloved queen, Mumtaz Mahal, and which on his death became his final resting place too. It is a very impressive structure, about that there can be no doubt, built by true craftsmen in a wonderful setting on the bank of the river, but whether it was something I could look at day in, day out, as Shah Jahan had done while a prisoner in the fort, I don't know. Perhaps that is not a fair comparison as, after all, it was his creation, for a very special purpose.

Delhi is a city that cannot be seen in a few days, but one immediately realises that it is a very well-planned and laid-out garden city, with its broad thoroughfares, clean, fresh-looking buildings and open spaces. One of the most impressive sights can be found on the drive from the India Gate along the Rajpath towards the President's Palace, first with the open parks and then the imposing government buildings. The city is a fine epitaph to its architects, Lutyens and Baker.

Friday was our last day and we now had to do, or try and do, everything we had missed earlier. One of the buildings Mike wanted to see before we left was the Laxmi Narayan Temple, a fairly modern Hindu shrine. It was rather a difficult place to find but nevertheless we got there in the end. While Mike had a quick look round, the children and I were entertained by a snake charmer. When Mike returned, he was just in time to 'snap' the cobra before he vanished back into his basket.

During lunch Mike suddenly realised that he had not seen the Qutb Minar. This tower is to Delhi as the Statue of Liberty is to New York, and one of the reasons why we had not seen it was that it stands some ten miles south of the city. I wanted to start the packing so I told him go alone later in the afternoon.

When Mike got back to the hotel he was not feeling very well, so I took his temperature and found it to be over 100°F. I decided to give him a couple of codeine tablets and to go to bed as tomorrow was going to be a long day. As the evening drew on he felt more feverish and started to sweat, and by midnight his temperature had reached 102°F. I decided that should it reach 103°F I would have to call a doctor. I then started to have visions of him being rushed to hospital, confined to bed for a week, leaving us stranded in Delhi without money and all sorts of other things; anyway he must have fallen into a fitful sleep, because the next thing I knew, it was six o'clock and the sun was just beginning to rise. Mike said he felt a lot better and his temperature was now normal.

On the 23nd November, by half past six in the morning, we were all up and putting the last touches to our packing, and by seven o'clock we were down in the dining room for our last breakfast. As we came out of the dining room we saw on the bookstall the newspaper headlines: *President Kennedy is dead.* He had been assassinated the previous day. We both took a copy and started to read the stunning news before we realised we had forgotten to pay for them. What a shock this news was; as we gathered ourselves we realised that several American women around us were crying, whilst others were trying to send off cables and wreaths.

This was not a good start to our long journey and was the topic of conversation for most of the day. We were ready to leave the hotel by half past eight. Mike thought he would be clever and miss the city centre by using the ring road. Little did we know that this existed more or less in name only and it was ten o'clock by the time we finally reached the Grand Trunk Road. We now had some 320 miles to cover to reach the frontier before the Customs House closed at sundown.

Fortunately, the road was very quiet and we were able to cruise along at between fifty and sixty miles an hour except for the tortuous crawls through Ambala, Ludhiana and Jullundur. The only stops we made were for petrol and calls of nature. It was about midday when we discovered that Tim had not got his teddy bear, his favourite companion. We usually left it out of the cases for Tim to play with on the journey. We could not stop long enough to make a thorough search and had to hope he was somewhere in the back of the car.

We finally reached the Customs House at half past four and were cleared through without delay, the only trouble being that they had sent the wrong car triptyque form away to their head office in Amritsar. Mike said he was not going to hand over the sheet that rightfully belonged to them until they could produce his section, otherwise he would never get his deposit back, so with that, we said farewell to India and drove into Pakistan.

As we approached the Customs House we crossed our fingers and hoped they would not ask to see what we had purchased in India – not that it was very much, but we were anxious to get home as we still had some 140 miles to cover, and as one of the headlights had burnt out we were a little anxious about the night's driving ahead of us. Anyway, like the Indian customs there was no delay, no questions were asked and there was no searching, just a case of endless paperwork, copying all the same information into another big ledger, stamping passports and then we were truly back in West Pakistan.

Once clear of the Customs House we stopped for a cup of tea from the Thermos flask and a bite to eat as we had decided to go straight home rather than stop at a restaurant in Lahore. By the time we reached Lahore it was dark and we had no sooner entered the city when we got lost. After a few enquiries and driving a little further on we recognised where we were and that we would soon be clear of the place. However, just ahead were two policemen on point duty, who signalled us to stop.

'Do you know that one of your headlights isn't working?'

'No,' Mike lied. 'It was perfectly all right last night.' He then twiddled the switch and dip button in the hopes that by some miracle it might come on.

'Where are you going to?'

'Mangla.'

'Well, I can't let you go straight on as our sergeant has just gone that way and might cause some trouble. Go down this lane, going off to the left, then keep right and that will bring you onto the GT Road.'

We thanked him profusely and drove off with a sigh of relief. We went down the lane as directed, which was very dark and full of tongas and bullock carts, none of which had any lights, which made driving quite hazardous. After about five minutes we came to two more policemen on point duty. We got as close behind the car in front as we could and hoped that we would be able to slip past them without them noticing our defective light. As luck would have it, they stopped our line of traffic and gave the side road the right of way.

Within seconds, the policeman not actually directing the traffic came over to the car.

'Hello, so you're back here again.' We just couldn't believe it. We were back at the same crossroads we had been stopped at ten minutes before. 'Anyway, you're lucky, the sergeant has gone back now so you can drive straight on.' So once again we thanked him and hoped that this time we would get clear of Lahore.

The remainder of the drive was uneventful until we reached the Jhelum Bridge, and as luck would have it the traffic signal was against us so there was nothing to do but sit and wait. After a few minutes the police guard came out of his hut and walked over to the car. As he approached he tapped the defective headlamp. He then came to the door and said something in Urdu and pointed to the lamp again.

Mike got out and went and had a look at the headlight, trying to show as much surprise as he could. 'It must have just gone out as it has been fine all the way from Lahore.'

The policeman then proceeded to give us a long lecture in Urdu; at least that is what we assumed he was doing, as our knowledge of the language was very scant, especially regarding the Motor Vehicle Act and car headlights. It was obvious he spoke no English, but Mike didn't know how much he understood so he had to be careful. So once again he played with the switches and opened the bonnet, muttering all the time that we were only going to Mangla and would fix the light first thing tomorrow. The officer was not really satisfied and obviously wanted Mike's driving licence. During this time, more traffic was queuing up behind us and very little was coming over the bridge, so we were hoping that it would soon be clear for us to move.

Shortly the light changed in our favour but the policeman told us to wait and waved all the other traffic behind us to move on. This looked bad and we felt sure he must have telephoned Jhelum for an English-speaking member of the force to come over. At last he reappeared and waved us on, and we hoped that we would make the last twenty miles without further incidents – we did.

As soon as we saw the twinkling light of Mangla we felt we were home. We drove straight to the office, which was always open as they were working twenty-four hours a day, as we were anxious to collect our mail, and there was quite a lot of it too. We got back into the house just on ten o'clock, having driven 476 miles since leaving Delhi that morning and exactly two thousand miles since we left Mangla eleven days before.

Tim's teddy bear was not found when we unpacked the cases and car, and as he was four years old he was greatly missed. Our only hope was to write to the hotel and see if anyone had picked him up there. In due course a reply came to say that Teddy was in the lost-and-found department and they would be pleased to have our further instructions. Luckily some people were going to Delhi and offered to bring him back. And so in due course Teddy returned to Mangla looking quite fit after his prolonged holiday in Delhi.

The weekend after our return we went into Pindi to get the headlight fixed, as we did not want any more brushes with the law, and to do some essential shopping while we waited.

Back at work, the drilling and grouting operation having been completed, Jim had finally given in his notice and was packing up for his return to Canada. After Jim left his house was occupied by the Copping family, with whom we are still in touch. The contractor was starting to work a three-shift twenty-four-hour day. Unfortunately, popular vote said they should change shifts every two weeks, which to Mike was not long enough for the body to adjust and it was this that made him decide not to stay when his contract came up for renewal, despite much pleading from Cox.

The day shift was from eight o'clock in the morning until four o'clock in the afternoon, and the swing shift carried on until midnight when the graveyard shift began and carried on until eight o'clock the next morning. Trying to sleep during the day with two young children in the house was not easy.

At the beginning of December, I started organising Tim's second birthday party, which although his birthday was on the 16th was held a day early, maybe because it would fall on a Monday. Anyway, it was a party to remember. I managed to hire a tonga to come up from Dina and got permission for it to come into the site. I then persuaded Ted Payne to dress up as Father Christmas and arrive on his sleigh pulled by a reindeer (tonga and donkey). Ted's daughter who was there suddenly realised who Santa Claus was when she saw his shoes. Her mother, when she realised what was happening, pulled her daughter aside and told her not to say a word! Nearly all the children on the British side were invited, but our special guests were Joyce Cammack and her daughter Lesley.

We made party hats for all the children and gift-wrapped a present for each from Santa. A lot of hard work went into the preparations and the party itself but it was well worth it to see the children enjoying themselves and hear their laughter.

Apart from our British friends, I had made contact with a number of Americans on 'the other side of the road'. One was a young Brazilian woman with a small child who was married to a man much older than herself and they were going through a bit of a difficult period, so we decided to invite them to lunch and show them what an English Christmas was really like. Earlier in the morning young Gareth Davies had come over with presents for Dinah and Tim and they accompanied him back with their gifts for him, Marion and the baby. Boxing Day was back to work.

Later in the month we received news that we now had our first niece, Caroline, born in Trinidad to Betty and Hugh.

As the weeks passed we started to make plans for leaving. I was worried about my parents in BG. Things were not going well there and Dad had been rather unwell, so we decided I should take the children and go and visit them, then we would meet up somewhere in Spain or Portugal and drive back to England having a longish holiday on the way once Mike had completed his contract.

Shortly before we left Pakistan we had a few days away together. We drove up to Peshawar and made Deane's Hotel there our base. Again, this consisted of a commercial city and a cantonment area. I liked the city with its bustle of buses, lorries, tongas, sheep and the populace as they made their way about their business.

On our first day we drove up the Khyber Pass to the Afghan border at Torkham. Some way out of Peshawar a modern-looking fort had been built together with a triumphal arch over the road before one reached the pass itself, which was duly announced on a board – *You are now entering the Khyber Pass* – where we had to stop to take a suitable photo to record the occasion.

As we wound our way up the gorge, sometimes alongside the railway line, which goes as far as the border, we saw plaques on the verges giving the names of the British regiments that had served and fought the tribesmen there. On the skyline could be seen the remains of the old forts and observation posts, and we could appreciate the difficult conditions our soldiers had had to contend with. In the middle of the pass we came to a small town, Landi Kotal, which we gathered was one of the centres for goods smuggled over the border. We were amused to see one building marked *Hotel and Restorant*!

Finally, we reached the border, which was marked by a chain stretched across the road and a huge pile of mailbags in the middle of the road, which, on closer examination, were from Moscow bound for New Delhi. Unfortunately, the border was closed as Pakistan and Afghanistan had broken off diplomatic relations, otherwise we would have arranged to continue our journey to Kabul.

It was while we were looking at the mailbags that Dinah decided to make an unofficial visit to the other side by ducking under the chain and trotting off westward. The armed guard, caught unawares, called out and we realised our predicament. A sharp word that we were leaving right away soon brought our errant daughter running back to the right side of the line.

The following day we visited a friend of an American friend at the US airbase outside Peshawar. It was from such a base that Gary Powers had flown on his ill-fated mission in his U2 spy plane to be shot down by the Russians, which caused such a rumpus between the two superpower leaders, Eisenhower and Khrushchev. After leaving the Hopsons we went on to visit the Warsak Dam which, we believe, was built by the Canadians. It was in a valley close by the Khyber Pass.

Mike decided he would make a detour to our return to Mangla by going south to Kohat through Pathan country. We passed through some pretty wild country and the Darra arms factory where the long barrel guns were produced which we could see lined up outside the shop-like factories that lined the road. We were making good progress when suddenly the engine died on us.

Our immediate thought was that once again we had run out of petrol, but Mike had made sure that this would not happen to us again, so the fault lay elsewhere. But try as he did he could not get the engine to start. We appeared to be miles from anywhere – there was no sign of habitation and the road was deserted. Just how long would we have to wait before someone came along who might be able to help us? We were almost at the point of despair when we saw, coming in our direction, a petrol tanker we had overtaken some time before.

We flagged down the driver and he and his mate came over after parking just behind us. They immediately took charge by disconnecting the fuel pipe, blowing it out and generally tinkering about under the bonnet. When everything was put back in place they tried the engine once again but still it would not fire.

We looked at the two men with dismay and said, 'What next?'

The two men had a few words with each other; then they opened the boot, took out some of the luggage and looked for the petrol pump to which, on finding it, they gave a hefty knock. We tried the engine again and this time it fired. In their halting English, they explained that this was the cause of the breakdown. With grateful thanks we repacked the boot, got back into the car and continued our journey without further trouble.

Shortly before I was due to leave I had lot of trouble with a tooth and the camp dentist, Dante Fransisco, a Filipino, decided that it should be removed, which he proceeded to do, not without some difficulty. The problem, however, did not go away as the wound would not stop bleeding. I had to go back to the hospital and Dante attempted to sew it up, a long and painful operation, which left me in a very weak condition for several days.

As we were entitled to first-class air tickets back to England we decided to go to the BOAC office in Lahore once we had the tickets, and change them to economy class, extending them to Georgetown, thus reducing the balance we would have to pay.

The day the children and I left, early in April, so did Mrs Martin, who was going back to Jersey on a short holiday. About two weeks later Arthur Martin had a serious accident. I can't remember whether Mrs Martin was back or not, but if not they soon had her back at Mangla. It had happened one afternoon as Arthur was supervising some concreting on the slope of the spillway when a concrete skip swung round out of control and struck him on the hip, fracturing his pelvis. He was rushed to the Baral hospital where he was to remain for many weeks with his legs in traction. Mike would visit him regularly, taking Mrs Martin and sometimes Doris Cox as well.

The days and weeks went quickly for Mike as he had still plenty of planning and organising for his own trip to do. There were all the necessary papers to secure for our trip through Europe, which took time as it all had to be done through London, added to which there were all the customs clearance forms to be obtained to get the car and baggage out of Pakistan.

By the end of June everything was falling into place. The one remaining question for Mike was how to get the car down to Karachi in time to catch the boat. If he sent it off too early it would be lying goodness knows where and if he cut it too fine he could miss the boat. In the end, he decided that the best way would be to drive down there, but it was quite a distance, almost a thousand miles, and it would be at the hottest time of the year. As luck would have it, Trevor Green, one of the bachelors on the site, on hearing of Mike's intentions, said he would like to go along with him. Mike was going to sail from Karachi to Gibraltar and then drive to meet us in Lisbon.

After two very long-distance flights I arrived at Trinidad with Dinah and Tim. I was met by Hugh, my brother-in-law, who said I was too tired to carry on to Georgetown that day so he took us back to his home for a good night's rest. Next day, well rested, we completed our journey to BG. It was good to see the family again – Dad looked older and not in very good health, Mum was about the same as when I last saw her and Auntie was looking older and not so well. Another 'aunt', Gussie, was fussing about as she always used to. Clive had grown and was said to be doing well at school.

What shocked me was the state of the country. There was hardly any food in the shops and most essentials were in short supply. This was all due to Burnham and his crazy policies, which were ruining the country.

After a few days' rest and with the children settled into their new surroundings we sat down to consider what we could do for the best, as things could not continue as they were. Dad always maintained that the colony was not ready for independence and things could only get worse. So, it was decided that I would go over to Barbados and find somewhere for Mum, Dad and Auntie to live. Gussie was undecided what she would do but thought she would go to the States.

After several days' searching I found a lovely little bungalow, right on the water's edge, near Hastings. I felt sure they would be very happy there. With this success, I flew back to Georgetown to give them the good news. I looked up old friends and enjoyed my stay but then it was time to make plans to rejoin Mike in Lisbon. I cannot now remember what date I had been given by Mike to arrive. However, I managed to get a direct Pan Am flight from Trinidad to Lisbon, which would save me having to change planes.

It was an overnight flight and the children were excited that they were going to see their daddy again. As we stepped off the plane I looked round and on a nearby rooftop I spotted Mike waving like mad.

I said, 'Look, there's Daddy up there.'

Dinah looked up and said, 'My daddy, my daddy.' Tim looked up, waved, and then turned to look at the plane that had just brought us all those thousands of miles.

With our luggage, we were soon outside and reunited with Mike. Moments later we were in the car and after asking about the flight and my family back in Georgetown told me about the problem he had had at Gibraltar.

When Mike reached the quayside on Friday 3rd July he was met by a man called Holm, who said he represented Blands Shipping Agency, who were handling Mike's car. He said he was very sorry to say that he could not release the car as the shipping costs had not been paid. Mike was dumbfounded and wondered what had gone wrong and asked what could be done as he had to get over to Lisbon to meet his family flying in from the West Indies. Mr Holm said he would need to go to Blands' office and see the manager.

Realising he would not be leaving Gibraltar that day, Mike made some phone calls to find himself a hotel. This done, he loaded his luggage into a taxi and made for the Bristol Hotel. After signing in he made his way to Blands' office to meet the manager, who was very sympathetic but said he could not release the car until the shipping cost had been met. He said the easiest way would be for Mike to telegraph his bank in London and give them instructions to settle the account. Mike then discovered that the following day was Saturday and Monday was a Bank Holiday in London, so he would be unable to do anything until at least Tuesday. He would be a 'prisoner' on the Rock. The manager said that he would get Holm to take Mike to the car to check it over and give it a run to charge the battery, but Mr Holm would have to accompany him – in case Mike tried to do a runner over the frontier!

Next day we drove north up the coast to Caldas da Rainha, a pleasant market town with the main square filled with market stalls selling fruit, vegetables, clothes, kitchenware and the like. From the map Mike saw there was a road running down to the coast to a place called Foz do Arelho. Following the road, we found we were running beside a river that discharged into the sea at Foz, which turned out to be a delightful spot. At the end of the road was the Hotel do Facho, where we had lunch. We were so taken with the place that as soon as the meal was over Mike went to the reception desk to see if they had any accommodation. We were in luck; they had a family room coming vacant the following day for one week. We took it immediately and we were back again within twenty-four hours.

The hotel faced west overlooking a wide beach onto which broke huge Atlantic rollers. The beach was very bleak and tended to be on the cool side as there was no shelter from the wind. Most people therefore opted to go to the river estuary, which was tidal and also sheltered from the wind. Dinah and Tim loved it there as the water was shallow with a sandy beach and they played there quite happily for hours on end.

We made several trips to Caldas da Rainha as we enjoyed wandering round the market stalls looking at all the fresh produce. During our first visit, we bought buckets and spades for Dinah and Tim and a hat for everybody as the sun was quite hot. Because of Mike's great interest in railways we would spend some time at the station watching the trains go by.

One afternoon whilst resting on the bed after lunch we noticed a parrot outside the window. He kept us amused for quite a while with his antics until he finally flew away. In the hotel was a French family with a daughter, Dominique, with whom the children played even though she was somewhat older than our two. We kept up a correspondence with her for a year or two until we lost contact.

The countryside around Caldas da Rainha was given over to the cultivation of grapes. The vines consisted of small bushes two to three feet high and had been sprayed with some white powder which was probably an insecticide. Just across the river from Foz is the delightful village of Óbidos, with its narrow, cobbled streets and small, whitewashed terraced houses, which features in Ann Bridge's *The Portuguese Escape*, which we had read whilst in Pakistan.

When it was time for us to leave, we drove down to the south coast and spent the night at Toures. In one place where we spent the night, the mattresses appeared to be filled with straw as every time we moved in our beds there was a deep rustling sound from below! From here we drove east to Val Real de San Antonio where we crossed the Guadiana River into Spain by a car ferry. Once in Spain we drove through to Alcala where we spent the night.

The following day we went back to Sevilla and did some shopping, and on our return to the hotel we watched the preparations for a big fiesta that was to be held that evening, and thanks to which we did not get to bed until two o'clock the next morning.

After what seemed a very short night we were up and off to Malaga. The road ran through a broad valley with high mountains on either side. In La Roda we stopped to buy some food to eat on the way. This proved rather difficult as we spoke no Spanish and the shopkeeper no English. All the goods were behind the counter so we could not help ourselves as in a supermarket. We finally got what we wanted by sign language and by making the noises of the animals whose products we sought!

In Antequera there was another fiesta in progress. Whilst at a filling station a crowd of boys and girls dressed in national costume rode past on horseback. Driving on through the town we suddenly saw two little children in national dress walking along with their mother. With a screech of brakes Mike stopped the car and jumped out with his camera and asked the woman in sign language if he could take a photograph of her and her two children, which she readily consented to after she had adjusted the children's dresses.

Once over a mountain range we were soon dropping down into Malaga, where we had tea in a cafe on the waterfront. It was quite warm here but because of a heavy sea mist we saw little of the town and its surroundings. From here we continued eastwards along a mountainous coastal road to Motril, where we arrived at a quarter to ten, by which time it was completely dark. We spent the night at the recently opened Costa Nevada Hotel. Having eaten on the way we had a hot shower and tumbled into bed.

The front tyres of the car were by now virtually treadless, and with the distance we still had to travel Mike decided that after breakfast, which we had served in our room, he would go into the town and buy two new tyres which were fitted while he waited.

Our road now climbed over the Sierra Nevada, which was quite steep, and in several places the road plunged into a tunnel, much to the children's delight. Once in Granada our sightseeing was done from the car as we did not have the time to walk round, plus the fact that it was very tiring for Dinah and Tim.

From Granada, we continued east through fairly mountainous country, the tops of the higher peaks being covered with snow. We put up at a small pension in Baza. After a rest, we had a walk around the town, looking at the shops, then returned for dinner with which a large carafe of red wine was served.

Whilst having coffee next morning a young French couple, whom we had not seen the previous evening, came down to breakfast. They had not been down long before a policeman arrived to make some enquiries about their passports. This led to a lot of shouting and gesticulating, which the Frenchman, at least, took as a huge joke. What it was all about we never found out, but we concluded they were on their honeymoon and the woman's maiden name had not been changed in her passport, or her husband had made a mistake on the police registration cards.

We continued to Mercia through some pretty bleak countryside, at one point passing through a village where the houses were carved out of a cliff face. By midday the weather had turned quite dull and overcast and by the time we reached Alicante it was pouring with rain and the roads were flooded. When we arrived at Benidorm the sun was shining and it was hard to believe that we had so recently passed through such a storm.

The sea here looked so tempting that we stopped for a swim – that is to say, Mike and the children went swimming while I sat in the car. After a very refreshing swim they returned to the car where they found me chatting to an English family who were on their way to Gibraltar. We spent the night at Seula.

Next day we continued, and after passing through Valencia we stopped for lunch on a beach. Whilst there, Mike had another swim. Beyond Tarragona the road turned inland and we came to Villafranca. Here we looked at a couple of pensions but were not impressed. In the market place a funfair was in full swing, so we took the children over to amuse themselves until we decided it was time to find somewhere to stay.

Not liking any of the places we looked at we decided to move on, although by this time it was getting dark. Nevertheless, we pressed on until we found ourselves in Barcelona. As it was dark we found it very difficult to find anywhere to stay. We tried several pensions but soon as we mentioned the family we were told there was nothing available. We got the impression that these were really residences for male or female students but not both together, and by the same token families were not accommodated. We eventually found a hotel at 10.45 pm.

We decided we would spend a week in the area before driving home, and so as we drove out of the city, which was very slow and tedious due to the volume of traffic, we saw a pension on the front at Monsolis. We drove in for a drink and whilst there discovered that they had a family room free, so we decided to take it.

The place was run by two young German women, one blonde, the other brunette. They were both very attractive and no doubt used their charms to entice customers into the small bar. It was, I believe, essentially a one-night motel-type establishment, as after we had been there a couple of days they kept asking when we were planning to leave. As we only bought bread rolls and other sundry items from them, and the bar showing no profit as a result of the Bennetts' stay, one can perhaps appreciate their desire to replace us with more lucrative customers. One of the drawbacks of the place was that the bathroom and toilet were at the far end of the corridor and always seemed to be occupied when we wanted to use them.

Between the pension and the beach was the main road and railway line. We were amazed how people wandered across the railway tracks instead of using the subways provided. The beach at this point was not very attractive so we would drive up to Masnou, which was a little further up the coast. On the second day of our stay we went into Barcelona by train, as we could not face the traffic on the road. After visiting the bank and collecting our mail at the post office Mike bought two maps of France so that he could plan our route home.

We wandered around the narrow streets, which were packed with fellow tourists, until we found an open-air cafe in a square full of pigeons, where we had lunch. The train journey back was not so good. The train was full and late leaving, with the result that it was very hot.

On our last day, we again returned to Barcelona, and this time we went by car as we wished to buy some souvenirs and other oddments. Parking was much easier than we had anticipated, almost in the shadow of a large statue of Columbus. After lunch we drove up to some higher ground overlooking the city and harbour. Here we found a cable car but it did not appear to be working while we were there.

We finally left on 31st August. By now the car battery was completely dead so it meant starting on the handle or leaving the car on a slope if there was one. The road along the Costa Brava was slow and tortuous although there was not a great deal of traffic about. In the more popular resorts large hotels were being built, while on the rocky headlands roads were being carved out for the development of holiday chalets.

From L'Escala we cut inland to Figeures where we had lunch. On our way there we saw a car and caravan on their sides in a field where they had obviously gone off the road. We felt very sorry for the man, who was trying to retrieve his belongings from the caravan.

Crossing the frontier at Portbou we had an anxious moment when I thought I had lost my watch, but as I got out of the car to look for it I discovered that I had been sitting on it. In Banyuls-sur-Mer Mike cashed some travellers' cheques and then drove on to Port-Vendres, where we had tea in a cafe by the harbour and did some shopping. We spent the night at the Hotel Fiton, which we found on the main road beyond Perpignan.

Next day we had a very slow start due to heavy traffic on the road, however once we got onto the N9 beyond Pézenas the traffic diminished and we made good progress even though the terrain was quite hilly. We drove all round Saint-Flour trying to find a bank, only to discover that they were all closed. Just north of the town we were delayed by some extensive roadworks. We finally found a bank open in Issoire. Having stopped, we decided to go no further that day.

Continuing north the next day, we reached Fontainebleau during the afternoon where we stopped and had a look round the château and gardens. We had planned to stay the night somewhere south of Paris but could not find anywhere suitable, and found ourselves getting closer and closer to the heart of the city, by which time it was quite dark and turning wet.

We saw a policeman on the corner of a street talking to two people, so we stopped to enlist his aid. As we drew nearer it became obvious that the two people he was talking to were two young 'ladies of the night'. Having asked if there was a hotel in the neighbourhood, there was a general discussion between the three of them; then the policeman gave us a set of directions which we then attempted to follow.

We drove round a few corners trying to follow the direction we had been given, and then I felt we were back where we had started from when we saw another policeman standing on a corner. We dared not go up to him in case he was the one we had just spoken to. Anyway, we continued along the main road and shortly afterwards found a very pleasant hotel with a couple of rooms on something like the eleventh or twelfth floor.

On looking out of the window the next morning we saw the majestic structure of the Eiffel Tower. Our hotel was somewhere on the right bank on the west side of the city. After breakfast, we drove round to the tower and studied it at close quarters. What a massive yet elegant structure it is. Having seen all we wished to, we drove off and found a street-side cafe where we had coffee and croissants.

Mike's intention then was to drive quickly around the city centre before making for Boulogne. The car engine, however, was not idling very well and kept stopping. Sometimes he managed to get it going again on the starter but once in a traffic jam on the Boulevard Saint-Germain it would not start, so, with much honking from the cars behind, he had to jump out and start it with the handle. After this we decided the sooner we got out of Paris the better, so crossing back over the river we got onto the Rue de Rivoli and past the Jardin des Tuileries onto the Champs-Élysées; then up past the Arc de Triomphe into the Place de l'Étoile. Shortly after this the road cleared and we were out of the city.

Somewhere near Beauvais the engine suddenly cut out and no matter what Mike tried he could not get it to start. Although the petrol gauge was showing that we were getting low on fuel Mike was quite sure that we were not out of petrol completely, unless, of course, the gauge was inaccurate. Fortunately, we had a can with us for such an emergency in the boot. So, with can in hand Mike set off back down the road to a filling station we had noticed as we came along.

Luckily, he had barely gone a hundred yards before a car came along and offered Mike a lift. The couple in the car were both middle-aged and spoke little or no English, but they managed to converse with Mike's limited French. They soon reached the garage and they insisted on running Mike back to the car once the can was filled – a very kind couple.

Back at the car and with the petrol in the tank, Mike tried to start the car. It refused to start on either the starter or the handle. He began to fear that something more serious was wrong with it; then we remembered the trouble we had had in Pakistan with the fuel pump. So, opening the boot, Mike gave it a sharp tap with a screwdriver and heard a few thuds from within. Closing the boot, he went to the front and swung the handle; the engine coughed and then settled down to a steady idling. Mike pulled out the handle, jumped in the car and made off, stopping only to fill up with petrol before we got to Boulogne.

Here troubles of another sort began. The queue for the ferryboats was a mile long. It transpired that one of the boats had broken down and it was anyone's guess when we would get away. We were relieved that we had actually reached the coast and were quite prepared to wait as long as was necessary. It did not really matter to us when we crossed, apart from the children's discomfort, as Mike had no job to return to. As on all such occasions rumours were rife as to what was happening and when we would get away. People got more agitated as time went by, but as far as we were concerned, que sera, sera.

Eventually we heard that the boat on the last scheduled sailing would make a further return trip to try and clear the backlog of cars. We finally drove onto the ferry at about half past seven that evening.

By the time we cleared customs at Dover it was close to midnight and we could not find a hotel that looked as though it was still open, so Mike decided that we would drive on to Guildford, thinking that this was the best way to spend the night. What Mike had forgotten was that, the roads being completely deserted, the journey would take only half the time that it would during the day, with the result that we arrived at London Road just before three o'clock.

As Mike's mother had a small flat, having sold the family home, we could not wake her up in the middle of the night so it was a case of sitting in the car until we thought she would be up. It was bitterly cold sitting there, sleeping fitfully. The children, however, were fast asleep on their mattress at the back and quite oblivious to our suffering.

At about six o'clock, feeling numb with cold, we drove out to the bypass in the hope of finding an all-night cafe open. We had not gone very far when the petrol pump began to give us trouble so rather than get stuck again we went back to the car park and then made our way to Mike's mother. Fortunately, she was up and soon had us drinking hot coffee and we were relating all our experiences while the eggs and bacon were being fried.

Mike on camel with Dinah

Tonga at party

Taj Mahal

Khyber Pass

Carpet makers –Swat

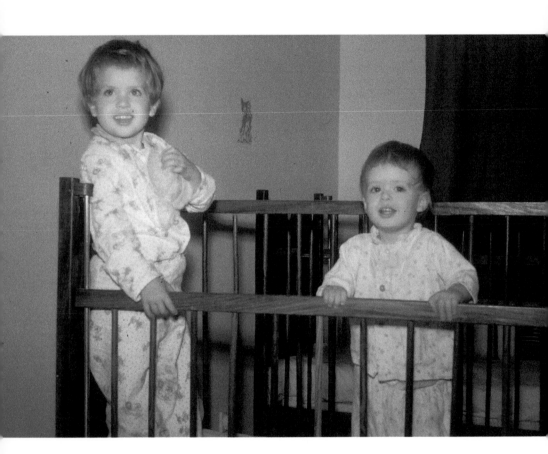

Dinah and Tim – Bedtime

House boat – Srinagar

3

Dibden Purlieu, Hampshire, England

1964

MAP 3

ENGLAND, SCOTLAND & WALES

Mike's mother had rented a house for us, Blackhouse Farm, for a month, during which time we had a look for somewhere else to stay and then think about finding a job. During this period, we had a short visit from Bernhard and Gisela, Mike's German penfriend and his wife, who were on their way home from a holiday in Ireland. As Tim was always playing with a toy aeroplane he earned the nickname of 'pilot man' from Bernhard.

After the war, a teacher from Mike's school went over to Berlin to set up a youth group. He asked a few of those who came along if they would like to correspond with a boy or girl in England as a way of building bridges between the two countries. Several said they would like to do this, so the master sent the list of addresses back to England and Mike selected Bernhard and they have kept in touch ever since.

After some searching we settled on renting a house from a vicar, at East Preston on the south coast near to Littlehampton. Once settled in, Mike set about answering advertisements in the press for civil engineers and after a week or so was called for interviews, most of which were in or around London. He was offered a job on the M4 motorway, a drainage job in Libya and several others, but the one that appealed most was with Rendel, Palmer & Tritton (RPT) on the construction of a power station at Fawley on Southampton Water.

The day after his interview we got in the car and drove over to Fawley to have a look at the site and register with some house agents. Lymington was considered a good locality in which to live so we started looking there, mainly at new houses nearing completion. To buy a house we would need a solicitor, so we called on the manager of the Midland bank and explained what we were looking for. He gave us the name of a solicitor, saying this was the firm the bank used and they had given satisfactory service when called upon.

As they were also in the main street we paid them a call and met Tom Rayner, who agreed to act for us when the time came. When he heard that we were considering Lymington he advised us to have a look in the Hythe area as the daily drive would be much less and Mike would not have to contend with the fog that descended on the forest from time to time.

We followed his suggestion and eventually settled for a detached house being completed in a small private development just beyond an estate built some years previously. We arranged for central heating to be installed. As Mike was to start work before the house would be ready he stayed for a couple of weeks in a hotel just north of Hythe right on the edge of Southampton Water; then moved to a guest house in Fawley.

When our house was finally completed we moved in on a Saturday on the understanding that the furniture and other items we had bought would be delivered the same afternoon. Our packing cases from Mangla had been in store in Guildford and had been delivered earlier, to the annoyance of the builder, even though they had been put in the garage. We waited and waited for the furniture to arrive, then realised that it would not be coming. So we all spent the first night sleeping on the floor in the small bedroom with the heating on for warmth as it was then mid-November 1964. The next day, when our next-door neighbours, Dot and Pete, heard of our plight they insisted on us having their settee-cum-double bed until our own goods arrived. We were very grateful for this. And so we spent the next four years living in Hampshire.

Pete was a foreman and shop steward at Monsanto Chemicals in Fawley. He was a tall, thin fellow with a touch of a West Country accent. They had two young daughters, Kay and Wendy. Our other neighbours were the Tharms; they were both schoolteachers with no children. Our house faced directly opposite the junction of Beverley Road with Heatherstone Avenue, so we had a lounge with something of a view and were not overlooked. We had a small garden with a thick hawthorn hedge at the bottom separating us from a small development beyond. The garden of a family named Jones backed onto the dividing hedge. Our section of the road finished three or four houses beyond ours, after which there was a smallholding, then the bypass to Fawley running along the edge of the New Forest. This new road had been built from Totton at the head of Southampton Water down to Fawley to facilitate the construction of the power station.

We enrolled Dinah at a private kindergarten school, Arnwood House I think it was called, on the road to Beaulieu, until she was old enough to go to the primary school nearby, where Tim eventually joined her. The Tilleys (my sister and brother-in-law) were still working overseas and during one of their home leaves had rented a house in East Preston during our time there. While on this particular leave, they bought a town house in Rustington to give them a base in England.

As the houses around us were finished we were joined by two engineers also working at Fawley, one on the corner and the other at the end of the road on the opposite side. On the other corner lived a young couple connected with the building trade; they had visitors coming and going at all odd hours of day and night and kept us entertained with all their activities. Two doors down from this couple a young family moved in. The husband had come down from Wales to join the Monsanto complex on Southampton Water. His wife was very class-conscious, another Doris Cox, and it must have been a bit of a shock for her when she discovered that one of her husband's subordinates was a shop steward and a close neighbour. She would not allow her daughter to play with any other children in the road apart from Dinah and Tim. One day she asked me where Mike worked.

When I told Mike about it he said, 'I hope you told her I was a road sweeper.'

We set about, as soon as we could, forming a garden out of the field in which the house had been built. Mike got some paving stones to form two strips for a drive and infilled between them with mortar. What there was at the front we made into a lawn edged with flower beds where I grew some wonderful dahlias. The back was divided into a small lawn and a vegetable patch by a path serving the washing line. In the middle of the lawn Mike built a swing for the children.

Our first winter in Hampshire was quite cold. I believe we had the central heating on in the house almost non-stop for the first few months to keep ourselves warm, and to dry out the house, which had been built during a wet summer.

Working on the power station Mike met several people who had had a connection with British Guiana. One was Jack Burton, who told Mike that both he and his brother had been born there, and that Tony Seaford was a cousin of his. Then there was a young engineer of Chinese origin with the contractor, who told Mike his father was a doctor in Mahaicony. Mike told him if his father lived in the GMO's (government medical officer's) house there he could remember having it painted in 1960. And yet another Guyanese was to come to site, Guy Grant. His father had been superintendent of transport and harbours. Although he came to site on a bachelor basis he was married to a Burmese woman living in Bedford.

In 1965 things were becoming increasingly difficult for Mum and Dad in Barbados where they had gone after leaving Georgetown, so we invited them to come over and live with us. With them came Dads journals, all beautifully handwritten in eleven, large, leather bound volumes each of 300 pages. These were the story of his life up until he left Government service and had been transcribed by him from numerous notebooks and diaries that would have carried with him during his work in the interior. When he had settled in, he had started to write his memoirs, based on the journals and illustrated with sketches and maps as he had done years ago in the journals.

When the summer months arrived, we would go over to Rustington for a weekend to look over the Tilley's' house and for a change of scenery, and we may have spent part of our annual holidays there.

In 1966 Mike's mother said she would treat us to a holiday in Italy and come down to Dibden Purlieu to look after Dinah and Tim with Mum while we were away.

It had been suggested that we went down to Bordighera on the Italian Riviera. We crossed from Newhaven to Dieppe and then used part of the route Mike, his mother and brother Antony had taken on their scooters in 1957 with Mike's friends the Hollands. We went at the end of the season when things were quieter so we had no difficulty in getting somewhere to stay en route.

We stayed at the Hotel Tennis Windsor for about ten days, making trips along the coast to the east and west into the French Riviera. We were sitting on the beach one morning when an obvious honeymooning couple came along and settled themselves down close to where we were sitting. They kept us amused with their antics in and out of the water.

When the time came to return, we crossed into France to Nice, then inland through Grasse, the centre of the perfume industry, we then struck north-west across country through Clermont-Ferrand to Cherbourg, from where we took the ferry to Southampton, passing the Needles, and saw the site at Fawley power station before a large red sun, as it was setting rapidly in the west.

Shortly after our return Mike made a Wendy house for Dinah and Tim out of packing cases that had been delivered to the power station.

Not long after our return from our holiday in Italy it was confirmed that I was pregnant, and in May, Fiona Ann was born in Southampton General Hospital. It was quite strange having a baby in the house again after a gap of six and a half years. As far as I can remember she was a very good baby, giving little or no trouble. She would sleep in her pram outside, flat on her back with both arms bent above her head as though in surrender. It was about this time that Dinah and Tim started getting up in the middle of the night and coming into our bed. Mike would have to wait until they had settled again; then carry them back to their own beds.

Dad had become so frail that the doctor decided that he should be admitted to Lymington Hospital. He seemed reasonably happy there. Mum would visit him every day and we would go over whenever we could. In the summer of 1967, a couple of months after Fiona was born, we went up to Scotland for a holiday, leaving Fiona in the safe care of Granny. We had heard a lot about Strathpeffer from Dad where he had spent some of his youth, and we were keen to see it for ourselves. Before he went to Lymington Dad had discussed the possibility of making the trip himself, but reluctantly decided that it would be too much for him.

First, we went to Wolverhampton to visit Dad's half-brother, Walter, and his wife and their family.

From there we drove up to Kendal along the M6 where, in those days, it terminated. Rather than climb over Shap we drove across to the Eden Valley, spending the night in Appleby before going on to Falkirk to spend a few days with George and Helen Smith and to see their son, Sandy, for the first time. During our stay with them we had a day in Edinburgh with a drive back over the Forth Bridge and various trips around Falkirk and Stirling.

Leaving Falkirk, we drove across to Dunblane and took the A9 up through Pitlochry to Inverness and Dingwall, then turned west to Strathpeffer. We stayed at a hotel which in Dad's day had been a private house and just opposite a house occupied by one of his aunts; it was also on the road down which he was riding on his bicycle when the brakes failed and he ploughed into the hedge opposite on the main road. Unfortunately, his cousins who still lived at the top of the village were away at the Braemar Games at the time of our visit.

Wandering round looking at the various sights Dad had told us about, we saw the railway station (now closed), the chemist's shop and the spa, where we were given a glass of revolting-tasting water said to be of great medicinal value. Here we discovered there was a ceilidh that evening in the village hall, so we decided we would go after our evening meal.

This turned out to be a bit of an embarrassment for us. The compère elected to have a singsong halfway through the proceedings with audience participation. When it came to the song *Daisy, Daisy, give me an answer do, I'm half crazy all for the love of you, it won't be a stylish marriage, I can't afford a carriage, but you'll look sweet on the seat of a bicycle made for two*, the compère came over to Mike as we were sitting on the front row and asked him to sing it again solo. Mike finally managed to get through to the end in his off-key voice, for which he was thanked by the compère saying, 'I think the bicycle got a flat tyre in the end!'

Leaving Strathpeffer we went south on a secondary road to Drumnadrochit, then along Loch Ness, passing the observation station on the west side where an almost continuous lookout is kept for 'Nessie', the loch's mythical monster, then on to Fort William and over the Ballachulish Ferry. From there we drove back across to Falkirk for another night or two before returning home.

Later, in October, we received a call from Lymington Hospital with the sad news that Dad had passed away during the night. As Betty and Hugh were still overseas all we could do was to send them a telegram to advise them of our sad loss. Walter and Alice came down for the funeral, which took place at Dibden Church where Fiona had been christened a month or so earlier. As we cleared Dad's personal effects away Mike started to read his memoirs, which fascinated him and in turn led him to start perusing his journals of life in BG.

It was then Mike started with the idea that one day he would edit Dad's journals and use them to effectively complete the memoirs that Dad had started just before he died. Every time we went up and downstairs at home Mike would look out of the window overlooking the garage and say to me, 'If I could build a little room out there as a study I could get on with my writing unhindered.'

The more we thought about it, the more the idea developed, and then I said, 'Well, if you're going to make a small room why not make it bigger and we can use it as another bedroom as well, which we will need as Fiona grows up?'

So, Mike set about drawing up some plans, which he submitted to the council for approval and received without any problems. He decided he would do as much of the work as he could himself, bringing in specialist tradesmen for the work he obviously could not tackle. He found a bricklayer who was willing to work on Sundays to put up the walls once the foundations were completed. With the help of a contractor on site he ordered materials with a trade discount including an extending ladder, and arranged for someone else on site to put up some scaffolding for as long as we required it. Within a matter of months it was completed and Mike and I used it as a master bedroom. The idea of a study got no further at the time but every night before going to sleep Mike would read some pages from Dad's journals until he had been through all eleven volumes. After many years of work editing the journals in his spare time, Mike eventually got them published in two volumes, entitled Vincent Roth, A Life in Guyana.

Dinah joined the Brownies run by a Miss Petty, who met in the church hall in Dibden Purlieu. I remember asking Mike to make a large Easter egg for them out of a wire frame covered with silver foil.

So it came as a bit of a surprise when one day Mike came home and said, 'Head Office would like me to go up to Ironbridge Power Station to look after an ash disposal scheme.'

4

Shrewsbury, Shropshire, England

1969

Mike was offered a new post at Ironbridge Power Station, Shropshire, in which he was most interested, and so a few months later he found himself in Devil's Dingle. Before finally committing himself, Mike and I went up to Ironbridge to have a look at the site and make enquiries about housing should we decide to move there. We stayed at the Happy Valley Hotel just outside the station for a couple of days.

We also saw Devil's Dingle, a dingle being a small wooded valley. This consisted of two small streams flowing down the hillside about one mile up the Severn Valley from the power station on the opposite bank. The wood had for the most part been chopped down during previous operations. A small lagoon with an outfall tower and access bridge had already been built under the power station contract on land once owned by Farmer Passey, whose house and buildings were alongside the site.

The power station was virtually completed and commissioning had started in a small way. Being a coal-fired station it had to have a means of disposing of the ash, and this is where the Dingle came in. The scheme was to create a lagoon into which the ash could be pumped with the surplus water and water entering from the streams flowing off through an outfall tower and down a pipe to the settling pits, to prevent pollution of the River Severn, the final outfall. This part of the work had already been completed, and Mike's task was to increase the size of the lagoon by raising the embankment using pulverised fuel ash (PFA) once the station started producing.

During one of the evenings of our stay Ron Williams, the engineer in charge of the power station, invited us to coffee at his house, a very nice place on a small estate just off the London Road on the south side of Shrewsbury. He told us he would be leaving soon and selling up, but thought his asking price would be above our means if we were interested.

It was double what we eventually paid and Ron sold his house to the new football manager for Shrewsbury Town. While we were there Mike asked what the correct pronunciation was for Shrewsbury – was it 'Shrews-bury' or 'Shrows-bury'? The locals called it by the former while the 'higher up and better off' used the latter pronunciation.

We looked at several houses and were very struck by a detached house with a largish garden on the Portland Estate backing onto the school playing fields, which would be ideal for Dinah and Tim. It had four good-sized bedrooms, a large entrance hall, a pleasant kitchen overlooking the road and a lounge and dining room separated by sliding glazed doors.

Back in Southampton Mike rang his head office accepting their offer and prepared to move to Ironbridge.

We continued to negotiate for the house we had seen in Portland Crescent and with property prices lower in the Midlands secured it for a sum less than for we sold Heatherstone Avenue. As there was not a lot going on at the site Mike came home every Friday, leaving after lunch and arriving home in the early evening. On one such trip he was suddenly aware of a low-flying dart-like aircraft passing across the road at a very low altitude and realised that he had just had his first view of *Concorde*.

Having moved to Shrewsbury and settled in our new house, Mike was able to set about his new job in earnest. Ron Williams had given him an old inspector, Hugh Macleod, who was close to retirement, and recruited two checkers, Roy Johnson and Les Gilmore, who were near retiring age. Roy was a great talker and would spend hours in Mike's office telling him about his life and the folklore of Shropshire. In his early days, he had worked on the railway as a signalman and later at a power station in the stores section. He had a son in Rugby whose wife was about to present him with his first grandchild. Les was a big, quiet fellow and lived at the site entrance in two cottages which he had converted into one house. He had quite a large family; one son was a fireman in London and there were several daughters at home. Their house had a large kitchen garden and on most Saturdays Mike was told to stop and collect a basket of fresh produce when things were in season.

With three growing children, we realised that our Riley, which had given us good service, was too small so we traded it in for a Morris Oxford. Getting to and from work used to take about twenty-five minutes and presented no problem, except in summer on Saturday mornings when the traffic on the A5 could be quite heavy.

Mike's office had a magnificent view over the Severn and across to the Long Mynd. On the opposite bank of the Severn was Buildwas Park.

Just before Christmas we received an invitation to the Fawley Dinner with accommodation kindly offered by Joan Funnell, the firm's secretary. We nearly didn't go as we had had our first fall of snow and road conditions looked somewhat precarious. However, on speaking to Joan she said it was quite mild with them and urged us to go. Fortunately, Mum was staying with us at the time so could look after the children.

We had a very enjoyable evening at the Beaulieu Hotel with several other ex-members of the staff present, including Ron Cleaver and his wife, who was wearing a trouser suit, something I had not seen before. Next morning, we were served a pot of tea in bed and, after a hearty breakfast, returned home via Shalford, where we called in on Mike's mother and brother.

Every year in the Dingle Mike had problems after the 'Glorious' 12th of August. The whole area was very popular with sportsmen who descended on the valley with their guns to 'bag' partridge, pheasant and grouse, a large number being bred and fed for this purpose in Buildwas Park. The trouble was that the shot birds often fell inside the site boundary, which resulted in people clambering over the fence to reclaim their prizes.

During Mike's stay in the Dingle he had two assistants, the first being Aszu Pishori, a young Tanzanian of Indian origin. His family, who lived near Arusha, had a coffee plantation and one of his brothers made meerschaum pipes, of which Mike was given a sample. His replacement was Chris Harris, a very tall, softly spoken lad who travelled about in a Mini.

One of Roy's hobbies was wood-carving, and one of the first things he made was a walking stick for everybody – he even made one each for Dinah, Tim and Fiona.

In the Wyle Cop in Shrewsbury we discovered an excellent model shop, so for Christmas we bought Tim a small 00 gauge Hornby electric train set which we installed in his bedroom. As he had the smallest room the layout was somewhat cramped and eventually we moved him and the railway to the other large front room, giving him more scope for the layout.

As we had space alongside the house we considered building on a self-contained room for Mum, and Mike drew up some plans and got them passed but never proceeded with the idea for one reason and another. When we sold the house, the new owners built a second garage instead.

Our neighbours were a mixed lot. Beyond where we planned to build our extension was a passage which one day would form an extra entrance to the school, and beyond this lived the Rochfords, who were related to the nurserymen of that name. They were an elderly couple and with them was their son, Terry, and his son, a little four- or five-year-old. Terry was separated from his wife. To look after the youngster a young girl came in each day and on occasions he would come over and play with Fiona on our swings or in the Wendy house.

On the other side was an elderly widow, Mrs Williams, whose married daughter, Mrs Hinchcliffe, lived next door but one at the end of the road. The Hinchcliffes were both doctors and had one daughter about Dinah's age. Directly opposite us were the Careys and their two children.

Between Mrs Williams and the Hinchcliffes was the Pierce family. Graham was a shift charge engineer at Ironbridge. Their daughter, Rhiannon, who was about Dinah's age, went to the Day Trust School in town. Graham and Margaret were actively involved in the Lions Club and periodically would have a party attended by club members, with the result that the road was filled with cars, making it very difficult for other residents to get in and out of their own driveways. We were invited to one of their parties shortly after our arrival. Later, we heard the couple had split up.

Around the corner in Allgold Drive, a cul-de-sac, were the Gradwells. Brian was an inspector with the police stationed in Wellington. They had two adopted children, David and Diane, as his wife Kathleen was thought to be unable to have children, until one day she produced a daughter, Sandra, who was six or seven years old when we first met them.

Further along our road was a family with four young children. He worked in one of the banks in town until one day he failed to come home; he had taken off with someone else, leaving his wife to cope with their young family. In another road, we befriended the Boardmans, who had two sons. He was an architect and his wife was recovering from a spell in hospital. They were a pleasant family and we used to exchange Christmas cards for a while after we left the district. Close to them was another couple with a young daughter, Nicola. They used to visit us, they said, because they liked Mike's dry sense of humour. Then only the wife came to see us, as she too had been deserted. It would appear that we were living in a district of errant fathers and husbands.

One couple who were somewhat older than the others were the Fords. He too was with the CEGB (Central Electricity Generating Board) at Ironbridge, and previously had been at Aberthaw Power Station in South Wales, during which time they had lived in Llantwit Major, which they had liked very much. It was with Gwen – I believe that was her Christian name – that we went to the Welsh Eisteddfod, which that year was held in Llangollen. It was a lovely warm day and we thoroughly enjoyed it, as the competitions were, in the main, held on open-air stages, making it very informal. It was very colourful too, with many dressed in national costume.

The first year we were in Shrewsbury we did not have a summer holiday as Mike spent the time repairing and painting the house, so the following year we decided to go camping in France. To avoid the summer crowds we went in May, perhaps a little early but we planned to head for the south where the weather should be warm enough. We spent a couple of nights with the Tilleys, who were now back in England and living in Tonbridge, as Mike had to go up to Bromley to borrow the tent and groundsheet from his cousin, Marlo.

The holiday could only be described as a disaster. During the time we were away a deep depression settled over France, bringing high winds and rain to all parts. We only learned this when we returned. We only spent three nights under canvas. On the first or second night we were flooded out, with the result that we had a wet tent and bedding to pack up the next day. The morning after our first night we had a job dismantling the tent. It appeared to be very heavy and difficult to control until we discovered that the problem was that Fiona was swinging from the top roof frame!

We drove down the eastern side of France, generally following the route Mike and I had taken when we went to Italy and heading for Divonne as we were anxious to try and find the old Roth mansion there. We did not allow ourselves enough time for serious research and so spent some time in the cemetery hoping to find some family headstones. All we picked up were some small pebbles, one of which Fiona managed to swallow. These stones were used to decorate the various plots.

From Divonne we went on to Geneva, where we sat for a while and watched the arrival and departure of planes at the airport. As the weather was so unsettled we decided to drive across to the west coast in the hope that it would be better weather there – it wasn't. In one of the hotels where we stayed Tim managed to lock himself in the room he was to share with Dinah! It was when we were going down to dinner that we found his door locked. Through the keyhole, we could see him fast asleep on his bed but nothing we did would wake him. We could not get the key out of the lock and the hotel management had no other means of getting into the room. So Dinah had to come in with Mike, Fiona and me and we had rather an unsettled night wondering whether Tim was all right. He awoke next morning bright and breezy, unaware of the worry he had caused.

As we had not planned to stay in hotels our funds diminished rapidly, so in the end we decided to return home as quickly as possible.

During our stay in Shrewsbury we had a number of visitors – one of these was Laura Francine, a middle-aged American, and a friend of the Roths'. She was over in England and phoned to say she wanted to come and see us. We did not get off to a very good start as we were late getting to the station to meet her, for which we got a telling-off from this feisty lady. We took her for several drives round the Welsh border country, which she enjoyed, and we parted on quite good terms.

When Mike's mother and brother came to stay, we took the opportunity to go over to Derby and see Mike's Uncle Denis, whom they had not seen for many years. We also went over that way again to Burton-on-Trent to see John and Bernice and their son Paul, who had left BG and settled here where John was teaching at the technical college. They had a pleasant bungalow which John had modernised and were the owners of a caravan, spending weekends fishing in the Derbyshire Dales. Mike's uncle and aunt, Jo and Tuk, called in when they were passing through the district. Jo, who was an old Salopian, was anxious to see his alma mater and the town again.

We had hoped to see Mike's old friends the Hollands, who were still in Lambley, and made tentative plans to meet in Derby or Lichfield, but for one reason or another never got around to it and we lost touch with them.

My friend, Grace Targett, together with her husband Brian and two daughters from Dibden Purlieu, also paid us a visit. I remember we had an inflatable paddling pool on the lawn and the children spent the day getting thoroughly wet.

As Mum continued to live with us and the Tilleys, when it was time for her to change her abode we would meet at Watford Gap service station on the Ml where the transfer was made. During one of her stays with us, Mum had spent a period in hospital, and while there had made several friends, one of whom was Mrs Wilkes, who we came to know quite well.

Mr and Mrs Wilkes were an elderly couple and lived in a small bungalow on the other side of the Wenlock Road. Their daughter was married to a teacher at Shrewsbury School and lived not far from us on the other side of the playing fields. Once or twice we took the Wilkes out for a drive in the country, and on one occasion when they had a relative to stay we went for a picnic near Whitchurch.

As a family, we would also go out and about at the weekends, and sometimes we would go to the site as Les and Roy were always asking after the children. The children liked to go to the Gilmores as they had a very talkative mynah bird. One event we looked forward to, was the Sleap Air Show, where there was a fly-past of all the latest aircraft.

Whilst we were in Shrewsbury it seemed a good time to get the dog I had always wanted. A visit to our local pet shop and I came home with a young terrier – Bimbo.

The children were really excited when they came home from school to find a small dog tearing round the garden.

We had not had him long before it was Dinah's birthday. Dinah took her presents upstairs and put them under her bed and joined her guests in the garden.

The party over Dinah went upstairs to look at her gifts. Soon she was running down the stairs saying 'someone has eaten all the peppermint creams'. Tim and Fiona denied all knowledge of the crime. We then noticed that Bimbo was drinking a lot of water and when I picked him up and shook him he sounded like a hot water bottle! The culprit had been found!

About this time, Fiona was into hamsters. As they only live for about eighteen months we had quite a lot of little graves in the flowerbeds. One night as she was cleaning out and feeding the latest 'Mousey' it managed to escape and ran over to the built-in gas fire and disappeared. Despite calling it many times, there was no reappearance. 'What are we going to do? she cried. I'm sure he will come out soon, I said. 'Phone Daddy, phone Daddy' said Dinah. In an attempt to calm things down I rang Mike, not that he could do anything being hundreds of miles away. He said he was sorry to hear what had happened and suggested we left the hamster cage open, as soon as 'Mousey' felt hungry he would come out and make for his home. We all went to bed hoping for good news in the morning. Sure enough, when we came downstairs there was 'Mousey'

running around on his wheel.

In 1972 Dinah had taken her eleven-plus and won a place at the Shrewsbury Girls' Public School. Tim and Fiona were at St. Giles. Dinah had attended a series of confirmation classes in the afternoons after school and on 18th June was confirmed in St. Chad's Church.

Not having made any plans for a summer holiday that year, we happened to see an advertisement for rented accommodation on the South Wales coast and wrote off for details. The outcome was that we booked a three-bedroomed bungalow in Saundersfoot for a week in July.

The holiday, however, started in Surrey. Ernie and Marjorie Reeve's daughter, Diane, was getting married on 15th July and we were invited to the wedding. Marjorie was the sister of Dad's long-serving secretary, Lilian St. Aubyn. On the eve of the wedding we drove down to Shalford and spent the night with Da. As the wedding was not until the early afternoon we had plenty of time to get over to Coulsdon.

The day dawned bright and sunny and stayed that way until sunset. At the church, we met up with my sister, Betty, and her family and other friends, some of whom we had not seen for over ten years.

The service over, we proceeded to a school about a mile and a half away where the reception was being held. The headmaster of the school was the bridegroom's father. After a very good time was had by all, especially Tim and his cousin Mark, we returned to Shalford.

Next morning Hugh Tilley came over to Shalford from Tonbridge with Mum, who was coming along with us to Wales. The journey was a little slow until we got to Reading and joined the motorway. After stopping at the Severn Bridge for lunch we reached Saundersfoot in the late afternoon.

The holiday was quite uneventful, most of the time being spent on the beach. Occasionally we would go into Tenby and during one afternoon, which turned out to be rather dull, we drove to Pembroke as Mike was interested to see the new power station there, one of the firm's other projects. Unfortunately, there was a sea mist on when we arrived so we were unable to see very much apart from a misty outline.

The following Saturday we returned home. Amongst the mail on the mat when we opened the door was a letter from the firm, saying they were looking for an engineer to work on a power station at Ahwaz in Iran. We all rushed up to Tim's room to look at the large *Daily Telegraph* map on his wall. After a hectic search, we eventually found Ahwaz in the bottom right-hand corner of the chart, about one hundred kilometres north of Abadan. We did not talk about much else for the rest of the weekend.

5

Ahwaz, Iran

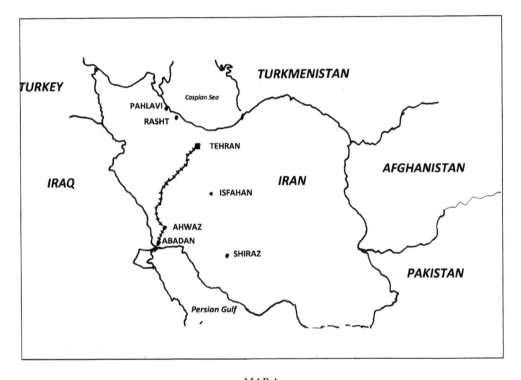

MAP 4

IRAN

When Mike started to make arrangements for us to join him at Ahwaz in south Iran early in 1973, I was concerned about Tim missing the eleven-plus exam. So I went to see Miss Lambert, the headmistress, and she advised me very strongly to let him take it even if he did not go on to a grammar school. Mike had said not to bother but I insisted on us staying back for six months to enable Tim to take the exam, which he passed. Tim got a place at the Wakeman School, which he attended before we went away.

Once in Ahwaz we registered Dinah and Tim with the International School, which was run by the Americans as most of the children attending were from the States. The only trouble was that their work was often marked as incorrect when they used the English way of spelling a word rather than the American. In the end, Mike had a word with the teachers, saying our children would be confused when they returned to England.

Dinah and Tim were very happy there. The school bus would pick them up outside the house at seven o'clock and bring them back in time for lunch. The reason being that after midday it was too hot to be outside. It was so hot you could fry an egg on the bonnet of the car! At school the malis (gardeners) would spray water on the areas where the children were standing as the ground became so hot.

When I first arrived, I could not speak a word of Farsi, the Iranian language, and one day in the commissary on the other side of the river I was wondering which cooking oil was the best to buy. Seeing a friendly-looking Iranian lady also doing her shopping I asked if she spoke English and could help me. This is how I met my lifelong friend Nina. She is really a lovely person; she would invite us round to lunch on a Friday when we would see her husband, Behrooz, and son, Sina, who was about

Fiona's age. It was through Nina that we met another Iranian family who befriended us and with whom we are still in touch.

One Friday afternoon after an excellent lunch of *fezanjan* at Nina's, Behrooz excused himself, saying he had to take Sina across the road to a birthday party. He was back in the space of a few minutes as his friends, on learning that we had three children with us, wished to invite them to the party as well. The invitation was readily accepted and they were off before we had time to ask the age of the child whose party it was. When they came back they were full of the time they had had, the things to eat and the film show which formed the pièce de résistance of the afternoon.

Thus, we made the acquaintance of the Morakabatis, who remain our good friends to this day. Morteza was very tall. Standing well over six feet and of slender build, he made a striking figure. He too worked for the National Iranian Oil Company, but in a different section to Behrooz. Giti, his wife, was also of slender build but of medium height only. Their two daughters, Shohleh and Mojdeh, were about the same age as Dinah and Tim, and likewise their son Reza was only slightly older than Fiona.

Several mornings a week after Mike had left for work and the children were away to school, I would spend the morning with Nina. If the fancy took us we would take a taxi and go into Ahwaz to do some shopping.

One day when we were returning home from such a jaunt the driver turned to Nina and asked, 'Why are you two ladies talking in English, are you students practising the language?'

'No,' replied Nina, 'my friend here is British and does not speak Farsi, that is why we are speaking English.'

Another time when we were out together, Nina drew my attention to the men dressed in long grey cloaks with turbans on their heads. 'You see those men, Audrey? They are mullahs.'(religious teachers or leaders)

Another engineer and his family (who had now returned home) had occupied the house we moved into. They had two small children and when I came to inspect the mattresses on the children's beds I saw they were quite badly stained, so Mike and I went straight away to the bazaar and purchased some new ones. I would never leave a house in such a state. One day when I went out to call the children in from playing on the street I saw Dinah was talking to the man who lived obliquely opposite. I went over and introduced myself. He said his name was Shanami and he spoke a little English as he had worked for the oil company for many years but was now retired. Unfortunately, he said, his wife spoke no English. We became good friends, they would come over to us and we would go over and pay them a visit.

One time when they came over Fiona came in and said, 'Buro Gomsha.'

Mr Shanami laughed and said, 'Fiona, where did you learn that word?'

'Oh, I've heard other children say it to me.'

I asked what it meant and was told it meant 'Go to the Devil!'

Mr Shanami told us that the previous family in the house had been there several years and yet had never even said hello.

The house directly opposite us and next door to the Shanamis' became vacant and the house agent told Mike that a young woman from Venezuela, whose husband was said to be old enough to be her father, was about to move in. She had told the agent that she wanted to be near to me as she had heard I was from South America.

The house being already furnished was a great asset and made life very much easier for us. There were, however, several things we needed to buy, so after a cup of tea and once Mike had returned home from work and the heat of the day was starting to abate we would all get into the car and drive down to the bazaar and make our purchases. The main bazaar was on Pahlavi Avenue and consisted of a continuous row of small shops on either side of the road. Some had plate-glass windows with an entrance door; others were just three walls and a steel roller shutter for security. Haberdashers and boutiques tended to be in the former category whilst greengrocers, bedding and mattress centres, hardware and plastic goods belonged to the latter.

On the north side were a couple of arcades which consisted mainly of jewellers, art galleries and the like. The streets off the bazaars were devoted to the repair of cars and vans and the sale of spares for them, furniture manufacture, plumbers, carpenters, metalworkers and almost every trade that one could think of. It was possible to obtain almost anything if one knew where to look.

The jewellers' shops were of great fascination to Dinah and me and we would spend hours gazing at the various trinkets displayed in the windows. After many visits and much window-gazing we befriended an old man by the name of Tawoosi, who received many commissions from us during our stay in Ahwaz.

Almost opposite each other were the two main handicraft shops. Here they displayed all the usual trappings – camel seats, marquetry work, brass work, coats, shawls and the like – and this was where most of the bartering was done. After half an hour or so of haggling one would retire gracefully, saying that you were going home to think it over. One then went to the shop opposite and started all over again. After sleeping on the offers made, one would return to the shop one thought would yield to the lowest offer. The shopkeepers were wily characters and would not hesitate to let you know that they knew that you were also dealing with their rivals across the road. If the truth were known, they probably all belonged to the same family.

Often in these shops would be an American couple stocking up with trinkets and souvenirs before returning to the States. The sums of money they were arguing about were usually much higher than we would ever contemplate offering.

It was often said the shopkeepers had one price for the Americans and another for Europeans. This may be so, as often after the customary 'Salaam Alaikum, Hali shoma chitore' they would say, 'Are you American, mister?'

While the family was out in Iran it was the intention that we should see something of the country before we returned home. There were two places we wanted to see: Shiraz and Isfahan. So, on a Monday in the last week of June we set off for Shiraz. To avoid the heat of the day we left home at five o'clock; it being still dark, the children and I soon fell asleep again. As dawn broke one of the children stirred and asked where we were and this break in the silence caused the others to sit up and take stock of the surroundings.

Suddenly Dinah said, 'Look, Dad, we're in the real desert. These humps are sand dunes. Oh, please let us stop and have a look, we might see a mirage.' Feeling like a break himself, Mike pulled off the road and the children were out of the car like a shot and disappeared behind the nearest dune.

While we were parked, we were conscious of a car slowing down and then moving off again in the same direction as we were travelling. We guessed he had seen our stationary car and assumed we had broken down and was slowing down to offer assistance, but on seeing us in the sand dunes had realised that we had no problems with the car. Anxious to be on the road again, Mike called the children and they reluctantly returned to the car.

As we neared the summit of the hill the gradient eased off and the road ahead was almost straight over quite long stretches. As we approached Bebehan we saw a filling station on the left-hand side and decided to top up the tank, as we were not sure when we might be able to refuel again. As we pulled up we saw there was another car at the other pump.

Whilst Mike was opening the filler cap with the key the driver of the car, an Iranian in his mid-thirties, came over and spoke to me.

'Good morning, you are English or American?'

'Hello, we're British from England.'

'You are travelling far?'

'Well, actually we're on our way to Shiraz. I wanted to fill up with petrol as I am not sure where we will find the next garage.'

'We are going to Shiraz too. Perhaps we will see you again a little later.'

'I hope so, cheerio.'

He returned to his car, paid the garage assistant and then drove off.

'*Chanta liter, Agha?*' asked the pump attendant.

'*Bist-o-panj,*' Mike said.

After passing through Gachsaran, we saw a windsock and realised we were alongside the local airstrip. It was here that we came to a road junction and for once Mike hadn't a clue which was the road we needed to take, so he turned onto an open area and stopped, then looked round to see if there was anyone to ask the way. We were out of luck: the whole place was deserted. Then we saw a car coming along the road from Gachsaran. As it drew nearer it slowed down, so by the time it was alongside it was moving at a crawling pace. In the offside front seat was a pleasant-looking woman and in the driver's seat was the man who had spoken to us at the filling station on the outskirts of Bebehan.

'The right-hand road is the road for Shiraz,' he called across as he slowly moved forward.

'Many thanks,' we shouted back after him, and turning to me, Mike said, 'That's a bit of luck, him turning up like that. As we know he's going to Shiraz we'll have to try and keep him in our sight.'

We managed to keep him in sight for a while but then he drew ahead when we had a stop for a drink and to answer nature's call. We also slowed down when we saw a rather strange-looking animal trotting along the side of the road directly ahead of us. As we got closer we saw it was a camel. It appeared to be alone and not the least bit put out by us or the other passing traffic.

Approaching a natural cutting in the landscape we saw that the cars ahead of us were slowing down and there was a chain across the road under the control of the gendarmerie, as the local police were called. As we drew up behind the car in front of us we saw, emerging from the car next but one in the queue, our friend from Bebehan followed by his family.

'Hello again,' he said, as he came up to me, 'we hoped you hadn't got lost again.'

'Oh no, thank you, we lost some time when we stopped for the children to look at the camel we passed some way back. If we hadn't seen you when we did I doubt if we would be here now. What's the hold-up for?' we asked.

'It is some form of traffic control. We shall be here for about half an hour. Come and see the spring, the water is very cool and refreshing. My name is Karami, Keramat Karami, and this is my wife.' Thus the introductions were made. The children had already run off together to where the stream was bubbling out from under the road.

Keramat was another employee of the oil company and lived in Abadan. He had left home earlier than we had and it turned out that it was he who had passed us when we were in the sand dunes near Aghajari. He and his family were going to stay for a day or two with his wife's family in Shiraz and then they were all going together to the family home in Abadeh, a town between Shiraz and Isfahan.

'Where are you staying in Shiraz?' he asked.

'We're not sure,' Mike replied. 'We haven't booked anywhere but we had in mind to try The Park Hotel when we arrive.'

'We would like you to come to my sister-in-law's house for a drink of something cool and we are sure they would like to meet you.'

Mike and I looked at each other. 'Thank you very much but we must go to the hotel and make sure we have a room for the night. Besides, we are very tired as we were up before dawn and we all need a good shower after all the dust on the road. No, thank you very much for inviting us, it's very kind of you but we can't.'

'Please come, Mr Bennett. If you come I will telephone the hotel and make a reservation for you from my brother's house. You can have a wash there and a drink and some refreshments, then I will take you to the hotel.'

The thought of someone offering to fix up our hotel accommodation was very tempting, and presumably if we could not get into The Park they would know where else to try which was more than we did, so after a quick discussion between the two of us we both said, without more ado, 'Thank you very much, we will certainly accept your very kind offer.'

To stop the children, who had spent the time playing together by the stream, from getting completely soaked, we called them over and explained to them what was happening, at which they were very pleased as they said they were getting on very well with the Karami children and wished to stay with them for a little while longer if they could. We all then made our way back towards our cars.

By the time we reached our car there was a lot of activity ahead and cars, lorries and buses were approaching us from the opposite direction.

'It looks as if the road is open again,' said Keramat. 'When we move off I will drive at the usual speed but will wait for you outside Shiraz and then you can follow me to the house.'

We returned to our respective cars and once the children had sorted themselves out we were off on the last stage of our journey to Shiraz. The countryside through which we passed was of little interest; gentle, undulating grasslands, extending to the horizon in all directions. Although it had been a long day I did not feel as tired as I thought I would. I think it was partly due to the knowledge that our accommodation in Shiraz was virtually resolved and very little effort would be needed on our part.

After about an hour we turned a corner and there laid out before us was the city of Shiraz. We then started a gentle descent onto the plain below. As we approached the first sign of habitation we saw the Karamis' car parked on the side of the road. Mike flashed his headlights and they pulled out in front of us and we started the rather hazardous task of following behind them.

We did not pass through the city centre, which was probably just as well as trying to follow a Paykan car on a road full of Paykan cars is not very easy. Eventually we reached a quieter quarter of the town where we were the only cars on the road. Here the roads were unmade and we had to pick our way very carefully. Soon the Karamis pulled up at a house on the corner of a street and a moment later we drew up alongside. The Karami children – there were two of them – were soon out of their car and ringing the doorbell, which brought the Shiraz Karamis to the gate.

Keramat's brother was more heavily built and older-looking and his wife, although very attractive, was obviously older than her sister. It is not often one meets two brothers married to two sisters. Keramat's nephew was only five or six years old and called Mazda. We were always to be reminded of him as we drove around, as there were a number of Japanese pickups on the road with the name Mazda on their tailboards.

We were soon ushered into the house and tea, freshly made lime juice and plates of fruit were offered to us. After a wash, we all felt quite refreshed. With so many of us in the one room it was almost like a party.

After many protestations and a promise that we would return the following evening, Keramat finally agreed to take us to the hotel, which they had booked during the evening. By the time we had settled in it was dark so we had little idea of the building and its surroundings.

The following morning after breakfast we set off to look at the city. The children were delighted at the size of the hotel swimming pool as it was about three times larger than the one at the Ahwaz Hotel.

At this time, the children had a craze for collecting plastic matchboxes which at that time were on sale in Iran. Being in Shiraz offered the chance of collecting ones not available in Ahwaz, or so they thought, so our walk consisted of a series of zigzags across the streets from one cigarette stall to the next.

After exhausting the cigarette stalls we found our way to the main bazaar. As usual it was a sea of people. The building was large with a high roof. The range of goods that were available for purchase seemed limitless. Plastic wares, carpets, clothes and the like. We must have spent well over an hour wandering round the various stalls and counters.

Across the road was another building that housed carpenters, blacksmiths and other tradesmen. Here, the building was of a low circular section and quite dark except for port-like holes in the roof that threw pools of light onto the floor like spotlights on a stage. The most interesting section was that where the ornamental plates depicting scenes from the poems of Omar Khayyám and Persian history were made. The noise was quite deafening. Both young and old men were employed here working side by side in their little workshops which lay on either side of the main passageway. There was a strong smell of bitumen with which the plates and salvers were coated to form the pictures. The pictures were marked out on the surface; then hammered with a series of metal punches.

In the afternoon, we relaxed in the hotel grounds while the children enjoyed themselves in the pool. Dinah made several friends, one of whom she corresponded with for a number of years. During our stay we also visited the mausoleums of Hafez and Saadi, Persia's other famous poets. These are set in beautifully laid-out gardens which were a great joy to walk in.

On the Thursday morning, we set off to visit Persepolis, the site of which is some sixty-five kilometres from Shiraz on the road to Isfahan. Thus we left the city by the road built by Iman Kali Khan, still lined with trees but obviously not the original ones, gradually climbing up into the hills. The end of the city was marked by an impressive stone gateway through which we passed. As the road levelled off we found ourselves in a shallow valley, and on either side of the road were large walled orchards. Soon these too were no longer in evidence and we were in the wilderness again.

After passing through Marvdasht we found ourselves on a small plain, the surrounding hills now being on the horizon. Seeing a herd of camels in the distance, we slowed down to have a closer look at them. There were fifteen to twenty of them, half of them being quite young animals, and with them were what we took to be a nomadic tribe as some of the bigger animals were laden with their belongings. One young woman was spinning wool taken from the sheep travelling with the tribe as she walked along on the side of the road. They may have been part of the Qashqai tribe who live in Fars province. In winter they live down on the shores of the Gulf, moving up into the Zagros Mountains south of Isfahan in summer; their main route being to the west of Shiraz. Andy Rusbridge, an engineer at Ahwaz Power Station, told Mike that on his way to Shiraz he had seen part of this migration, which was quite a sight. Hundreds of sheep, goats, camels, men, women and children all on the move together.

Soon a sign indicated that we should take the right-hand fork at the junction ahead. The road onto which we had now turned was better than the highway we had just left. The reason, no doubt, being that the road had been rebuilt for the celebrations held here in 1971. This was the spectacular display put on by the shah, and to which the heads of state from all over the world were invited to celebrate the 2,500 years of monarchy in Iran. It must be remembered that the monarchy in Iran is not the same as is found in other democratic countries.

The Pahlavi dynasty only commenced in 1925 when the Reza Shah was elected king by the Majlis, the Iranian Parliament. The title *Shahanshah*, King of Kings, is rather grandiose, but is one that has been used throughout Persian history and would seem to imply that the king was the king of the various kingdoms that made up the empire.

As we approached we saw the huge columns rising from the complex that formed Persepolis. Directly in front was a broad flight of steps leading up to the plateau on which the ancient city is set. On the right were the tent-like buildings that had been erected to house the visiting dignitaries in 1971. Since then they have been used for conferences and other such gatherings.

After parking the car we paid the entrance fee and climbed the stairs and started to explore the ruins. Persepolis was created by Darius in 518 BC almost as soon as he completed his palace at Susa to the west. It was set on the spur of Kuh-i Rahmat, not as an administrative or commercial centre but as a shrine for the celebration of Nouw Rouz, the New Year.

While Dinah, Fiona and I went to get a drink and buy postcards, Mike and Tim climbed up the hillside behind the ruins to the rock tombs of Artaxerxes II. From here they had a panoramic view of the ruins, the tented city with the flat, arid plain behind.

After a fairly extensive tour we were beginning to feel tired, so we decided to return to Shiraz, stopping on the way to eat the packed lunch provided by the hotel.

Part of the evening we spent with the Karamis at their home. During the general conversation after we had related our day's activities, Keramat said they were going to their family home in Abadeh and suggested that we went along with them and, having had lunch in Abadeh, we could then go on to Isfahan. On the way to Abadeh we would call in at Naqsh-e Rustam and Pasargadae.

The idea was that we should settle with the hotel the previous evening as they planned to leave Shiraz at five o'clock in the morning. This we duly did. We also asked Keramat to telephone the hotel at half past four to arouse the night porter, as we could not rely on him to being awake at that hour to give us a call.

Although we packed the previous evening and went to bed early it seemed only a matter of minutes after we had fallen asleep before the phone was ringing to wake us. We were soon up, washed and dressed and were just making our way down the hotel steps to the car when the Karamis drove into the courtyard.

After we had greeted each other and loaded up the car we were soon on our way through the deserted streets of Shiraz heading towards Persepolis. Dawn had already broken and the sun was climbing rapidly into the sky to herald another fine, hot day.

The roads being traffic-free, we made good progress. As we had travelled this road only the day before the distances seemed much less and it was not long before we could see the columns of Persepolis outlined against the backcloth of Kuh-e Rahmat. This time, however, we kept to the main road and were soon entering a small valley leading off the plain.

This turned out to be only a narrow passage leading through to another plain. We were now close behind Keramat's car and in a short while he was turning off onto a minor road which led towards the nearby hillside. As we continued it looked as if we were going to visit an old quarry.

The road ended abruptly at the foot of a wide stone stairway. On the left-hand side was a small wooden hut. The car in front was slowing down and finally parked alongside the hut and we pulled up behind them. We had arrived at Naqsh-e Rustam.

As we had left the hotel long before breakfast was served, we were all feeling decidedly hungry. The Karamis had brought some food and drink along with them, which they very kindly shared with us. The womenfolk were soon busy laying out a spread on the bonnets of the two cars. Meanwhile Keramat was at the little hut, which was now open, paying the entrance fees for all of us. His brother, whose name we could never remember but referred to as KB, Keramat's brother, had produced a small tape recorder, which he then switched on. It was a dialogue in English, giving the history and details of Naqsh-e Rustam. The idea being that visitors carried them along as they wandered around the site and thus could learn the details of the various points of interest. Similar recordings were available in French, German, Italian and other major languages of the world.

Having eaten an adequate breakfast, we packed away the cups and plates and then climbed the stairs to look at the wonders beyond. Naqsh-e Rustam was chosen by the Achaemenid kings as a necropolis and the tombs of Darius II, Darius I, Xerxes I and Artaxerxes I are hollowed out of the cliff face of Kuh-i-Hosayn.

Left of the tombs are two open-air Sassanian fire altars cut out of the rock, pyramidal in shape but unequal in size. Opposite the cliff face was a square building known as the Ka'bah-I Zardusht, where the sacred fire was preserved. The structure stands on a triple base of large blocks of white stone. The walls are decorated with rectangular hollows set out in a chequerboard pattern with black niches that look like bricked-up windows.

As we walked back to the cars, we looked out over the plain. Here once stood the town of Istakhr, where in the Sassanian period were crowned the kings of that period. Today nothing remains, the town being destroyed during the Arab conquest in the 7th century AD.

Back in the cars we soon rejoined the Isfahan road and headed northwest for Pasargadae. The road wound its way through narrow gorges, then across the wider plains in shallow valleys. Pasargadae, about seventy kilometres from Persepolis, lies on the Morgag Plain and was the first of the two great Achaemenid capitals to be built in Fars. Skirting the village of Madar-i-Sulaiman and crossing a wide-open stretch, we saw the tomb of Cyrus rising from the ground.

The tomb consists of two elements, a gabled tomb chamber and a majestic plinth of six receding tiers. The body of Cyrus was said to have been placed in a gold sarcophagus. This shrine was visited twice by

Alexander the Great; the first time just after his conquest of Persia and again six or seven years later to punish those who had violated the tomb. About 1,500 years later the tomb gained further fame when the mortal remains of Solomon's mother were interred here, from which fact the modern local village takes its name. The shah performed the opening ceremony to the 2,500-year celebrations here.

Time did not allow us to visit the site of Pasargadae as we were expected in Abadeh for lunch and still had two hundred kilometres to cover. The scenery was much as we had seen before reaching Pasargadae; the road, however, became busier as the day progressed.

After a while the valley widened and we appeared to be on a high plateau fringed on two sides by a low range of hills. We passed through several villages and finally reached Abadeh. We drove slowly through the town centre, which was quite busy both with traffic and pedestrians.

On the northern outskirts of the town we turned off to the left and headed across an open space towards a settlement of houses, each of which was surrounded by a high wall. We then made our way through a series of narrow lanes until the car in front pulled up before a set of large double doors. KB got out and opened the gates and the car moved forward into a driveway whilst we followed slowly behind. The noise of the cars brought the grandparents out of the house, followed by two unmarried daughters.

The introductions over, we were taken into the house, which was very much like a pre-war bungalow in Britain except that like all houses in Iran it had a flat roof. We had a quick wash to remove the worst of the dust and dirt and then we all sat down to a huge lunch.

After lunch as we were finishing our tea I told the children to start to get ready so that we could be on our way again as we did not want to be too late in arriving in Isfahan as we had no accommodation booked there. There was then a lull in the conversation and Keramat turned to us and said they would like us to stay the night with them. We thanked them but queried whether they could really cope with us considering the great influx of people there had been that day. They said provided the children did not mind sleeping on the floor they could manage quite easily. It transpired that there was another house next door that belonged to them.

Within the walls of the property there was a fair-sized garden with a *jube (open drainage ditch for rainwater)* flowing through it. After sitting in the shade of a large tree for a while it was suggested that we visited their orchard. We were quite a crowd, there being about fifteen to twenty of us including the children. The orchard lay on the north side of the town in the middle of the plain and was like another town in that all the orchards of the more affluent citizens were grouped together, each one surrounded by its own high brick or clay wall and approached along narrow lanes formed by the walls. These lanes were crossed at regular intervals by little streams used to irrigate the various allotments. The wide ones caused some merriment when the female members of the party failed to reach the opposite bank as they jumped across.

We finally reached the Karami orchard and made ourselves comfortable on the grass in the shade of one of the larger fruit trees. Grandpa and Grandma Karami busied themselves collecting pomegranates, apricots and other fruits for us to sample whilst the children ran off to explore the further depths of the orchard.

When we left we did not retrace our steps but continued on the lane we had come along earlier. Emerging from the lane we found ourselves in a wheat field. The wheat had already been cut and threshed and the bales of hay stacked in the middle of the field, where a small boy sitting on a donkey was guarding them. The perimeter of the fields was marked by low mud walls used to retain the water during the growing period.

Beyond the fields was a barren area on which were a series of low mounds. As we approached them Dinah ran ahead and started to climb the nearest one.

Suddenly Keramat ran after her, shouting, 'Dinah, don't go up there – they are dangerous.' These were the famous qanats.

As Dinah came down Mike and I climbed up the bank to have a look for ourselves. Looking into the crater we could see the open shaft leading down to the subterranean passage. Picking up a stone and throwing it down the shaft, we could hear it ricocheting off the sides before the 'plop' as it hit the water. Qanats are gently sloping underground channels or tunnels constructed to lead water from the interior of a hill to a village below

The qanats are constructed and maintained by *moqannis*, as the qanat workers are called. The subterranean passages are many kilometres long, and form the lifeblood of the villages they support. Excavation first

156

started at the site of the proposed village or settlement and the heading continued towards the nearest hills until the water-bearing strata were reached. The vertical shafts were sunk at intervals to facilitate the removal of the spoil from the tunnel and to provide easy access for the *moqannis* during construction and subsequent maintenance. The spoil was built up round the shafts to prevent animals and children falling in. The *moqannis* use a wooden windlass, which they set up over the shaft to gain entry to the tunnel, to haul up the spoil (waste material) and their fellow workers at the end of the day's work.

The next day, after a breakfast of boiled eggs, bread, cheese, honey and yoghurt we set off for a walk around the town. On leaving the house we were taken down a narrow lane and into a small building. When our eyes became accustomed to the gloom after the bright sunshine outside we saw three young girls in the process of weaving a carpet. We were told that they had been on it for about a year and the carpet was only half completed. The main strands were stretched between two frames at either end of the building with the girls sitting on the floor working the shuttle across the strands. With the door held wide open Mike was able to take a photograph of the work in progress.

Leaving the girls to continue their work on the carpet, we made our way to the town centre. Going down a side street off the main road we entered a courtyard of an old caravanserai (roadside inn). The sides of the yard were surrounded by a low two-storey building. The ground floor had been used as stables for the mules and horses while the upper floor had served as resting rooms for the travellers.

One of the main industries in the town was the manufacture of *givas*, the canvas shoes worn by the poorer classes. The soles are of rubber and in some cases are made from old motorcar tyres. We then moved on to a cafe where we had a very cold soft drink each, then returned to the Karamis for lunch.

The meal for some reason was served in the other part of the house and as far as I can remember we were joined by some other relatives or friends.

While over there Keramat happened to see my eyes resting for a moment on a picture on the wall of what looked like a large mausoleum. 'That's the main centre of our church in Haifa; you see, we are Baha'is.'

After thanking the Karamis for their hospitality we set off for Isfahan, promising Keramat that we would visit them one day. The journey was quite uneventful. One interesting place we passed through was called, I believe, Yezd-i-Khast. It is a large fortified village with the buildings perched on the edge of a sheer cliff face above a river. After crossing over the river, we stopped to take some photographs of this very unusual-looking place.

It was dusk as we approached Isfahan. On the south side of the city we passed the site of the large steelworks which was being constructed by the Russians. It was an awkward hour to arrive, as the streets were busy with evening traffic making driving very difficult in a strange place. We were unable to get in at the Shah Abbas Hotel so we settled for the Irantour Hotel on Kheibar Abbasabad. It was a pleasant place; the building was only one or two storeys high but tended to sprawl over the grounds in which it stood. Most of the meals we had there were al fresco. After supper in the balmy Isfahan air and a shower we were soon in bed and fast asleep.

It has been said that 'Isfahan is half the world' by its inhabitants and the poets of Persia, and its origins date back to the 5th century, but it was the beginning of the 17th century when it reached the height of its importance when Shah Abbas the Great settled there in 1598 and made it his capital. Under constant threat from the Ottoman Empire, the Persian capital had, for strategic reasons, been moved from Tabriz to Qazvin and now it was to be located in Isfahan on the eastern side of the Zagros Mountains. The splendour of Isfahan continued until the dawn of the 18th century when it was sacked during the Afghan invasion. After Nadir Shah's victory over the invader, Isfahan reverted to a provincial capital and its place was taken by Mashhad.

The Isfahan of today is due to the work of the early Safavids and Shah Abbas the Great. The principal street, Khiaban-e Chahar Bagh, the Avenue of Four Gardens, runs from the north of the city down to the Si-o-Se Pol, the Bridge of Thirty-Three Arches, over the Zāyandé-Rūd and then on to Shiraz. To the east of the Chahar Bagh is the famous Maidan-i Shah, with the Ālī Qāpū on its western side, the Masjid-i Sheikh Lutfallah opposite and the great Masjid-i Shah on the south side of the square. The Bazaar-e Bozorg lies some distance to the north of the Maidan-i Shah.

Having spent a day in Abadeh we now had to 'do' Isfahan in one day instead of two as originally planned. This meant an early start. Getting the children up and having breakfast all took precious time. At last we were ready and set off down the road to Chahar Bagh, having a look at the Shah Abbas Hotel which is situated at the junction of the two roads. Before Mike knew what was happening the children and I had popped into a souvenir shop. As we had bought several things in the bazaar in Shiraz Mike had hoped that we had collected enough for one trip already. We did not leave empty-handed. Then Dinah found a sweet shop selling *Gaz*, a mixture of nougat and nuts for which Isfahan is famous.

We crossed the road and made our way northwards. Stopping for a moment outside a mosque to wait while the children tried to buy some of the matchboxes they were collecting at a kiosk, Mike was approached by a man.

'Mister, you want to take some good pictures of Isfahan? I help you.'

'Yes,' replied Mike, 'I would like to take some good photographs, but how can you help me?'

'If you come with me I will take you up onto the roof of this mosque and you will get a good view of my city.'

Guessing that he would not get something for nothing, Mike asked, 'How much?'

'One hundred fifty rials.'

'One hundred and fifty rials,' Mike repeated, 'that's a lot for a photograph or two when I don't know what I shall be able to see. I'll give you a hundred.'

'All right, I take.'

As Mike paid him the money the girls and I went through into the courtyard of the mosque. Tim and Mike followed the man through a small door and climbed a dark, narrow, winding staircase which led to the roof.

Taking them to the edge of the roof and pointing eastwards to a large dome, the man said, 'Masjid-i Shah.'

It was indeed an impressive sight, the vast expanse of blue tiles of the King's Mosque reflecting the rays of the sun. Perhaps it was worth a hundred rials. On reaching the pavement again, Mike saw the man hastening off to accost two middle-aged American tourists, to whom the starting price no doubt would be three hundred rials.

After taking some photographs of the family around the pools of the mosque courtyard we moved on to the Maidan-i Shah. Standing at the south end of the square in the shade of the mosque we tried to imagine what the scene must have been at the time of Shah Abbas.

The Ālī Qāpū, Gate of Ali, is a tall structure, but what catches the eye is the terrace on the side facing the square covered by a shallow roof supported on eighteen slender columns. Here the shah would sit and watch the races or his courtiers in their high pointed hats playing polo, as depicted in the pictures in all the souvenir shops on the square below. The women of the harem would also watch, but only through the Venetian blinds covering the windows of their suite.

The Ālī Qāpū also served as the entrance to the large park that lay behind the buildings and stretched back as far as the Chahar Bagh. In the park were the royal palaces to which foreigners were not invited, all foreign dignitaries being received in the resplendent rooms of the Ālī Qāpū itself. Alas, no longer could one hear the sound of thundering hooves on the baked ground or the click of mallet on ball, only the roar of 20th-century traffic.

After a quick walk round the square it was time to wend our way back to the hotel for lunch. In the afternoon, we returned to the square and then on to the bazaar. Although the streets, or rather the pedestrian precincts, were narrow there was a feeling of spaciousness due to the high roof which consisted of a series of cupolas, the tops of which were glazed to let in the sunlight in much the same way as in the Shiraz bazaar.

On our way back, we stopped for tea and ice cream in the Chahar Bagh and then made our way down to the Zayandeh Rud and the Pol-i-Khadu or Khaju Bridge. This is a really impressive structure, two storeys high consisting of a series of arches and arcades with a large pavilion at its centre. The bridge also serves as a dam with sluices set between the piers to supply water to the *jubes* in the gardens on both banks of the river.

Due to our unscheduled stay in Abadeh, the next day found us on our way again. According to the map there was a secondary road running almost direct from Isfahan to Khorramabad but no one we asked knew anything about it, so we decided to err on the side of safety and stick to the main roads even though the distance to be covered would be much greater.

Starting early, we managed to clear Isfahan before the morning rush hour began. The road north was generally straight and with little or no traffic about we made good progress. Although the day was sunny it did not feel unduly warm as we were still on the central plateau. We passed through several villages where we had to reduce speed due to the increase in traffic and the number of pedestrians. These villages all appeared to be of a similar design, a series of two-storey blocks on either side of the road, each containing a number of shops with living quarters above.

Eventually we reached the main Tehran-Abadan road. From what I can remember there was no town or village at this important road junction, just a petrol station. From the distance travelled since leaving Isfahan we were probably not far from the holy city of Qom.

Once on the main road and travelling in a south-westerly direction we at last felt we were heading for home. The countryside changed and the surrounding hills were less stark and appeared to be of more gentle slopes, and large areas were covered with what we took to be coarse grass. Coming over the brow of a hill we were suddenly aware of the city of Arak over which there appeared to be a dusty haze, no doubt due to the large cement works located here.

Travelling along the main highway that links the Gulf ports with Tehran we saw many huge lorries that transport the vital imports around the country and the disasters that can befall them. On the more mountainous stretches of the road, we could see at the foot of the steep slopes the remains of the vast juggernauts that had gone over the edge and fallen to their destruction. Some mangled remains were visible on the roadside, the victims of head-on collisions. The more numerous were those that had simply broken down and had been abandoned where they had stopped. Usually a line of stones or boulders would start about fifty metres behind the vehicle at the roadside and form a kerb around the stricken vehicle as a warning to other motorists of the hazard ahead. Sometimes this kerb would be formed from parts of the vehicle stripped out by the driver during his search for the fault. Once the cause of the breakdown had been located the driver would hitch a lift to the nearest large town to buy a replacement part or have it made up in the bazaar, and as a result may have to abandon his charge for several days. The magnitude of these roadside repairs is quite unbelievable.

After Arak the scenery again changed as we reached the Zagros Mountains. The rolling hills gave way to rocky outcrops and everywhere had a more rugged appearance. If the hotel had given us a packed lunch then it had been eaten a long time ago and we were all feeling hungry again.

The road began to twist and turn as the rock outcrops encroached on the road and we had to reduce our speed in anticipation of what we might encounter on the next bend. As we knew we were not far from Khorramabad we decided we would stop there and find somewhere to eat.

Soon we found ourselves descending, and rounding a bend saw the flat roofs of the houses forming the township. Suddenly on the left-hand side of the road we saw a very modern-looking building with a sign indicating that it was a restaurant. We pulled over to the other side of the road, parked the car and entered the building.

At the end of a wide, long corridor was a large room with a rostrum at the far end, where one could imagine an orchestra or band playing. Around the perimeter of the room the tables were stacked one on top of the other, creating a large, empty space in the middle of the room. The place appeared deserted. The air in the room was stale as though there was no free ventilation, but there was an aroma as though food had been recently prepared. Apart from two doors bearing symbols indicating male and female toilets there were several other doors leading from the room in which we were now standing.

On opening one of these unmarked doors we found a youngish man in the process of getting up from a mattress on the floor. In the gloom beyond I was conscious of others taking a siesta.

'*Salaam Alaikum*,' Mike said. 'Is this a restaurant?

'*Bale*, yes,' replied the man as he continued to rub the sleep from his eyes.

'Good, you have some food for us?' I asked.

'We are closed. It is late,' he muttered, looking at a watch dangling from his waist.

'Please, we are very hungry; we have driven all the way from Isfahan. The children are very thirsty too. Surely if you are closed you should lock the doors.'

By this time the other recumbent forms on the floor had woken up and come over to join us. After a hasty discussion amongst themselves they reluctantly agreed to provide us with some lunch. A table was laid and a jug of iced water placed on it, and we all sat down in hopeful anticipation. Then a plate of Barbary bread and butter was brought in and soon devoured – we were also ready for the water jug to be refilled. Finally, large plates full of steaming rice were set before us with *chelo* kebab, and as one might guess, it was not long before the plates were empty.

It must have been about three o'clock when we left the restaurant. For the rest of the afternoon the scenery was quite fantastic. We continued the gradual descent with the cliffs becoming higher, the gorges deeper and the river wider. Labouring their way up on the other side of the road were cars, lorries, buses and tankers. Mike longed to take his eyes off the road for a minute to take in the scenery but knew such a momentary lack of concentration could be fatal.

Eventually we crossed the river for the last time and emerged onto a flat plain, leaving the Zagros Mountains behind us. Soon on our right we could see the line of telegraph poles marking the route of the railway from Tehran to the Gulf. The road was again straight and we were able to increase our speed and before long we were on the outskirts of Andimeshk.

We passed what appeared to be an army camp as there were a fair number of soldiers walking around the compound. Shortly after this the road increased in width and we were almost in the centre of the town. Seeing some pedestrians close by, we drew up and asked them where a hotel was. From what we were told we understood there was one just a little further ahead on the right-hand side of the road.

Sure enough, at the next corner there was a building which from the outside looked like a large cafe. We pulled into a side street and parked the car and Mike went in to see if they had a room for us. We were lucky; they had one largish room with sufficient beds for all of us. After a wash, we found there was a large dining room on the first floor in which we sat down and drank ice-cold Coca-Colas and watched the life of Andimeshk through the windows.

After supper, we had a walk round the shops, not that there was much to see, and finished up at the railway station where we were just in time to see the night train to Tehran. By the time we got back to the hotel it was dark so we decided to go straight up to bed as we wanted to be on our way early the following morning, and to try and get home before the heat of the day.

We had no sooner entered the room when there was a cry from one of the children – the room was full of hurrying cockroaches. An intensive cockroach-crushing programme was put into immediate effect and in a short space of time their numbers were greatly reduced. The invasion seemed to stem from the bathroom, with the result that everybody was reluctant to take a shower. The children decided that all the beds should be pushed together to ward off a possible night attack by the creatures and before long we were all in bed. Whether sleep came easily to all members of the party I am not sure.

We were up shortly after dawn and it looked as if it was going to be a hot one. Whether we could get any breakfast at that hour I am not sure; I seem to remember we had to make do with a cup of tea each. We were soon on our way along the deserted streets and before long had left Andimeshk behind. After about half an hour we turned off to the right to visit the small village of Shush. It was not really the village we had come to see, but Daniel's Tomb.

The most distinguishing feature was the tapering spire which formed the roof of the tomb, a change from the usual tiled dome of the mosque. As it is a Muslim shrine we were not allowed to enter but from the entrance it appeared to contain a large dark-coloured stone edifice surrounded by a wrought ironwork fence. Outside was an open courtyard in which there were several families sitting about, and from the litter of sunflower seeds, pistachio nuts, paper, Coca-Cola bottles and the like it looked as if they had spent the night there waiting for the shrine to open. After a brief look round, we were soon back in the car and retracing our route back to the main road.

As we continued our way south we saw signposts indicating the sugar cane project at Haft Tappeh, Seven Hills. By this time we were back on the flat plain of Khuzestan and it was getting hotter by the hour. At last we reached the turn-off and a short while later were crossing the toll bridge over the Karun. Looking down into the water I saw, standing on one leg on a small sandbank, what looked like a pelican. Five minutes later we were back in Zeytoon.

A day or so later I noticed that the house opposite was now occupied, so the woman from Venezuela had arrived. I had heard about her from Mike as she had been living at the Ahwaz Hotel as her husband, Jack, had to spend most of his time in the desert oilfields. She had a dog, a lovely poodle called Bo-Bo who went everywhere with her. Esther spoke quite good English but with an accent. She became quite friendly with the children as they were often at the gate looking out at the activities on the road.

She started visiting, which I didn't mind as I knew she was lonely, like most of us who go to a new country. In the end the constant bell-ringing became a little too much so I would go upstairs to my peephole to see who it was. One afternoon she came over and we were all sitting at the dining table making paper hats for Fiona's birthday party when she suddenly announced she was four months pregnant.

I said, 'Esther, have you seen a doctor yet?'

'No, I don't need to.'

I said I thought she should see a doctor to make sure all was well. As time passed by I asked her again if she had seen a doctor yet. Again, I got a negative reply, so I asked her if she had got any clothes for the baby, and again she said no.

I found this quite unbelievable. 'But Esther, what happens if the baby comes early as they sometimes do?'

'Oh, Mike will take me to the hospital!'

It was not long after this that her houseboy came knocking at the door to say the baby was on its way. Mike immediately drove to see the wife of Jack's boss, whom he knew.

She told Mike not to worry. 'These people are quite used to having their babies on the floor.' Anyway, she took her to the hospital where she had a bouncing baby boy.

As Jack, the proud father, knew nothing of what was going on, Mike and I went to visit her. We found her sitting up in bed, beautifully attired in a lovely nightgown with manicured nails, each with a star on them, looking as though she was on her honeymoon!

When I asked if she had sufficient clothes and nappies for the child I got the usual reply: 'No.'

I went over to see my friend, Nina, who very kindly offered to go and get the essentials for her. Back home, Esther was forever coming over asking about this and that for the baby, and in the end Mike said, 'She might as well come and stay with us' but I was quite against this. Esther told me she couldn't cook so I had to show her how to make some simple meals. She told me the nuns only taught her how to crochet, but not to cook.

Eventually when her husband finally came home he came over to thank us for all that we had done for Esther and admitted that 'she was quite a handful'! He even offered to pay us for all the things we had bought for his wife.

Time was passing and it would soon be time for the children and me to return to England. We were keen to make the trip to Abadan before we left, so Mike wrote off to the Karamis to try and fix a date. After about two weeks a reply came back saying they would be pleased to see us on a particular Friday.

When the appointed day arrived, we were up at dawn and on our way by half past six. The journey, which was quite uneventful, took just over two hours. There was little or no traffic on the road and apart from the odd village that we passed through there was nothing to see at all, just flat, sandy desert. As we neared Khorramshahr the road for Abadan veered off to the left, crossing over first the railway, then the River Karun. Continuing south and looking westward we could see the funnels and masts of ships in the port of Khorramshahr.

Soon we saw trees ahead and the start of the residential area of Abadan. Then on our right we passed the airport and Hilton hotel. The cars on the road were now more numerous and we felt we could not be far from our destination. The road then turned right and we found ourselves on a bridge crossing a stretch of water. Once on the other side we were on the island on which Abadan is situated. We crossed to the west side of the island, where the road was lined with date palms as it ran alongside the Shatt al-Arab waterway, passing what looked like a power station, and then we were in the city centre.

We stopped to enquire where the NIOC (National Iranian Oil Company) housing area was and were soon on our way again. We now found ourselves on the edge of the refinery and stretching as far as the eye could see were row upon row of oil storage tanks. After enquiring again as to which road to take we were soon in the residential district, and with little boards indicating the house numbers we soon found Keramat's bungalow. The bungalows were similar to the ones occupied by the Kafis and Morakabatis but much older-looking, probably having been built by the British of the old Anglo-Iranian Oil Company. Here, the gardens were divided off by thick hedges.

As soon as we rang the bell the door opened and we were being greeted by the whole family. KB, his wife and Mazda were also there, so we were quite a large party again. Once inside the house we were offered drinks, fruit and pastries as we related our activities since our last meeting.

I was anxious to do some shopping in Abadan so it was agreed the children would stay in the bungalow whilst we went with Keramat into the city. By the time we got there it was quite busy considering it was a Friday. On our return most of us, I am not sure if all the Karamis joined in, went along to the oil company swimming pool. The children, as usual, thoroughly enjoyed themselves. Mike did not enjoy it but at least it was an experience. The water was so warm it was like trying to swim in a hot bath. After a few strokes he was exhausted but coming out of the pool was the greatest agony of all – the concrete was so hot that one had to literally sprint into the changing room.

On our return to the bungalow there was a terrific spread of typical Iranian food awaiting us, which we soon tucked into. After we had eaten our fill we retired to the lounge for tea and a chat. KB told us he was thinking of going to England with his family and wondered about finding some suitable accommodation. From some of the remarks made he would have liked to have had the use of our house knowing that it was lying empty, but forgetting that we would be occupying it ourselves again shortly. Anyway, Mike said he would write off to some estate agents and see what they had to offer, which he did when we got back to Ahwaz. In some of the papers he produced, which KB had to fill in before he could leave Iran and enter Britain, it appeared that he had been married before.

They tried to persuade us to stay longer but Mike was determined to be home before dark, having heard of an American family, half of whom had been killed after running into an unlit lorry parked on the road between Abadan and Ahwaz. We had an uneventful journey back and arrived before dusk.

It was becoming evident that Mike would need to stay in Ahwaz for approximately two months after the children and I returned to England. I was worried as to how he would manage on his own with the washing, cooking etc. Mike assured me he would be quite all right and it would not be the first time that he would have had to fend for himself. I was also sure that Nina and the Morakabatis would make sure he was all right. We also felt that we should tell Bettala, our 'bargee'(the Iranian term for a home help), of our plans so she could look for another job. So one day I told her of our position.

'Bettala, at the beginning of September the children and I are returning to England so I am afraid we shall not need you after that. You have been very good and I will try and find another job for you if you like with another expatriate family.'

She looked a bit upset at the news, then said, 'Is Mr Bennett going as well?'

'No, Mr Bennett will be staying here for another month or so after we have gone.'

'Who is going to look after him then?'

'Well, no one, he will look after himself.'

'But his washing and ironing, what about that?'

'He says he can do it himself. Actually, Bettala, we would have asked you to stay on and do this work but you once said you could not work with only men in the house.'

'Yes, I know, but that was with American men. Mr Bennett is different.'

'So, I am different in Bettala's eyes,' Mike said. 'Well, I only hope I am not too different!'

'Mum, Dad, Dad, Mum,' cried the children one Thursday as they dashed into the house from the Ahwaz Hotel pool. 'There's a man at the pool who is drinking champagne out of a large bowl and eating plates of caviar and buying everyone drinks. He says you are invited to have lunch with him tomorrow.'

It struck us both as being rather a strange invitation, but quite plausible.

'Well, I am not going,' Mike said.

'But why?' I asked. The children suddenly looked very disappointed.

'He's very nice,' they said. 'You'd like him, Dad, really you would.'

'I can't accept a blind invitation from someone I have never met just like that. Maybe he is very nice, but he will probably be gone by tomorrow, the hotel having run out of champagne and caviar if he is devouring them in those proportions.'

So the subject was dropped for the time being. Friday morning the children went off to the pool as usual, Mike and I staying at home to do some odd jobs around the house. When they came back at lunchtime they reiterated the invitation from their newfound friend, who was obviously still in residence.

'He says you must come and have lunch with him,' they said.

'I think we ought to go,' I said. 'After all, he may be very nice and it looks bad if we don't go to see him, even if we only have a drink and a chat with him.'

'All right, I'll go.'

'Oh good!' was the cry, as Dinah and Fiona dashed off into their room to dress for the occasion.

When we arrived at the poolside our host was just leaving a table littered with empty bottles, glasses, plates and an ashtray full of cigarette ash and crushed stubs. With him were a young expatriate couple and their small daughter.

'Hello,' he said, 'I was afraid you weren't coming. As you can see we are just going in to lunch. Anyway, now you are here I bid you welcome. My name is Mansur.' He was a big man, tall, with thinning hair. He looked as if he tended to obesity, no doubt caused by excessive eating and drinking, possibly more so the latter, judging from what the children had told us.

After we had introduced ourselves we moved into the restaurant where a long table had been reserved for us. As we sat down the waiters were fussing around the table bringing plates of caviar, lemon and thin slices of hot toast.

'Now then, Audrey, what can I offer you to drink? How about a glass of this champagne? I can thoroughly recommend it.'

'Thank you, that would be very nice,' I said, and he proceeded to pour me a large glass of bubbly.

'And Michael, can I offer you the same?'

'Thank you very much, but if you don't mind I would prefer a whisky,' Mike replied, having caught sight of a bottle in the hands of one of the waiters. 'I am not very fond of champagne at the best of times.' The children settled for a variety of soft drinks.

As we gave our orders Mike tried to find out what our host, Mansur, did for a living. It seems he was a senior fire protection officer in Tehran and an oil well had recently been put down very close to the hotel, and the hotel management considered it to be a hazard and had called him in to advise them. They were obviously hoping he would assist them in a claim against whoever had decided on the location of the well, hence the very lavish treatment being afforded him. He had only to raise his hand and Farouk, the head waiter, came rushing over to the table.

He was clearly well connected, judging by the stories he shared.

The meal passed without incident, but by the end Mansur was the worse for drink and was becoming increasingly loud and boisterous in his manner. We decided that the best thing we could do was to take him home and sober him up on black coffee.

'Well, Mansur,' Mike said, 'thank you very much indeed for a most enjoyable lunch, one we shall remember for a long time to come. And now we would like you to come to our house for coffee.'

We thought he would politely refuse, wishing to continue his hospitality at the hotel, but to our surprise he almost jumped up, saying, 'Audrey, Michael, thank you very much. Let's go.'

As we had walked round to the hotel we had to return by the same means. Mansur slipped off for a minute to tell his chauffeur to drive behind us at a discreet distance. He obviously did not wish to walk back by himself, or was afraid he might get lost.

It was clear he was enjoying his present assignment, where he was being treated like royalty. About five o'clock we managed to persuade him it was time he returned to the hotel. After the heavy lunch and a rather trying afternoon we felt like a breath of fresh air, so we went for a drive in the desert wastes near the railway line, letting Tim take over the steering, much to his delight. When we got back home I started to prepare for a coffee morning I was having the following day. I had decided to liven it up a bit by laying on a bowl of rum punch.

Next morning as she was getting up, Fiona complained of a sore ear so I decided she should stay at home rather than go to school and have problems there. It was probably some infection she had picked up in the pool. Mike went off to work and Dinah and Tim went out as soon as the school bus appeared outside the house.

I set about my usual chores so that I could then concentrate on my party. About eight o'clock I heard a bang on the outside gate; the bell and loudspeaker system were still not working. On opening the gate, Bettala having not yet arrived, who should I see standing there but Mansur?

'Good morning, my dear, how are you?' he asked.

'Very well, thank you, and you?'

'I'm feeling very much better this morning, thank you, and I wish to thank you for your very kind hospitality yesterday afternoon.'

'Oh, that was nothing,' I said, 'after your wonderful lunch.'

'My pleasure, my pleasure. I now wish to invite you to join me for breakfast at my hotel.'

'Thank you very much, but I am afraid Fiona is ill in bed and I cannot leave her, and also I am having a coffee morning which I still have to prepare for.'

As soon as he heard about Fiona his manner changed and he showed genuine concern and asked to see her, and said he would send his car for a doctor if I so wished. We went to see Fiona who, on seeing the fuss being made about her, said she was feeling much better already and the pain was not as bad as it had been when she woke up. After a few more minutes' chat I managed to persuade Mansur to return to the hotel for a solitary breakfast and let me get on with my preparations.

As with all such things, time sped by and before I knew where I was the first of the guests was knocking on the door. There was quite an expat crowd when we were all seated. Betty Kitson, her daughter Leonie, Jean Wright and Chic Griffin were among those that turned up. The rum punch was a great success and was in danger of running dry; the Iranian rum appeared to be having a strong effect on some who were not used to it.

The sudden appearance of Bettala in the doorway leading to the hall brought a sudden silence to the gathering as she announced that a gentleman was here. I was still halfway across the room on my way to the door when who should stride in but Mansur, dressed in a white boiler suit and rubber boots, followed by his chauffeur carrying bowls of caviar and bottles of champagne.

'When I heard you were having a party I could not resist the temptation to come along. Don't worry, I've brought my own refreshments which I want to share with you, especially you, Audrey, as you were unable to join me for breakfast.'

I did not know what to say, so hastily started introducing Mansur to everyone, hoping that they had not heard his last remark and wondered what was going on between us!

Mansur soon settled himself down and started to ply everyone with caviar and, for those that could stomach it, champagne. Time sped by and, remembering that Mansur had said he was leaving on the two o'clock plane, and realising that time was getting on, I said to him, 'I thought you said you were going back to Tehran this afternoon?'

'I am,' he replied.

'Do you realise it is going on for two o'clock now and the plane leaves at two?'

Although his boiler suit looked clean apart from a small coffee stain and a speck of caviar, wellies were hardly the shoes to fly up to Tehran in.

'Don't worry, Audrey, the plane will wait for me.' And it did. Such was the power of a senior fire prevention officer of Iran.

The early evenings we used to spend visiting the Kafis and Morakabatis or down in the bazaar looking for souvenirs to take home. Quite often a visit to the Morakabatis included a swim in one of the oil company's pools. The big one next to the Naft Club was usually very busy, whereas the older, smaller one was hardly ever used. Occasionally we would be planning to go to bed when there would be a knock on the door; it was the Morakabatis wanting to take us to the club now that it was a little cooler. The children were soon up and raring to go.

As the time drew near for the children and me to return home we started the job of getting the suitcases out and packing them. Because of all the baggage we had and the problems of getting on a plane to Tehran, we decided that Mike and Tim would go up by train and take the bulk of the luggage with them, leaving Dinah, Fiona and me to travel up in comfort by plane.

On the appointed day, everything went according to plan and there were no hitches. Tim, a railway enthusiast, enjoyed his trip up by train but as there was no moonlight he was unable to see any of the remarkable scenery Mike had witnessed previously.

One of the evenings we were at the hotel, we invited Bob, Zena (one of Mike's colleagues and his wife) and one of their sons who was over on holiday to dinner at the hotel. It turned out to be a very merry occasion.

On the night of departure, to get to the airport involved two taxis. Everything went well until we got to Mehrabad Airport when, as soon as the cars stopped, porters descended on us in droves, heaving the cases out of the taxis and onto trolleys and starting to dash off before we had time to tell them which flight we were connecting with. We were booked to return by Qantas and to the children's delight the plane was a jumbo jet, but were not too happy with the confusion these planes create at the end of the journey when three to four hundred passengers jostle to collect their luggage and personal effects at the carousel.

The flight was delayed on its long haul halfway across the world and so we suffered a longer agony before our separation. Somehow Mike had managed to get into the departure lounge and we were able to wander round the duty-free shop, which was full of Aussies replenishing their supplies of liquor and cigarettes.

At last the time came for us to part and so, with a final kiss and a wave from us all, we left Mike and made our way to the plane for our long flight home.

Mike eventually arrived home just before Christmas. He had left Tehran and flown to Athens, where he spent a few days before taking a train to Munich. From there he flew to Berlin to spend a few days with Bernhard and Gisela and then made his way back to England. We were all very glad to have him home again.

Persepolis

Fiona's 6th Birthday Party – Ahwaz

6

Largs, Ayrshire, Scotland
1975

After a few days of adjusting to life at home again Mike rang the firm's personnel officer to see where his next job was to be. There were suggestions that he should return to Devil's Dingle. This would have been ideal from a domestic point of view, but as the bulk of the engineering work had been done, Mike was hoping something more interesting might be offered.

Then came a phone call – would Mike be prepared to go to Aberdeen on secondment to the Harbour Board there, where the firm had a lot of work on upgrading the various quays? Mike asked a few questions and was told that further details would be put in a letter. The proposal was acceptable and Mike moved to Aberdeen.

When he met the harbour engineer, Malcolm Chapman, he discovered that Malcolm had recently had an accident. He had been on the roof of his bungalow to fix or adjust his television aerial when it had started to rain, and he slipped and fell off the roof. As a result of the accident he had been told that he had developed multiple sclerosis and needed to walk everywhere with a stick.

Mike's contract allowed him a return ticket to London once a month. This enabled him to come home to Shrewsbury on a weekend return every fortnight as the fare was much cheaper. He would leave Aberdeen on the 9.30 am Glasgow train and I would meet him about teatime at Shrewsbury station.

There was only one serious hitch in the fifteen months that he made this journey, and that was at Easter on the trip home. For some reason the train was held up for over an hour and a half just north of Preston, with the result that Mike missed all his connections by the time he finally reached Crewe. The only train was one leaving just after midnight bound for south Wales. I was really worried when I arrived at the station and Mike was nowhere to be seen. We did not have mobile phones in those days so I had to return home and hope that he would phone and let me know where he was. Fortunately, I got a call from him about midnight to say he was stranded at Crewe but hoped to be on his way shortly and not to worry. The train's departure was further delayed when the driver failed to turn up and a relief had to be organised.

So about two o'clock on the following morning Mike arrived in Shrewsbury and started to walk home, there being no taxis about at that hour of the night. He had not gone far when he became aware of a car pulling up beside him and then driving along at the speed at which he was walking. Mike looked round and saw it was a police car.

The front nearside window was opened and a voice said, 'Where are you going to?'

'Portland Crescent,' Mike said, and wondered what sort of figure he cut with his old holdall and very creased raincoat. By this time, he and the police car had both come to a standstill.

Hop in the back then and we'll take you home.'

'Thanks very much, it's very kind of you,' Mike said as he climbed in. 'I've been travelling since half past nine yesterday morning and was not looking forward to foot-slogging it home.'

'Where have you come from then?' asked the driver.

'Aberdeen,' said Mike.

'And it's taken all this time?' the driver asked in a rather doubting tone. Mike then explained about the delays at Preston and Crewe. As they turned into our road the driver asked, 'What number are you?'

'Number 80,' Mike said, 'right opposite Inspector Gradwell.' He thought he might as well inform them that he was already 'known to the police'.

I must say I was very relieved when I heard the front doorbell ring.

Because of Malcolm's illness and absence from the office – he was only coming in two or three times a week – Mike could not see how he was going to get away for a summer holiday.

One day, talking to George McGowan, the contractor's local manager, Mike happened to mention his predicament and he suddenly said, 'Why don't you bring your family up here and take a holiday in the area and come into work two or three times a week?'

When Mike asked if he had any ideas where we might stay he said his father had recently retired to a large house in Ellon, a town some twenty miles north of Aberdeen, and in the garden some outbuildings had been converted into a cottage for his married brother but the brother had left home and the cottage was now empty.

And so it was that we spent five weeks of the summer in a small but comfortable cottage in Aberdeenshire. The weekend before we were due to take the cottage Mike came home as usual but returned with Fiona and me in the car. Dinah and Tim had gone off to spend time with their cousins in Kent.

Once on the motorway the route was clear and quite fast, but this was only as far as Dunblane where the dual carriageway ended. After that the road was slow and tedious, busy with the large, refrigerated lorries of Christian Salvesen carrying fish and the like to the south and the trucks with barrels of whisky travelling north. As a result of this we broke our journey at Auchterarder where we stayed in a very pleasant little guest house in the main street.

Shortly after we were established in Ellon, Dinah and Tim came up by train to join us. As might be expected Mike was not able to get as much time off as he had hoped. Most days we would go down into Aberdeen at lunchtime or in the early afternoon and we would all go home together in the evening. Occasionally we would stay in Aberdeen until nightfall. Tim and Mike enjoyed a round or two of 'pitch and putt' while the girls and I spent our time and money in the nearby amusement arcade.

Weekends we would go up to Fraserburgh where the children would have a swim, but even for them the water was too cold to stay in long. They reckoned the water off Aberdeen and Balmedie beach was even colder.

The weeks flew by and soon it was time for us to return home and Mike to his hotel. While we were up in Aberdeen we had looked for a house to buy, as there were indications that the firm wished Mike to stay in Aberdeen for some time as more work was being given to them. We did in fact find a very nice house near the zoo at Hazelhead belonging to a fishing boat captain, but the price being asked due to the oil boom and American presence was beyond our pocket.

Mike had not been back in Aberdeen long after the Christmas and New Year holiday when he had a letter from Head Office offering him a job at Hunterston on the Clyde, as deputy resident engineer on a new jetty there.

After a long discussion, Mike decided to accept the job and we would be a family together again. This meant a trip down to London for Mike to meet the Head Office engineers dealing with the project.

Having finally agreed to go to Hunterston the next task was to find a house there as the job was due to last for at least two years. Mike managed to take a week off and we drove up to Largs to have a look at the locality and find somewhere to live.

We stayed at the Marine and Curling Hall Hotel, an imposing name for a small, modest hotel, but considered to be the best in Largs. It is situated right on the front at the south end of the town and overlooking the island of Cumbrae. The hills rise steeply behind the town, thus giving it little room for expansion.

We started looking for a house in West Kilbride and Fairlie as these places were closer to Hunterston, until we discovered that if we lived there the children would have to go to school in Ardrossan.

Coming into the hotel one lunchtime, Mike found a telegram waiting for him with a message to ring Head Office and speak to the senior partner. What on earth could this be about? Well, the only thing to do was to phone up and find out.

Mike did just that. He got through after lunch and after the formalities of the switchboards etc. he found he was speaking to Mr Irwin Childs.

'Ah, Mr Bennett, good of you to ring so quickly. I am sorry to trouble you when I know you are busy looking for somewhere to live for your move to Hunterston but we urgently need an answer. We are looking for someone to go out to Port Hedland in Western Australia for about nine months on a dredging and reclamation job and your name has come up. It would be on a bachelor basis, I am afraid, but I can assure you the salary would be very attractive.'

Well, that was the gist of what he had to say. He gave Mike a day to think it over. We did not know what to do. Mike had been away from home for over a year in Aberdeen and we wanted to be together as a family again. He was very tempted but knew the job would last more than nine months – they always did. It meant we would be separated again for at least another year, which was what we were trying to avoid by moving to Largs. Anyway, after sleeping on it, we decided against it and continued our house-hunting.

The problem with looking for a house in a small town is that there are very few on the market at any one time. After several visits, we had almost given up hope even though we kept in constant touch with the estate agents. We had looked at two possible ones which turned out to be too small, and were wondering what to do when we called in at one of the agents' shops and were told of a bungalow that was being put on the market that day. It was in fact a Saturday.

We were without the car as Mike had come down from Aberdeen by train and I felt I could not drive all the way up from Shrewsbury. This time we were staying at the Springfield Hotel on the north side of Largs and quite close to where the bungalow, we were looking at, was situated. We went straight back to the hotel to ring and make an appointment to view. After several attempts, it became obvious that the owners were out, so we decided to go and have a look from the outside.

It was a bright, sunny day as we walked to the bungalow. We found it right on the corner of a newish development, wedged between the road and a trout stream, beyond which were open fields. It looked ideal, with a well-established garden.

The problem was how to see round the property. We had to return to our respective homes the following day and the only train left at just after ten. We spent the afternoon and evening trying to get through to the owners – we eventually made contact at ten o'clock in the evening. The lady who finally answered said they had gone out for the day, never thinking that anyone would want to view so quickly as the agents were not even sure that the notice would be ready for that day. We explained our predicament and she said she could show us round at half past nine in the morning before she went to church. So, we finished up literally dashing around the place. The taxi we had ordered to get there was late coming, thus reducing the time we had available for viewing.

We just caught the train for our journey home, and recovered our breaths as we were arriving in Glasgow. We finally got the bungalow and moved in just after Easter. Buying property in Scotland is quite different to the system used in England. In Scotland one makes a bid for a house or flat and if one's offer is accepted then one is legally bound to take it, whereas in England it is possible to make offers for several properties at any one time and only when contracts are exchanged does one become the owner of the property.

Having settled the housing problem Mike could settle down to the remainder of his stay in Aberdeen. The long journey home and back again every fortnight in the cold winter months was acceptable as an end date was now in sight. But then there was a hitch.

The Hunterston job had a delay of about six months on its start date, so they wanted Mike to go over to Loch Fyne to work on a site for the construction of an oil rig platform.

When Mike asked his friend in the Glasgow office exactly where the site was he said, 'Well, it's rather hard to pinpoint the place. Actually, it's on Loch Fyne almost opposite Tarbert and the nearest village is Tighnabruaich.' As Mike was planning to leave Aberdeen at Easter anyway it was agreed that if he did go to Portavadie, as the site was known, he would be allowed to go home every weekend. He decided to accept.

So, in mid-March Mike left Aberdeen for the last time and drove over to Loch Fyne. During his time on this project he stayed at the Strachur Hotel owned by Sir Fitzroy Maclean. The hotel, a small, delightful place right on the edge of Loch Fyne, was on the north side of the village of the same name. The laird's house was situated between the hotel and the village.

As the hotel was not large enough to house everybody, some of the engineers were billeted at Sir Fitzroy's house, an impressive stone-built mansion with panelled walls, long corridors and wide stone staircases.

Because most of the hotels and guest houses in the area had been taken over by the contractor, it meant that the usual summer visitors were barred from the area. One enterprise that was affected by the project was a sailing club that used to give courses during the summer. Without pupils, they faced a bleak year, so it was decided that people on the project should be encouraged to go on the course. Mike volunteered to go along with several others. They went once a week after work and spent about two hours on the water. After about half an hour's lecture on the theory of sailing with the aid of a model on dry land, they took to the boats. There were usually four in a boat plus an instructor, with one in charge of the mainsail and tiller and the other on the spinnaker. They all enjoyed it but there were moments of anxiety and misery. As the wind usually dropped about sunset they were often becalmed and would have to sit and be patient until a puff of wind would come along to take them back to shore. However, on some occasions they had almost gale-force winds and squalls to contend with. There were one or two minor collisions but no serious damage done.

Mike's worst memory, he said, was of the time they had to learn how to cope with a capsize. This meant plunging into the icy waters of the Kyle and then getting the boat back on an even keel. Another was the thousands of midges that attacked them as they came ashore. They all used to change as quickly as they could and then jump into their cars and drive off at top speed.

So, to start with Mike spent a week at Hunterston and a week at Portavadie until permanent site offices at the former were completed and he moved over for good.

One of our concerns at the prospect of moving up to Scotland had been the effect this would have on the children. We thought that Dinah, being the eldest, would find it the hardest to adjust but as it turned out it was Tim who rejected the move the most. He was very attached to Shrewsbury and almost refused to visit the town when we passed through on our way south. Mike said an accent of any kind marked one as a stranger, and so too did the children on their arrival in Largs and, in particular, at school. Dinah and Fiona soon acquired a 'Scottish' accent, and as time passed so did Tim to a lesser extent. Fiona's was the most impressive. Taking her and a local friend of hers out in the car, listening to them both talking, I could not tell which one was Fiona.

One feature of our bungalow was the double garage. Being only a one-car family there was plenty of room for all our junk. As soon as we moved in Tim and Mike decided that the far end of the garage would be screened off to form an area for their model railway. The previous occupants had left a huge workbench in the garage, which formed an excellent top on which to lay out the track. Most evenings when Mike came home he would find Tim in the garage, hammering and sawing away at some piece of scenery or new platform.

Shortly after starting at Largs Academy, Tim discovered that he was the only boy in his class that did not possess a set of golf clubs. Every town in Scotland has a least one golf course to its name and Largs was no exception, in fact it had two. Mike's mother, who had always been a keen golfer herself, gave Tim a set of clubs. He had a course of lessons at the recreation centre and then sallied forth on the municipal course at Routenburn.

During our stay in Largs we came to know Glasgow quite well. We found the famous Sauchiehall Street and visited Marks & Sparks in Argyle Street, and also, in this same street the female members of the family would vanish into a shop with the enticing name 'What Every Woman Wants'. Tim and Mike, on the other hand, would gravitate south over the Clyde and through the Gorbals, now largely rebuilt, to a shop that sold model railway requisites.

Then in the summer of 1976 the Morakabatis wrote to say they were coming to England for a holiday and would like to come and see us, which they duly did. We met them at Largs railway station and took them home. It was very nice to see them all again.

One afternoon I had just collected the children up from school and had turned left into another road and was just starting to pick up speed when a car shot out of a side road on the right. I jammed on the brake, Dinah getting a nasty bump on her head from the windscreen as he hit me on the side wing. He was going so fast that he bounced off our car and into another car parked on my side of the road. A woman came out of her house on hearing the crash and came over and asked if we were all OK.

'We're fine, thanks, a little shaken up I guess.'

'Please come to my house with the children and I will give you all a cup of tea and phone your husband.'

The kind woman left a message at the office for Mike, who soon arrived to take us all home. After discussing the accident and its aftermath for a few more minutes we then thanked the people who had taken me and the children in and made our way home. From there Mike went to the garage and had a look at the damage to the car. The foreman reckoned it would take about six to eight weeks to put it back on the road once they got the go-ahead from the insurance company.

The following evening the driver of the car who had wrought such havoc came to the house, and apologised for his actions. It transpired that he lived on the estate behind our house. I can't say I had ever seen him before, and after this one meeting I never saw him again. We put everything in the hands of the AA, the Automobile Association, and they gave us excellent service, including the use of a car until ours was back on the road.

Every Christmas the contractor gave a dinner dance to which we were all invited. The first two years it was held in the Marine and Curling Hall Hotel in Largs, sadly no more, having been subsequently pulled down and replaced with old folks' homes. The last occasion was celebrated at the Seamill Hydro Hotel on the road to Ardrossan.

During the summer of 1977 we were invited to spend a week with Betty in Tonbridge. The children had gone ahead to spend longer with their cousins so Mike and I were left to travel down on our own. This gave us an excellent opportunity to drive down the spine of England and visit some of Mike's old haunts that he wanted to show me.

We set off from Largs one Saturday morning and headed south-east across Ayrshire to Dumfries and then onto the motorway at Carlisle. We continued south until somewhere above Kendal, where we turned off and headed for Settle and Skipton.

As we motored along towards Keighley Mike told me that this was one of the roads they had come along as children on small bikes and trikes; in fact, Mike had had to tow his brother, Antony, part of the way when he had become too exhausted to pedal any further.

In Keighley, instead of carrying on straight through the town Mike turned off and made his way to the back of the station as he was anxious to see what he could, if anything, of the Keighley and Worth Valley Railway. As luck would have it we arrived just in time to see a train departing.

Continuing on our way we soon reached Crossflatts, after which I was given a running commentary. 'This is where the trolleybuses, or "tracklesses" as they called them, from Bradford used to turn around. That road there is Lower Sleningford, where we used to come along to cross the railway on our way to school. Look up there to the left, that's where we used to live, and here on the right is the grammar school.'

As we entered Bingley Main Street, what really captured Mike's attention was the eyesore of the head office building of the Bradford & Bingley Building Society and the fact that they had demolished the family doctor's house to build it.

It was now time to find somewhere to stay for the night and Mike was not sure that Bingley could provide it without going well beyond Cottingley Bridge, so after a quick trip down the high street and off on the Harden road to have a look at the River Aire we turned back and made our way up Park Road.

The toyshop was still there just opposite the entrance to the station, then we started to climb up past the fish and chip shop which Mike used to frequent for 'three penn'orth' of chips after Scouts.

'That's the Baptist church where our Scout troop used to meet.' Was the dentist still there on the left? No time to look, we were now passing Smailes' house, Mike's headmaster, then past the end of Hall Bank Drive and so on up past the park. 'I can't see anywhere here to stay,' Mike said. 'We'll have to go on to Ilkley where there's bound to be somewhere.'

We drove on through Gilstead, then past Dick Hudson's, a lonely pub on the edge of Ilkley Moor, and then a few minutes later we were skirting the moor itself.

'Many's the time I've cycled along this road on my way into Wharfedale and beyond, and it's mentioned in John Braine's celebrated book *Room at the Top*,' said Mike. 'Those rocks there are known as the Cow and Calf Rocks.'

Once in Ilkley we had no difficulty finding somewhere to stay and I remember we had a typical old-fashioned English breakfast the following morning.

We did not delay any longer as Mike was anxious to be on our way. We retraced our route as far as Dick Hudson's, but instead of turning left for Gilstead we carried straight on and went down past the old brick kilns where they used to collect frog spawn. The ponds, Mike noticed, were now covered with derelict cars. Passing the old teacher training college, which was well known to many women schoolteachers, then the lower side of the park, we were soon in Gawthorpe and going down the hill and into Beck Lane.

The one change Mike could not miss was that Falcon Road, where Mike's cousins, Marlo and Richard, had lived, was no longer a cul-de-sac as we could now continue round a crescent of houses that had been built since Mike was last here on the field where they used to play. We continued to Fairfax Road and parked the car just by Number 2, where Mike and family used to live; the only difference being that a driveway had been added to the front garden.

Leaving the car, we walked down to the Leeds and Liverpool Canal and had a look at the five rise locks where Mike used to help the barges in exchange for a ride up to Crossflatts. We walked down to the bottom where we found a pleasure boat about to enter the first lock. Talking to a woman who was opening the gates, we learned that they had hired the boat in Silsden, where they were now returning.

Returning to the car we made our way down into Bingley and then on to Bradford, passing through Saltaire and Shipley on the way. Descending into Forster Square, Mike recognised the station but that was all, and after passing the Town Hall we were lost – somehow the streets with their new buildings looked quite different and Mike had to carefully watch the signposts for directions. I was surprised how quickly we reached the M62 motorway and before long we were on the Ml and watching for the turn-off for Derby. Mike had decided that as we were in the neighbourhood we would spend the night here and call in and see his Uncle Denis again as we had not been over since we were living in Shrewsbury.

As the job progressed the question of where do we go next came up, as people started to think a bit more about the future. People were still required for Libya and the Thames Barrier, but nobody wanted to go to these places.

Talking with a colleague in the Glasgow office one morning, he asked Mike if he had seen the circular about staff wanted for Iran.

Mike said he hadn't. 'Whereabouts in Iran is it, and what sort of job is it?'

'It's for a marine job somewhere on the Caspian. I tell you what; I'll put a copy in the post for you.'

When Mike got the circular, he was very interested in what he read. It was for some sea defence works at Bandar Pahlavi and whoever went would be seconded to Irendco (Iran-Rendel Company) . As we had not been able to get up to the Caspian and the power station project at Gorgan had fallen through Mike was determined to return to Iran if it was at all possible. I was keen as it meant I would be able to see my dear friend Nina and her family again, and the Morakabati's.

Mike made an immediate application to the personnel office and heard no more except for the excuse that they were waiting to hear from Tehran. As time went by Mike still had no news, but happened to see an advert for a civil engineer in North Iran for the supervision of some grain silos. It was not quite his cup of tea, not liking heights, but it was in the right location so he wrote off for further information and started to consider the prospect of leaving RPT, as such a move would entail.

Mike cannot remember the details now but seems to recall that the person organising the silo project had some connection with Ben Dixon-Smith of Irendco, and when Ben heard Mike was making enquiries on the other job he soon responded to London and Mike was made an offer for Bandar Pahlavi ensuring he remained with RPT.

7

Bandar Enzeli (Pahlavi), Iran

1977 – 1980

Mike went ahead to Iran and then moved up to Bandar Pahlavi with his assistant, Shimiari. They settled in at a hotel until they could find somewhere more permanent. Mike found a nice ground-floor flat, with Shimiari's help, overlooking the sea and a hotel, just outside the town.

When it was time for Fiona (now ten) and me to join Mike, Mum came up from Betty's to look after Dinah and Tim (now sixteen and fifteen respectively). Fiona and I arrived at Tehran at 11.30 that evening and Mike was waiting there to meet us. He said it had turned very hot in Tehran recently and it was still very warm when we arrived. It was great to see Mike again.

Our next spot of adventure was on our way back to Pahlavi. We were in the mountains beyond Qazvin when the engine died on us. No, we had not run out of petrol and Mike could not find out what was wrong. We were fortunate as while he was still peering under the bonnet a motorist stopped and asked if he could help. After tinkering about for some time, he said it was the petrol pump – we never seem to have much luck with petrol pumps. He offered to go off and get a replacement from a garage he knew of not far away.

Eventually the man came back with a new pump and fitted it in no time and after Mike had paid him for the pump and his trouble we continued our way without further incident.

Fiona and I had not long settled into the flat when Dinah joined us for the summer. Ben had met her at Mehrabad Airport and she travelled down to Pahlavi with Monsef, from the office, who was coming down for a meeting.

On Friday, we usually went over to the Hotel Bozorg for lunch and, as a result of these visits, Dinah was offered a part-time job there as a receptionist, but not for long. Shortly after she had started work Mike came home with Shimiari, who was saying we had to go to the police station.

'Police station, whatever for?' I asked.

'I don't know but I think it is about your daughter.'

We walked over to the station that was just behind the office. We went upstairs to a senior officer's room where Shimiari and the officer had a long discussion.

'He says your daughter cannot work at hotel as she does not have work permit. She must stop right away.'

Mike said he was sorry for any trouble caused and would tell her to leave at once.

Zarobi, the contractor's manager, had brought his wife back with him one weekend and they set up home in a holiday village, on the other side of town near the Sefid Kenar Hotel. Zarobi was always behind Mike to move there as well.

'Michael, your wife would be company for my wife, she is lonely there during the day.'

We had been to his house but did not like the place, there were too many trees (although we love trees), and it was some way from the sea, so Mike had to make all the excuses he could think of for not moving there.

Shopping in our usual grocery store one afternoon we were surprised when a lady came in and started looking round the shelves. We continued to discuss what we needed and then the woman came over to me and said, 'Excuse me, but do you by any chance come from British Guiana, as I can't mistake the accent?'

'Well, yes I do, do you know it?'

'Yes, my name is Lorna Adolphe and I was born in Kitty.'

'Good Lord,' I said, 'fancy meeting someone from BG in Iran. I'm Audrey Bennett. I was a Roth before I married – you may have heard of my father, Vincent, he was director of the museum and zoo.'

We spoke for a few minutes; then she took us outside to meet her family. Her husband, Kelville, was from Trinidad and was seconded to the navy in Rasht as a computer technician. They had two little girls and a boy. We learned that they lived in Dekadeh Saheli, a very pleasant private

192

resort on the coast to the east of Pahlavi. They invited us to visit them the next Friday.

They had a very nice house quite close to the beach, where we spent most of the day under a large umbrella. It was here that Fiona and Mike had their first swim in the Caspian. The beach and water were very clean and there was hardly anyone about. We were very envious of the Adolphes and we paid them several visits at the weekends.

After Dinah had been with us about a month, Tim arrived from Leighton Park for his summer holiday. A few days after his arrival Zarobi invited us all to a circus that was visiting Rasht. We had ringside seats and quite enjoyed the evening's entertainment.

During one of our visits to the Adolphes we were telling them that we were not very happy with the flat we were living in. They said, 'Why don't you move here?' Mike then reminded them that he had tried earlier but with no success, being told the place closed in the winter.

'Well, there's a bungalow between here and the beach that has just been completed and it may not have been rented out yet. Why don't you ask about it?'

We did just that. We saw a Miss Bahpayma, a very friendly young woman in the office, and a week later we arranged to move in. It was like paradise.

Dekadeh Saheli was well organised: rubbish was collected every day and when we required *naft* (paraffin) for the water heater and stoves we ordered it through Miss Bahpayma and it was delivered within hours. The monthly rent was also paid to her.

One day in her office Miss Bahpayma said, 'Oh, now we have the two Bennetts together.' A man about Mike's age had come into the room – yes, he was a Bennett. He turned out to be the resident engineer on the new pipeline under construction for the supply of gas to Russia. We got to know him and his wife, Penny, quite well. In fact we also got to know a Canadian Bennett working at CHUKA. This was a complex to the west of Bandar Pahlavi serving the timber industry.

Between our house and the beach was a single row of bungalows. The one directly opposite us was occupied by the Richards, pronounced with a French accent. He was a wealthy businessman in Tehran and was intensely proud of his wife, Lily. Mike got into conversation with him one Friday morning.

'Mike, you must come over and meet my wife when she gets back from Europe, she is really beautiful.' He had his mother-in-law, a Mrs Azzisi, who stayed with them, together with a teenage niece who came over periodically to see Dinah and Fiona.

As the work on site developed Mike discovered that a senior manager, Fallahi, and a director of Boussa, the contractor, Golchen, also had properties in Dekadeh Saheli and they invited us round for dinner once or twice during our stay. Another family we got to know through the Adolphes was a Canadian one, the Sandfords, we believe they were called. He also worked at CHUKA.

We were all on the beach one Friday and one of their younger children started to climb under an upturned boat. When Mr Sandford saw what the child was doing he yelled out, 'Get the hell out of there!' It was a phrase we used in a jocular way for quite a while afterwards.

We saw quite a lot of Miss Bahpayma in the early days after we moved in as the house had not been finished – for one thing there were no wall light fittings in the lounge and Miss Bahpayma was having problems contacting the landlord as he was on a visit to New York. We believe that for some reason, he was supposed to supply curtains as well, so to bring the matter to a conclusion, she told us to go ahead and buy what we needed and she would reimburse us.

We went into Rasht and selected some light fittings and had the curtains made. The estate workmen fixed them for us and Miss Bahpayma reimbursed us the costs we had incurred.

One would have thought that would have been the end of the matter, but no, apparently, the landlord, when he returned to Iran, was not happy with what we had bought on his behalf and a big meeting was held in Miss Bahpayma's office. In the end, whatever was agreed did not affect us.

While walking round the market during one of our visits to Rasht, we saw some day-old chicks and could not resist buying two, whom we christened Henry and Henrietta, regardless of their sex. To start with they lived in a shoebox but they soon learned to fly out of it and wander round the house. They found the terrazzo floor hard going as they slipped and slithered all over the place. When they learned to fly properly and could get onto the table when we were eating we decided other arrangements would have to be made.

Mike found a large sheet of plywood washed up on the beach, which he turned into a house for them. In the Shambeh Bazaar we bought some chicken mesh and strips of wood, out of which we made a run to attach to the house. The Shambeh Bazaar was where the weekly market was held every Saturday.

One day Shimiari asked Mike if he would like some fish.

'What sort is it?' Mike asked.

'It's very good fish, Mr Bennett, es-sturgeon.'

'How do we cook it?'

'It's very nice if you cook it over charcoal.'

At the time, we did not know that we could buy charcoal in the bazaar, so Mike collected some driftwood and made our own. The es-sturgeon was nice but tended to be rather meaty and heavy. Having got a grill we had chicken barbecue on a number of occasions.

Coming home from work one day, Mike was greeted by the children who were in a very excited mood. 'Guess what, Dad, we've been water skiing.'

'How did you manage that?' Mike asked.

'We were on the beach when this man in a speedboat came up and asked us if we would like to go for a trip in his boat. As we were all together we saw no harm in it. When we got into deeper water he asked us if we would like to try water skiing and whether we had done any before. So we did. It was great, and he's coming for us again tomorrow.'

As it happened the next day was Friday so we decided to go along as well and see who this newfound friend was. His name was Zia and he told us that he was related to a king who had ruled over part of Persia in the 17th or 18th century. We had an enjoyable morning.

When it was time to return home for lunch Zia invited us to dinner that evening at his farm on the road to Rasht. The farmhouse was more like a ranch than a traditional farmhouse. As far as I can remember the only other person there, apart from the servants, was a niece. After the meal, we watched the television or a video. Zia was a well-built man and must have been at least forty years old, and as far as we could make out he was unmarried.

The next morning there was more skiing and then it was time for Tim to return to school. Dinah would be following a week or so later as she was starting University.

Going to work every morning as he crossed the Mian Poshteh Bridge, Mike could see how the pile driving operations were going. On a number of occasions, he saw no activity, and on arriving at the office he would find out what the hold-up was.

'Good morning, Zarobi, how are you? No piling this morning I see. What's the problem?'

'Good morning, Michael, how are you? *Nein, Kein* piling just now. *Die draht von der Tchosh ist* broken. Ve send to Rasht *fur ein* other.'

Poor Zarobi, he was obviously worried again at the delay, hence an explanation in three languages.

On another occasion when there was no activity, the first person Mike saw was Shimiari.

'Hello, Mr Shimiari, why is there no piling today?'

'Ah, Mr Bennett, the crane driver has gone to Abadan.'

'Gone to Abadan?' Mike said incredulously. 'Why on earth has he gone there?'

'Big trouble there. A cinema full of people there catch fire and the driver thinks his son may have been there, so he's gone to find out.'

This was a big mystery at the time, and a terrible catastrophe. There were said to be over four hundred people in the building when the fire started and when they fled to the exits they found all the doors were locked from the outside.

Before Dinah left we decided to have a party to return all the invitations we had received during the past months. Somehow, we had the feeling that Zia and his mother would not come, and when we made some remark to this effect to him, he said he would not miss it for anything.

When Fallahi and Golchen arrived, they brought with them a gift of a beautiful carpet, which was a bit embarrassing for us as they were the last to arrive so the presentation was made for all to see. The party was a great success.

Dinah flew up to Tehran and was met by Behrooz, and when she came to leave for England he took her to the airport to see her off. It was just as well that he was there as things were going from bad to worse in the country as a whole and in Tehran in particular. In fact, the night Dinah left there was a huge demonstration in Tehran that ended with troops firing on the crowd, resulting in many casualties. She was lucky to be on one of the last civilian planes out of the country as the revolution began. Zia took Dinah to dinner in Tehran that night, and, as we later discovered in a letter from Dinah, he had proposed marriage to her. He left Iran shortly after she did and visited her in Edinburgh where she was studying. She declined his offer.

It was about this time that Zarobi's parents came to Pahlavi on a visit and we were invited to dinner at the Sefid Kenar Hotel to meet them. They were an elderly couple; he had been a governor of Khuzestan at one time, stationed in Abadan. During the evening his mother told us she was desperately hoping that her son would start a family and thus cement the bond between the couple.

After Dinah and Tim had departed, we had a number of trips to CHUKA as we had decided that Fiona should join the school there as the work would be going on for at least another year. The Adolphes' two girls were already enrolled there. When school started Kelville or Mike would take them to the Sefid Kenar Hotel, from where a school bus took them the rest of the way. In the afternoons after the classes were finished for the day the system worked in reverse.

Fiona started school, leaving her little time for swimming. The Richards opposite packed up and returned to Tehran, as did their neighbours, a pleasant young couple whom we had got to know through our trips to the beach as the path passed their garden. Although politics and the Shah were taboo subjects in all conversations we gathered from these two families that things were not well in the country and they were considering leaving for the West.

It was about this time that a notice was put up in all conspicuous places around the town. Mike had one stuck on one of the office windows.

It was an announcement from the Shah that he had come to realise the excesses that the Pahlavi family were enjoying from their involvement in large business deals and he had ordered that these should cease forthwith. This was to counter the growing discontent among the public at the behaviour of the royal family. It had really come far too late to have any real effect.

Through the autumn, the discontent continued and there were a number of opposition marches in the town. These were followed by pro-Shah demonstrations said to be made by soldiers in civilian dress. Shah supporters were asked to drive with their car headlights on, and as dusk fell every driver became a royalist. We decided to follow the majority, believing in the safety in numbers!

One wet evening Mike was sitting in the lounge reading by the stove; at that time we only had one in the bungalow. Fiona and I were in the kitchen feeding and changing the chicks' nesting box. Suddenly the fridge jumped and plates in the sink rattled.

I shouted in a very loud voice, 'What on earth is happening?'

'I don't know,' Mike said; then as he looked through the swing doors leading to the dining alcove, he saw the lampshade over the table swinging to and fro.

'That was an earth tremor.'

I said, 'Let's get out of here before there's another one.'

'And where can we go in this rain? We're better off inside,' said Mike.

'But supposing the roof comes down on us, we'll all be killed.'

'That's very unlikely; the roof is only timber and corrugated iron and should be pretty stable even if there is another tremor. The best place is in the bedroom, away from the main roof and the chimney.'

So, with quick sideways glances at the roof and ceiling we closed up and went to bed. Fortunately, there were no further tremors. Rumour had it that the tremor was much worse at CHUKA, and that the plant, which was virtually completed, had been badly damaged; it was said that it had not been designed to withstand seismic disturbances.

As the troubles in the country continued we were able to keep in touch with Nina and the Morakabatis further afield by means of the Adolphes' telephone. Occasionally in the evening Lorna or Kelville would come over to say there was a call for us. When we got to their house and answered it was either Kafis or Morakabatis to see how we were and in guarded words advise us as to what was happening.

We were glad when December finally arrived as we were going home for Christmas. We spent the festive season with the Tilleys in Tonbridge, Mike's mother and Antony coming over for the day; then we went up to Largs for the rest of our leave. During our time in Britain we watched the situation in Iran very carefully.

Geoff Kempton, from Irendco in Tehran, had also come home for Christmas but had left earlier than we had, with the result that he was due to return before we did. Mike kept in touch with him over the holiday and asked him to let us know if he thought it would be pointless for us to return.

Early in the New Year the weather became colder and there were falls of snow. The news from Iran continued to be bad and then on the 16th January we heard that the Shah had left for Egypt in the hope that his temporary absence would cool the situation as it had done in 1953. Mike heard that Geoff was leaving Tehran, so it looked as though we would not be returning for the time being.

Then Mike had a phone call from John Munro (a Partner of RPT). 'Mike, you must get back to Tehran and Pahlavi, even if you have to go by camel. Your job is still going on and they need you there, however, in view of the situation you should go on a bachelor basis.'

'John, if I have to go I'm taking Audrey with me. We have already discussed the possibility of me having to go back alone. She would be driven frantic here not knowing what was happening to me as it would be practically impossible to keep in touch.'

Munro was not at all keen on this arrangement, but finally relented.

The day we were due to leave Largs, the airport at Glasgow was closed due to ice on the runway and British Rail had decided to have one of their one-day strikes, therefore it was impossible for us to get to London. We had to change our plans and discovered that the only airline flying into Tehran was Swissair, so we had to go down to Heathrow and fly by Dan-Air to Zurich to get the flight there. During our transfer, Mike met a quantity surveyor working on the Lar Dam (a project near Tehran) who was also trying to get back to his job.

The flight left just before midnight, arriving in Mehrabad shortly after sunrise. We had one intermediate stop at Damascus. The plane was quite full, which was surprising; I did not think many would be travelling to Iran with all the turmoil there. The cabin staff were very attentive, issuing us all with blankets after the meal had been cleared away.

The airport appeared somewhat untidy and deserted. We got a taxi to the Commodore, where we had to be admitted through the large double doors at the street entrance, which were closed. The hotel seemed deserted with very few guests in evidence. The large Persian carpets that used to cover the reception area had been taken up. We were given a room at the back on the sixth floor. It was cold and the heating was not working. We went to bed in an effort to get warm and to catch up on our lost sleep. We dozed off for a while; then Mike got up and made his way to the office.

Ben was pleased to see us back and was keen that we should go up to Pahlavi as soon as possible. However, with things as they were it did not seem that we would be able to stay as the situation was still very volatile. The plan was that Mike and I would drive down to Pahlavi with Monsef and Shimiari as soon as it could be arranged and Mike would formally hand everything over to Monsef.

I had phoned Nina, who was very surprised to hear that we had come back and invited us to stay with them until we left for the Caspian. We spent about a week at their flat. Each morning Mike went with Behrooz to his office, from where his driver took Mike on to his office. In the evenings after a meal we sat chatting and listening to Sina as he practised on the piano.

Then came the day for our departure. Mike phoned me and told me to take a taxi and come down to the office. Monsef, Shimiari and Mike sat around waiting for me to arrive. I had set out for the office but had been unable to get through, as there was a large demonstration in progress and the taxi driver had refused to go on, so he took me back to Nina's where I phoned Mike and explained what had happened. Mike said they would drive up to Mirdamad to pick me up.

Nina was very concerned for our safety and gave us a picture of Khomeini to carry and show if we were stopped at any time during our trip. As we left the flat we were made to walk under a copy of the Koran, a custom to grant us a safe journey. A very nice gesture, we thought.

Our farewells over, we got into the car and set off for Bandar Pahlavi. By driving around the outskirts of Tehran we avoided the city centre and any disturbances that might be taking place there, and were soon on the Expressway to Karaj and Qazvin.

As we settled down to the three- to four-hour journey, I related my experiences earlier in the day.

'It was awful. The streets were crowded with people and traffic and we could hardly move, then there were these lorries with men on the back holding up huge white sheets. I did not know what they were for.'

'They are es-shrouds which they use to wrap the dead in,' said Shimiari.

The journey was quite uneventful; we made a short stop for Monsef to buy something in Qazvin and a second one miles from anywhere for a call of nature. This was a little embarrassing, but resolved by me going first with the gentlemen keeping a strict 'eyes front'.

It was growing dark as we drove into Dekadeh Saheli. The whole place looked deserted as we drove to our old bungalow. Leaving me there to pack up what I could, Mike and the others went over to the office to settle the account and to inform them that we were leaving for good. As luck would have it Miss Bahpayma was there so they were able to explain our case more easily.

Once inside the house I was told I could only take the bare essentials and a nice Persian rug. Our elderly gardener then turned up and I told him to take our two chickens, Henry and Henrietta, and started to give him some of Mike's shirts and jackets but he said he would not be allowed to take them out of the compound, so I brought him into the hallway and told him to put as many on as he could and cover them with his coat. I also started to load him up with all the kitchen utensils and the like we had acquired until other workers on the estate started to come up to see what was happening, so I had to ask the gardener to leave and close the door.

When the others came back to the house we put our suitcases in the car and drove off to the office. When we arrived there was no one about except for the watchman who opened the door for us. We stayed just long enough for Mike to hand over to Monsef the various files and to collect his personal bits and pieces from his desk.

Leaving the office, we drove through the town and out to Zarobi's bungalow where it was planned we should spend the night before returning to Tehran. In the end we finished up by spending two or three nights. Zarobi and his wife greeted us nervously as everybody was very tense.

On the following day as we were about to leave it was announced that the road between Tehran and Qazvin was closed as a result of two opposing groups marching towards each other, so it was decided that there was no alternative but for us to remain where we were. The Iranians spent most of the day watching television, which appeared to be an ongoing report of events in Tehran. They were not very communicative as to what was happening; whether they were embarrassed or were not really sure themselves, I don't know. They did call us over to watch as some elderly men covered in blood and wearing dirty shirts and trousers were brought out of what looked like a cellar. These included the former Prime Minister and generals from the army who had been beaten up during questioning.

Although it was bright and sunny outside it was quite cold so we were forced to stay in the bungalow. There was little for us to do so we spent most of the time in our bedroom trying to decide what to do. The only bright moments were the phone calls from Behrooz. Initially he said they were looking forward to seeing us back in their flat when we returned, but then just before our departure he advised us against this.

'Michael, I'm very sorry but for your own good I think it would be better for you to return to your hotel. The reason is, the revolutionary guards have set up sentries on every street corner and are stopping all cars and questioning the drivers and passengers. Anyone they are uncertain about is taken to an office. While I don't think they would trouble you, it could take you a very long time to reach us. So, please understand and we will come and see you when you arrive.' Rather depressing and worrying news.

The morning we finally left we all posed outside to take some photographs for old times' sake. The road to Tehran having been opened, it was decided that Mike and I should return to Tehran by bus as Monsef and Shimiari wanted to stay a day or two to discuss the continuation of the project with Boussa.

Monsef and Shimiari came to see us off; they bought the tickets and saw our suitcases being loaded onto the coach. As we drove into Pahlavi Monsef had said, 'I would advise you not to speak to each other on the bus. We don't know who will be travelling with you and if they hear a foreign language they may be tempted to report you to the police or revolutionary guards.' For me, that was one of the quietest five hours I had spent for some time! With muted farewells, we climbed aboard the bus and settled in our seats. The coach was reasonably full so we heeded Monsef's warning and kept quiet.

It was a bright, sunny day with little traffic on the road so we made good progress. The rhythm of the coach drumming along the road soon lulled me to sleep, which was a blessing. Mike was quite happy to watch the passing scenery.

Somewhere up in the mountains we made the usual halt for a meal. Having foreseen this difficulty, we had brought some food with us so only left the coach in turn to pay a visit to the toilets. After about half an hour the other passengers rejoined the coach and we continued on our way.

The only awkward moment on the journey was in Qazvin. There was a lot of traffic here and our progress was reduced to a slow crawl. Occupying the seat in front of Mike was a small boy. He was becoming fretful and restless and finally stood up on his seat and turned to look at Mike. Mike smiled at him and then, remembering Monsef's warning, wondered what he should do if the boy started talking to him. Mike then remembered the old World War stories of escaping prisoners who managed to travel on trains or buses but could not speak a word of the language and did not wish to become involved in conversation with fellow passengers. They feigned sleep, so Mike did just that!

As we drove through the outskirts of Tehran we saw the results of some of the recent riots. There were stones and bricks littering the streets, burnt-out cars, and on a number of the street corners were youths armed with automatic rifles. The Commodore Hotel was cold and empty-looking and very uninviting. We phoned Nina to announce our safe arrival.

We had been told that arrangements were being made for our evacuation and we were to stay where we were and await further instructions. It was early in the afternoon on the following day as we were resting after lunch that the phone rang. It was Ben.

'Hello, Mike, Ben here. I've just heard from the British Embassy. They want you to go up to their place at Gulhak where they will give you details of the evacuation plan. Please contact the others in the hotel and give them the details, and I suggest you get off right away.'

Mike told me what Ben had said and contacted everyone by phone and arranged to meet them in the foyer in ten minutes. When we got downstairs we found John sitting in one of the easy chairs across from the reception desk.

Just then a tall young fellow smoking a large pipe joined us. 'You must be Mike Bennett, I'm Richard,' he said in a haughty voice. 'What's all this about going to the British Embassy? I'm not leaving here until I've seen Ben and been paid what I'm owed.'

'I'm not keen to leave either,' said John. 'I've got to sort out my income tax with the authorities before I can think of going.'

Mike then repeated what Ben had said over the phone so there was no misunderstanding. 'That's what we've been told to do and I think that's what we must do. It's up to you two what you do after that.'

After some muttering from the other two we made our way outside and tried to find a taxi. Some failed to stop; others, as soon as we spoke to them in English, drove off without a word. Several, on hearing the intended destination, professed ignorance or, again, just drove off.

'Where exactly is the British Embassy, Mike?' I asked.

'To be honest I don't really know apart from the fact that it's in Gulhak. I've passed it once or twice but I couldn't direct anyone there. We'll just say Gulhak and look out for a building flying the Union Jack.'

This did produce a taxi that was willing to take us and we all piled in. We set off up Pahlavi Avenue and after a while reached what we assumed was Gulhak as the driver slowed down and looked at us questioningly.

'British Embassy,' we said, but he just looked at us with a vacant expression on his face and said, '*Nemidenam*' (I don't know).

'Let's stop here and I will get out and ask,' I said. 'I can pass for an Iranian.' I got out and asked a number of people who were passing by. They just shrugged their shoulders and moved on. Eventually one started pointing in the direction from which we had just come, and so I returned to the taxi.

'He reckons we have passed it. He says he thinks it's about a kilometre down the road on the left. It has a pair of large gates, so he says,' I told them.

The driver, who seemed to have followed some of the conversation, turned around and made his way back down the road. A few minutes later we saw a pair of large gates leading into a park-like area. We told the driver to stop and I got out, crossed the road and went up to the gatehouse. After a minute or so I signalled that I had found the embassy. They paid off the driver and crossing the road, joined me at the gate.

We walked along a short roadway to what turned out to be the English school that was situated in the grounds of the embassy. The main embassy is in the centre of the city but in the heat of the summer the ambassador and his staff operated from a second embassy at Gulhak. The staff houses are located in this large park or embassy garden.

On the blackboards in the various classrooms to which we had been directed were a long list of names. The idea being that once we found our names we would be dealt with in that particular room. This done, we were soon being interviewed by a member of the embassy staff. We produced our passports and helped fill out a form, which in effect said we would reimburse the Foreign Office the cost of our repatriation. We were told to return there the following day with one small suitcase each. Having completed these formalities, we joined up again with John and Richard and returned to the hotel.

We collected our keys from reception and told the clerk that we would be leaving the next day; then made our way to the lifts. As we moved away we were approached by middle-aged Iranian in a dark blue suit. He was clean-shaven and wore a pair of rather thick glasses.

'Excuse me, but I couldn't help hearing you tell the receptionist that you would be leaving tomorrow and, as you spoke in English, I assume you are British and perhaps going to England?'

'Yes,' Mike said, 'we are, but I don't see—'

'My family is in England,' he interrupted, glancing nervously around as he spoke, 'and I want to get a message to them. I want to leave here too but I'm having a little difficulty with the authorities to get a visa. Could you possibly come to my room after dinner and I will give you a letter to post to my wife when you arrive in England, if you would be so kind?'

'No,' I said quickly, 'you write your letter and bring it down to our room, which is 812.'

'All right, I'll do that. Thank you very much.' And with that he moved away.

As we travelled up in the lift I said, 'Well, what do you think of that? I wasn't going to go up to his room. I was right, wasn't I? We don't know what trouble he's in and they may be watching him. We don't want to get involved any more than we have to, do we?'

'No, you're right. I reckon some of the other people staying here are in the same predicament as he's in.'

Later in the evening Mike was having a shower when there was a rattling sound outside.

'What's that noise, Mike?' I shouted out.

'It's nothing; it's the garbage collection. I always used to hear it when I was staying here but it was usually in the morning.'

'I can't believe that,' I shouted back. 'I'm looking out of the window and can see a stream of little lights in the sky.'

'OK, those must be tracer bullets,' Mike replied.

'Then they're firing. It's not safe up here. Hurry up and get dressed and let's get out of here. I'm off.'

'Don't panic, you're quite safe up here. That's miles away.'

'A minute ago, you said it was the garbage collection, now you say it's firing.'

Opening the door, I looked down the corridor and saw several men coming out of the rooms opposite, all armed with guns. They looked really angry. I slammed the door shut and ran back into the room.

'What are we going to do now? I'll phone Nina and see what she thinks.'

I was able to get through without difficulty and more or less repeated for Mike's benefit what Nina was saying to me. 'They're all lying on the floor at the moment as the firing is close to them. Nina says they are attacking the radio and television station.' I then told Nina of my experience with the armed men outside, and that I thought the firing was probably a signal for them to move out.

Next morning Behrooz, Nina, Sina and Maryam came to say goodbye and to bring a suitcase we had left with them when we went to Pahlavi. They did not stay long as they were anxious to get home again.

I remember Sina saying, 'Don't stand out here, Auntie Audrey, please go inside.' I could see the children were a little nervous.

No sooner had they left than there was a knock at the door. It was the Iranian man with his letter. 'I have left it open so you may read what I have said in it,' he said. 'I have also put a telephone number inside so you may give my wife a call if you would be so kind, as soon as you arrive, and tell her that a letter is in the post. Thank you very much.' And with that he left.

We closed the door and I sat down on the bed and read the letter. After a few 'ums' and 'ahs' I handed the letter to Mike, saying, 'What do you think of this?'

He read it through several times. From what the man said it was possible that he had worked for the Shah, and asked for forgiveness for what he had done. He had two children, a boy and a girl, both at very good public schools, and suggested his wife used a certain bank account to cover running costs until he was able to join them and sort things out.

I was very worried about it and could talk of nothing else for the rest of the evening. 'We can't take it. Suppose we are searched at the airport. They could arrest us and make us identify the man,' I argued. After a lot of discussion, I copied the phone number down on a piece of paper, tore up the letter and flushed it down the toilet. 'I only hope he doesn't come back for it,' I said.

'We'll just say it's hidden away for safety and we can't get it out,' Mike said.

When I got back to the UK, I phoned the number I had written down and passed on the contents of the letter to the man's wife

Next morning, we finished our packing, had breakfast and waited for Behrooz to come and collect a case we had agreed to leave with them as we had more than we would be allowed to take with us. When he rang to say he was downstairs Mike took the case down to him and saw him off. It was very sad saying goodbye.

After signing the bill for Irendco to settle we made our way to

Gulhak. We did not see John or Richard again. At the Embassy there was quite a crowd gathered already. We reported in, handed over our cases and then stood around and waited. There was one well-dressed woman with a young daughter, having a long argument with an official about a huge trunk she had arrived with. He was maintaining that they were only allowed one small suitcase each and her large trunk did not meet this requirement. What was she to do? It had all her possessions in it. It was suggested she left it with someone who was not leaving, but this suggestion was not received at all well.

We stood around for ages waiting for something to happen and then we were all called over to a large house in another part of the grounds. As we all congregated, we saw Ben and Pamela, his wife, over at the far side, although we knew they were not leaving just yet. An official then came out on a verandah and announced that the planes coming to take us out had been turned back. The authorities had stated that the arrangements made with the airport manager were void as the manager concerned had been arrested and so new negotiations were having to be made and it was now hoped we would get away tomorrow. We were therefore requested to return to our homes or hotels and return early tomorrow morning. Those who had nowhere to go should raise their hands.

I immediately put up my hand. 'Put yours up as well,' I told Mike.

'Why?' Mike asked. 'We can go back to the hotel.'

'I'm not going back there – suppose that man asks us for his letter?'

Mike agreed and raised his hand, wondering what Ben must be thinking if he saw what we were doing.

As those who had somewhere to go drifted off, we homeless ones were rounded up and taken to houses in the compound, the occupants having left earlier for home. We were allocated a nice bungalow with three others, two women and a man, and told to make ourselves comfortable. We did. The women set to in the kitchen with tin openers and knives while Mike and his colleague opened a bottle of whisky and selected a couple of bottles of wine to have with our meal. The evening was passed in a very relaxed mood, despite the fact that we did not know what tomorrow would bring.

After a good breakfast we tidied up the place as best we could and made our way over to the school where several buses were waiting to take us to the airport. We were told that two aircraft were expected, a Royal Air Force VC10 and a Hercules. Most of the women and children were to travel in the latter plane.

We eventually boarded the buses and made our way to the airport. It was a bright, sunny day and everyone was in a cheerful, hopeful mood. Mehrabad seemed to be under the control of a group of youths, all armed with automatic rifles slung over their shoulders. We were led into the building and told to wait in an area next to one already occupied by Americans, who were also waiting to be evacuated. Their area was covered with expensive-looking cases, dog kennels and cat boxes. Women with furs draped over their shoulders strolled up and down as they exercised their poodles and other pets.

The British settled down to wait. Some read paperbacks, others sat and smoked while others sat in small groups and chatted in subdued tones.

'This is your evacuation leader,' blared a loudspeaker in the American area. 'We've just heard that the first of our planes is approaching the runway. Isn't that great, folks?' A big cheer went up. 'We'll keep you posted with news as it comes in.' The young guards wandered about the building but did not appear to speak to or interfere with anyone from what we could see.

There were more loudspeaker announcements and more cheers from our neighbours, then as they moved off for emigration and embarkation the area became quiet and we had the place to ourselves. Eventually we heard that our aircraft were on their way and we picked up our hand baggage and moved forward in single file towards the first checkpoint.

It was while we were standing here that I suddenly felt something sticking in my back. I swung round and found that it was a gun belonging to a youth. He had been pushing his way through the crowd, not realising the menacing impression his rifle was giving.

'Pardon, please, lady, come back to Iran,' he muttered with a smile.

We presented our passports, our names were checked against a list and we were issued with Royal Air Force boarding cards. After this we were separated into male and female queues. When Mike's turn came at last his passport was again checked and his body and briefcase searched. He was a bit apprehensive as they rustled through the papers as he had a lot of receipts in Farsi with him and feared they would want to read through them all. But they were not interested. He was then free to go and he caught up with me again. I had had no problems but a woman next to me was involved in a long argument with the officials when they discovered her American Express Card.

As we moved forward we found we were almost on the airport apron. There before us was the welcome sight of a VC10 with *Royal Air Force* written along its side. We joined a small queue that was waiting to board the plane and were soon on our way up the stairs ourselves. The unusual thing about the plane was that all the seats faced the rear of the aircraft, it being a military aircraft.

As it was a military plane there were no stewardesses to greet and serve us, just happy and smiling aircraftsmen. I had a window seat; Mike the centre, while a newspaper correspondent occupied the aisle seat. Once we were all aboard the pilot lost no time in starting up the engines and moving off to the end of the runway. After a short wait we were soon hurtling down the concrete and then we were airborne. We had no sooner left the ground than we suddenly veered to the south, followed by a correcting swing to the north.

As we were sitting on the port side we did not get a chance to have a last look at Tehran and the Elburz Mountains. The important thing was, we were on our way home. Once we reached our cruising altitude we were welcomed aboard by the captain, who gave us our flight time and one or two other details. He apologised for the rather erratic take-off but said that it had been necessary as there had been a warning that the plane might have been fired on from the ground.

We were served with soft drinks and some refreshments. As we flew westwards a glance through the window showed patches of snow on the ground, which thickened as time passed.

The pilot was speaking to us again. 'I'm pleased to announce that we have just left Iranian airspace.' There was a large cheer from all the passengers and the level of conversation increased considerably as people expressed their relief at having got away at last. We passed over part of Turkey; then we saw the blue of the Mediterranean and started to lose height and the island of Cyprus came into view. I caught a glimpse of Limassol harbour as we were landing at the British base of Akrotiri.

Leaving the aircraft, we made our way to the airport buildings where we were free to wander round until the slower-flying Hercules arrived. We heard from those that travelled on this plane that they had found it very noisy and quite cold. We had been lucky to come on the VC10. We then boarded a fleet of buses and were taken to the British base, where we given a cooked meal. This over, we returned to the airbase where we joined a specially chartered British Airways plane bound for Heathrow. During the flight, we were served yet another meal.

We finally arrived at Heathrow about ten o'clock after a very hectic and eventful day. We took a taxi to a nearby hotel where, as soon as we were settled in our room, we phoned home to let them know that we were back. Next day we flew up to Glasgow and from there took a taxi home to Largs. It was good to be home again even though we had had to leave some very good friends, and, quite a few of our possessions, behind.

8

Khartoum, Sudan

1981 – 1985

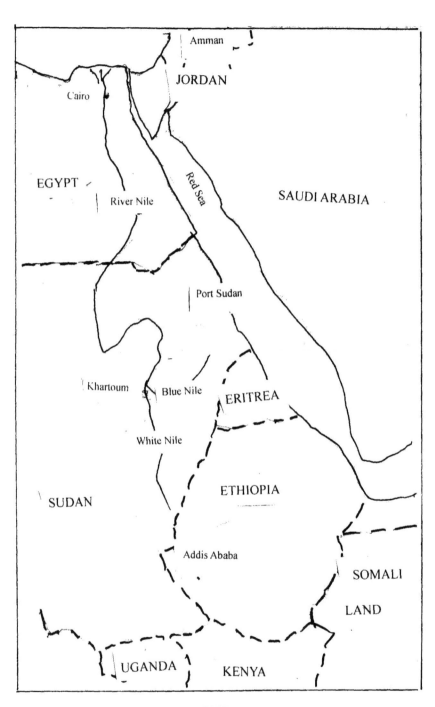

MAP 5

EGYPT, SUDAN & JORDAN

The day after our arrival back in Largs, Mike phoned Head Office to report that we had returned safely. He then flew down to London to discuss his future with John Munro, now a partner, and Bill Adams, the personnel manager. John Munro had been in charge at Fawley when Mike first joined the firm. It was agreed that he would work on the Thames Barrier.

When Mike started work in Head Office he stayed in Shalford with his mother and brother until we could find a house, travelling back to Largs for a weekend every fortnight. Now, both Dinah and Tim were at University.

Trying to find a house three hundred miles away from where we were currently living was not easy and in the end Mike took a week off, during which time we made a concerted effort to find somewhere to live. We had in mind to find somewhere in Tonbridge close to my sister, Betty, but house prices were very high in the area within walking distance of the railway station and moving further out presented problems of getting to the trains. We then discovered house prices were lower in Tunbridge Wells even within a reasonable distance from the station so we started the hunt in this locality and eventually settled on a house within walking distance of the station.

Then on 4th April 1979 my dear mother died. She had travelled down from Largs a day or two earlier to stay with the Tilleys and was taken ill during the night. The children and I travelled down the same day and we all stayed with the Tilleys until after the funeral. The day after we went back to Largs we started preparing for our move to Tunbridge Wells.

As we had no car at the time, and it would be well into the afternoon before the removal firm would have packed up, we hired a car in Glasgow and drove down to Tunbridge Wells, breaking the journey near Dumfries. Mike handed in the car at Gatwick Airport.

One evening Mike came home with news which was quite different from the usual matters of what he had had for lunch, the travel problems etc. He had had a phone call from Head Office asking if he would be interested in going to Khartoum as the engineer's representative on the construction of a power station there. It did not take him long to make up his mind – he hated commuting and the weather in winter, and he was not particularly interested in what he was currently doing.

The power station was being built using a grant from the British government. Ewbank and Partners were in overall charge, and RPT (Rendel, Palmer & Tritton) were to check the contractor's design and supervise the construction.

When Mike finally arrived at Khartoum Airport in 1981, there waiting in a minibus was Bill, resident engineer for Ewbank's. He was a tall, well-built fellow with glasses and greying hair and a trace of a North Country accent. We subsequently learned that he was sixty-three.

They were both staying the Grand Hotel, which was situated on the south bank of the Blue Nile just before its confluence, downstream, with the White Nile. One evening, during dinner Bill and Mike got onto the subject of their families. Bill, Mike learned, was married to a Jamaican, Pat, some twenty years his junior, with one son, Trevor, who was hoping to go to Birmingham University. Bill had worked in Saudi Arabia, Grenada and Jamaica.

'As Pat is coming out shortly I have decided to take a room in the annexe at the back of the hotel on the ground floor. It's quieter there than here by the main road and handy for the swimming pool. I'm taking Room 136 and suggest you have a look round there for yourselves.' Mike did and settled for Room 134. It was a largish room with a television and a refrigerator, neither of which worked very well, and nor did the air conditioner and water heater. There were two small windows that overlooked a lawn between the two buildings.

I was planning to fly out with Fiona at the end of July when she broke up from school, but after the royal wedding, which she wanted to be at home for. Fiona had been expressing a wish to go to a boarding school and her wish was about to be granted. As there were no suitable schools in Khartoum there was little alternative but to enrol her somewhere in

England and as a result we had booked her to start the autumn term at Bedgebury.

Fiona and I arrived at the same time as Pat and Trevor. Fiona was duly settled in Room 133 next to ours and we communicated by banging on the wall or calling each other on the telephone. On the first Friday Mike took us new arrivals on a grand tour of the three cities (Khartoum, Khartoum North and Omdurman) in the Land Rover, leaving Bill to draft some more of his telexes to Brighton. In the New Extension, near the airport, vast areas were still covered with sheets of water from an earlier storm. Fiona would arise in time for a late breakfast, after which she would go for a swim in the pool then lie on one of the loungers and soak up the sun.

Because of the rather slow postal service it had been decided the firm would use one of the worldwide courier services to handle the private and business mail. Every week RPT sent a package to Brighton which Ewbank's enclosed in theirs, and a day or so later it would be with us in Khartoum. Because of these slow delivery times, people returning to England would be asked to take a letter or small parcel and post it on when they arrived. We heard that a teacher at the international school was asking people to take a small parcel at regular intervals to England. It turned out that his 'small parcels' were drugs! He was eventually caught and punished.

One week Mike received a cost-of-living survey sheet to complete. The idea being that each month we would visit certain shops and find out the cost of various commodities given on the list. I volunteered to do this and got Pat to help me. As soon as Bill saw it he made a copy and sent it off to Brighton saying he and his staff should also be included in the survey.

George Mathieson, the RPT project manager, when he came out on the first of his regular six-monthly visits, realised that Mike was not able to spend as much time on the civil engineering aspects of the project as he should do due to the amount of work he was having to do in helping Bill to get things off to a good start. As a result, he arranged for two engineers to come out and assist Mike.

Friday afternoons and in the early evenings I would wander around the hotel verandah and lounge in the hope of meeting someone new in the hotel. On the front, patio tables were set out where snacks and tea were served. One Friday afternoon I met a young woman, Eugenia and her husband Gurgis, a Sudanese with a thick black beard. Eugenia, I learned, was from Yugoslavia and had met her husband, when he was studying to be a vet in Zagreb. They lived in part of the home of his three unmarried sisters. The highlight of their week was walking to the Grand Hotel for a cup of Turkish coffee.

In a similar way, I met the Elias family. One evening, Mike having gone to the telex room, as I passed into the lounge I saw three people sitting outside the entrance to the dining room.

I smiled and said, 'Hello.' An elderly lady, Mrs Elias, and her daughter Alice and son Wahid. Wahid was an anaesthetist working in Zambia and due to return there in the next day or so. Alice was in her forties and unmarried. They lived in a house just off the city centre and to break the monotony we would go to visit them every ten days. If we did not go Alice would phone up to see why we had forsaken them. During one of our visits, we met a near neighbour of theirs, Frieda Debs.

Frieda was a widow with two sons living and working in Paris. She was a petit lady with a bad hip that caused her to walk with a pronounced limp. She worked at the French Embassy as secretary to the ambassador. Frieda was Lebanese, as was her husband, and they had come over to Sudan many years before. We became very friendly with her. During the period of the Condominium, many Lebanese, especially lawyers, had been employed in Sudan, as most had been educated at the American University in Beirut. Frieda's sister-in-law, Mrs Malouf, was the mother of Charles Kfouri's wife, and it was her house that had been seized by the government and given to the British for their club, the famous Sudan Club.

Bill became very interested in the Kfouris when he heard they were big landowners with a large house on the bank of the Nile near Khobar. He invited them to visit the power station and to dinner at the Grand, and after a while, they were invited back to the Kfouris'. When the Kfouris visited the site, Mike had to be on hand to answer any technical questions that might floor our resident engineer, and also accompany them on a guided tour as Bill didn't know one building from another, referring to the workshop as the administration building.

Then when someone asked why such a building had such large approach ramps, Bill would turn to Mike and ask the same question, to which Mike would have to reply, 'Because it's the workshop, that's the admin building over there.'

One day a young couple with a small boy arrived at the hotel. She was a small, blonde haired woman, while he was tall and dark with a trim moustache. Fariba and Farouha were Iranians from Ahwaz. After the introductions Farouha said everybody called him FF for short. They had lived in the Riad section of Ahwaz, and we must have passed close by their house many times when we used what we called the 'back way' home to Zeytoon. Theirs was quite a remarkable story. After the revolution as the guards clamped down on all social activities they had become prisoners in their own home. Finding things becoming unbearable, they decided to escape to Pakistan. They made their way over to Zahedan where they found a small open truck with a driver that was willing to smuggle them over the border. The journey was hot, rough and dusty as they were driving along old riverbeds and animal tracks to avoid the border guards, in case they were caught or stopped by bandits.

Once inside Pakistan they had to make their way to Islamabad to get their passports regularised. FF, who was in the oil business, had got an introduction to a Sudanese oil company that he was trying to follow up. Fariba was finding it hard to entertain their young son Farzad all day in the hotel, so they bought him a tricycle that he rode round, much to the annoyance of the waiters, with whom he was in constant collisions.

Within a few days of their arrival I was being introduced to their first newfound friend.

'Audrey, this is Shamsi,' said Fariba. 'She's Iranian too and her husband's the chief chef at the Hilton.'

This resulted in a rather disastrous dinner when John Munro called in to see us on his way home from a business trip to South Africa. He took all the RPT staff and their families to a meal in the Ivory Room at the Hilton, and Shamsi's husband, hearing there was a large party in the restaurant, came out to advertise his specialities. That night it was seafood, which he managed to sell to most of us. Next morning Munro apologised for giving us such a poor meal and Mike had to make out we hardly knew this new chef at the Hilton even though he greeted us like long-lost friends.

One day we heard Bill was moving to the Friendship Palace Hotel (a KLM Royal Tulip hotel) across the river where he had taken a suite, and he had talked the Clarks into moving over there as well. When John asked Bill, 'And what about the Bennetts?' Bill had replied, 'Oh, they don't want to move.' How right he was – for a very different reason. At last we would be free from his frequent, annoying interruptions. Bill, we believe, hoped to drive a wedge between John and Mike, but John remained loyal and foiled his intentions.

When the Clarks' child, a girl, whom they christened Alexandra, was born in a private hospital in Khartoum run by a Welsh woman doctor and her husband, Mike gave John three days off to be with Sally and the baby, for which he was grateful and even referred to in his letter of resignation. After all, they had done the same for Mike when Fiona was born.

In Khartoum, there was a British firm who were having some problems with their telex machine, so they asked if Mike would send some telexes for them. When I went to collect the messages, they asked if I would do some typing and general office work for them, which I was very happy to do as time was beginning to drag while we were waiting for the housing situation to be resolved. Here I met Zeinab, a typist employed there. Zeinab was Sudanese, a lovely woman.

It soon became apparent that we would not be in our own house or flat for Christmas, and we were planning to bring the family out for the festive season. We had Christmas with a crowd of others on the lawn at the Sudan Club, where we also saw in the New Year. The day the children left to return to England we were all invited to lunch with Eugenia and her family at their home.

Fed up with living in hotels, we decided to bring the accommodation fiasco to a head. Mike sent a telex to George Mathieson, the project manager, saying the situation was becoming untenable, and Bill told the embassy he was thinking of resigning and that no doubt others would follow. This brought Chris Haywood from the embassy up to the site, where he tackled Mike on the subject.

'Bill tells me he might go if things are not resolved with regard to your accommodation. Would you go too?' he asked.

'Well, it's all right for Bill to talk, he's always saying how rich he is, so no doubt he could afford to quit. I can't, but I'm certainly fed up with the Grand and I have told RPT so, and I hope something will be done about it pretty soon.'

Things began to move fairly quickly after that, and it was finally agreed that we should take unfurnished accommodation and Ewbank's would order furniture in the UK and have it shipped out as soon as possible. With this settled, we set about looking for somewhere in earnest.

We decided we wanted somewhere in Khartoum North or Khobar. New Extension, where most people lived, was always without power and crossing the river morning and afternoon was a nightmare, so that was out. Discussing the problem with Alice during one of our visits, she said she had an uncle with a large house in Khartoum North and he might be interested in renting out the upper floor. I went with Alice to have a look at the house and found it to be almost ideal; the only problem was that it had only one bedroom. There was another large bedroom and bathroom but this was part of the ground-floor complex, and if we could get them to give us this extra facility then it would be ideal. The flat was situated just over the old Blue Nile Bridge on the road leading to the Friendship Palace Hotel. We could not hope for a better location. So it was a case of going round to see the Habishis and negotiating with them. This proved difficult, as they never seemed to be in when we called.

Fariba and FF managed to rent a house on the far side of the airport from the city. Once or twice a week we would go to see them, when we would be invited to take supper with them. By this time we hardly ever ate at the Grand as the food was dreadful, so it was either the Hilton or the Sudan Club. FF was having problems with his employer and wanted to move over to a more attractive job with the Chevron Oil Company, and was glad for Mike's advice on drafting his letters, for which he was rewarded with large glasses of whisky.

Through them we met Homa, another Iranian, married to a Sudanese, Abdel-Salem, with two young children, Javid and Jasmine. Homa had met her husband-to be while he was studying at Cambridge.

Mike discovered that Abdel-Salem had worked for Mitchell's at Fawley Power Station for a short while just before he went there. We also met another Iranian couple whose names I can no longer remember. As a result, when one of them held a Nouw Rouz party it was more like being in Iran than Sudan.

We eventually tracked down Wadi and Watiba Habishi and started negotiations with them for the flat. We would sit out on the front lawn drinking glasses of cool Karkadeh (sorrel) drink, while their puppy, Lassie, dashed about with a rubber bone. Wadi was one of the 'old school', as he referred to himself; he was a small man with grey hair and could pass for a European. He had been the Minister of Agriculture before he retired. He was a charming fellow and very interesting to talk to as we sat discussing the flat and life in general. They were a very pleasant couple who treated us like family.

I was conscious that the house was very close to the railway line and the flight path to and from the airport, so there would be plenty to occupy Mike should we be fortunate enough to get the flat. We were. Wadi had the screen moved to give us access to the master bedroom and bathroom; then it was a case of waiting for the furniture to arrive.

The British government sent officials to visit the site at regular intervals, however, after the initial meetings they delegated their inspection role to an independent, Edward Judge. As the senior civil engineer on the site Mike used to have long discussions with him about the problems they were encountering and the general progress of the project. Mike soon learned that he was an electrical engineer by profession and had been at Mangla, arriving just after we left. He knew the Coppings well as Jack had been the resident engineer on the powerhouse that had been Edward's section of the works as well. Mike told him we still corresponded with them and had met Carol since our time as next-door neighbours.

On the following evening, we would invite the visitors to a meal at the Sudan Club, after which Edward Judge and Archie Reeve, the contractor's man, would entertain us by playing duets on their guitars, Edward using an instrument lent to him by Archie. They had many practice sessions before 'the night'.

Just before we finally left the Grand, Zeinab and some friends invited us to visit Tuti Island with them. From the hotel, we walked some quarter of a mile down the road to the ferry crossing, the boat being an old tank-landing craft of World War II vintage. Once on board with the other passengers and the odd car and cart the journey time was only a matter of minutes. Walking ashore up a dusty unmade road, we came to an open-air bus; that is to say, it had a roof but no windows. We all clambered aboard and settled down on the hard, wooden seats. When at last we got underway, we had no sooner started than it was time to get off again as we had arrived at the one and only village on the island. We walked along the streets towards the west end of the island to an open field where a crowd of youths were finishing a game of football. As we stood watching, the red ball of the sun was rapidly sinking in the west, so by the time we reached the ferry it was quite dark. The island is basically a market garden for the three cities, having some very rich, fertile soil.

At last the furniture for our houses and flats arrived on site. One set was from Heal's and the remainder from some other supplier. To us, the set from Heal's was far superior to the others and had been allocated to us. On Saturday 15th May we finally departed from the Grand, our home for almost a year, and set ourselves up in the flat above the Habishis'. Once we knew the furniture was on its way, we went in the evenings to buy such items as a cooker, part-gas, part-electric; a washing machine; a carpet and a sun lounger for the verandah, which we had been told were not included in the package from England.

To start with, we had agreed with the Habishis that we would take on their houseboy, Jack, in the afternoons when he had finished their work. Jack, whose forehead was covered with a line of cicatrix, a custom among some Sudanese tribes, whereby small stones were placed beneath the surface of the skin, worked well initially but as time went by it was clear he couldn't work between the two houses so eventually we replaced him with someone else.

We soon settled down to a routine. In the mornings, Mike would make his breakfast and take it out onto the verandah where he would be in time to see the 6.50 a.m train which ran about three times a week, either to Wadi Halfa, on the Egyptian Border, or Port Sudan, and the odd plane that might be taking off or landing. On Friday mornings when he had breakfast somewhat later, he always tried to be outside in time to see the Air France flight take off, as the plane was one of the new Airbuses. There were three or four weeks in January when it was too cold to sit and eat outside so he had to remain indoors and listen to the BBC World Service instead. Work normally finished at four o'clock and Mike would return home to a high tea, after which I would go off in the car to do some shopping or visit Alice or Frieda, returning in time for our evening meal, after which Mike would lie in his hammock on the verandah and study the stars, which on most nights were very clear, and the lights of the odd high-flying aircraft as it passed overhead.

At the beginning of June, we experienced our first haboob, a strong wind from the south bringing with it clouds of dust from the desert. One could see them coming – a heavy brown cloud like smoke from a fire – and if the wind was strong and one was unfortunate to be out in it, the grains of sand stung like hailstones. When we came back off our first leave we found the flat covered in thick dust from the haboobs that had occurred during our absence; we literally swept up half a bucket of sand out of the lounge-cum-dining room alone. This was partly because the rooms had, in addition to ceiling fans, air coolers. These consisted of a fan set in the wall with the outside opening lined with straw that was saturated by a supply of water. They were very efficient but did create an opening through which dust and dirt could pass. We learned our lesson and on subsequent leaves sealed all the openings. At the airport, aircraft that were not currently in use had large covers placed over their engine intakes to prevent the ingress of sand.

On July 1st 1982, we went off on our first leave to England. In order to arrive at Gatwick, we flew KLM via Amsterdam. We should have left just after 9am but it was midday before we got away. The plane had been delayed on the outward flight by a faulty oil seal in one of the engines, and the crew could not fly again until they had had an eleven-hour break. When we finally got off our first meal was breakfast even though it was by then early afternoon. The cabin crew apologised for this, saying that was all they had on board.

During the stopover in Athens they decided to have another look at the oil seal. That delayed us even more, with the result that it was about 10pm when we finally reached Schiphol. We had obviously missed our onward flight to Gatwick. Fortunately, we were in fact staying the night in Amsterdam, taking advantage of the Dutch Tourist Association promotion 'Stay on the Way', whereby they offered free accommodation to any business-class passenger arriving from outside Europe. Putting most of our luggage in the left luggage office, we caught a shuttle bus to Amsterdam station, from where we took a taxi to the Hotel Pulitzer. It was so late we went straight up to our room. As we explored our quarters we opened one door and found ourselves about to enter someone else's room! The occupier, a man, was just entering by another door. We hastily explained what we were doing and retreated quickly, locking the door as we went. We could have burst in on quite a different scene. The bed was a strange affair; it turned out to be two wicker settees put together side by side to form what was like a large dog basket, in that we had to climb over the back to get into it. Nevertheless, it was very comfortable and we slept like logs.

Next morning, we went down to a huge buffet breakfast, one of the largest spreads I had yet seen anywhere. The hotel was located on one of the famous canals, along which we wandered on our way to the main shopping centre.

We came home again on two other occasions with an overnight stop in Amsterdam, and on the first of these we stayed at the Hotel Sonesta quite close to the city centre. This must have been in 1983 as I remember we watched the British general election on the TV in our room. During our first stop we had taken a trip around the canals which I enjoyed so much, especially a cat hospital on an old barge.

Shortly after arriving home we went down to Bedgebury to see the headmaster, John Delany, for a report on Fiona's first year at the school; then at the end of term we would go again to collect her and her belongings and attend speech day and the prize-giving ceremony. It was during this visit that I discovered the daughter of Sonny Ramphal, the Commonwealth Secretary, was at the school and I reminded Mike that Sony had been a senior lawyer in BG.

When we got back to Khartoum, Bill was away and was only coming back to collect his belongings. Different engineers came out to 'hold the fort' until a permanent resident engineer, Dave Piggott, was available. With all these changes of staff Mike acted as linkman, having been there from the commencement of the project. Sometime after Dave had taken up his post, the next time Hugh Pyper from Ewbank's came to site, they entertained Mike and me with dinner at the Hilton, in appreciation of the help Mike had given them.

As time went by the number of power cuts we suffered was on the increase, with the result that we started to lose food in the refrigerator, so it was decided to give each one of us a small portable generator. They were very noisy but effective and our neighbours were rather envious. When ours first arrived, Mike could not get it to start so he had to ask John, a young Ewbank's engineer, to come round and sort it out. Later on, we were supplied with a deep freezer each, which was a great boon. The problem with the power cuts was we never knew how long they would last, so we would spend hours debating whether it was worth putting the generator on or not. In the summer when it was really hot and there was no power, we took the single beds out on the verandah with mosquito nets and slept under the stars. During the power cuts we appreciated the fact that our cooker worked in part by gas so we could still boil water and cook.

One day, to our horror, we found a rat in the kitchen. As soon as it saw us the rodent shot behind the cooker. As we had nothing with which to catch or kill it we called downstairs for Mr Habishi's boy, Jack, to come up and help. He did not have much success either; then Mike remembered the old saying '*If you can't stand the heat get out of the kitchen*', so we put the oven on and sure enough after a while out came the rat and Jack was able to chase it away.

When we moved from the Grand we did not see so much of Eugenia, although she did call occasionally to see us. One, fairly regular, visitor was John; being a young bachelor, I think he was lonely. On Fridays, he would go to the post office to collect the mail and if there was any for us he would bring it round to us.

In the evenings, Mike would try and pick up the BBC Overseas Service on medium-wave, as he was not into short-wave transmissions in those days. One evening he discovered that there was a war going on in the Falklands but found it very difficult to follow with no maps to know where the various places mentioned were in relation to each other. To us it all seemed very far away.

At the beginning of a New Year the government would increase the price of flour, rice, bread, sugar and other basic commodities. That led to riots by students and others and brought the army out. One day, trying to get to the Sudan Club or the Grand, we found the main road closed and the smell of tear gas so we had to take a different route to avoid the trouble and get to our destination.

Most Friday mornings were spent shopping. First, we would go to the market in Khartoum North for fruit and vegetables, trying to avoid the meat market, which was always swarming with flies. For our meat, we went down to a butcher in the New Extension who had a shop below a flat occupied by Jill. She was a freelance journalist. We invited her to dinner one night; I had got to know her as she often dropped into the office where I was working. Having seen her name in articles and heard her on the radio, she could still be out there.

During a crisis when Libya was threatening to invade Sudan, Mike saw an AWAC aircraft circling in the sky. It looked rather strange with the huge radar antenna on its roof. Another incident was one Friday afternoon; returning home from brunch at the Hilton, we heard a series of loud explosions – these had been caused by some bombs that had been dropped near the radio and TV station in Omdurman. Who dropped them remained a mystery; the Sudanese said it had been done by Libya while others said Nimeiry, the Sudanese President, had organised it in order to put the blame on Libya.

While on the subject of aircraft, I recall some other incidents concerning our flights with KLM. Going home on leave, the plane was a DC8 of Surinam Airways on loan to KLM. As we took our seats we found the aircraft unusually hot and after a while people started to complain. The cabin crew told us the air conditioning was not working but would be operational once we took off. We could only hope they were right. Take-off was further delayed as we were taking some fifty Ethiopian refugees to Athens. By the time we took off Mike's shirt was wet through, but fortunately I had spare in my bag so he changed as he sat in his seat. Once off, Mike could literally wring the sweat out of his shirt. The second one became pretty wet too. The air conditioning did work once we were airborne.

I started toy-making, with other expat women, for local charities. The ones I made for myself, there was the problem of getting them home. Some of the characters were too large to pack so we had to carry them as part of our hand baggage. As the aircraft were never full we used to put them in the spare seats, much to the amusement of the cabin crew who insisted on fixing their seat belts round them. A stewardess even asked if she could take a photograph of them.

Returning to Khartoum one time we found we could not make a connection from Gatwick to Amsterdam on the same day. Mike phoned KLM and explained our dilemma. They said this was no problem and fixed us up at a hotel near Schiphol. On another occasion I took some artificial flowers back with me. As we boarded the plane a stewardess took them from me, saying she would put them in the refrigerator 'to keep them fresh'.

One night after seeing someone off at the airport, we were aware of a lot of unusual activity after the plane had departed. As Mike was on the viewing gallery roof he saw another plane in the sky, so he waited to see it come in. It turned out to be a Boeing 707 of TEA (Trans-European Airlines). We learned later that this was part of the secret evacuation of *Falashas*, Ethiopian Jews, to Israel. On another occasion returning from the airport in the middle of the night we found the bridge over the Nile completely blocked by hundreds of sheep being driven to market. There were so many, we had to wait until the road was clear again.

During our stay we saw President Nimeiry but once. It happened when President Mubarak of Egypt came on a state visit. On the Friday morning, they planned to drive over our bridge to Khartoum North, so we walked down to the main road, which to our surprise was lined by tribesmen on camels brought in for the occasion. In due course the two presidents drove by in an open car and we had a good view of both leaders. After they had passed the camels and riders set off behind them in hot pursuit. Quite a spectacle, although a somewhat dusty one.

The press reported that the Sudanese government, ever short of money, went on a begging mission to Saudi Arabia. The Saudis were sympathetic but said they were only prepared to help if Sudan followed more closely the tenets of Islam, which resulted in the introduction of sharia law. Bars and liquor stores were closed and hotels relieved of their bottles. Nimeiry made a show by strewing beer cans on the road near the Grand Hotel, then having a road-roller run over them until their contents flowed into the Nile. We saw army lorries passing the flat, loaded with crates of beer and inebriated soldiers after depleting the Friendship Palace of its stocks. The British Ambassador saved the contents of the bar at the Sudan Club by having the cellar sealed as a bonded warehouse until better times prevailed. It was said later that black-market alcohol and beer could be bought at a price. New gallows were installed at Khobar Prison and most Fridays a stream of people could be seen making their way there to witness an execution or amputation. A British journalist seen up a tree with a camera was spirited away and put aboard the next flight home before the authorities could lay hands on him.

Fiona came out for Christmas as usual and Tim was due to join us just before the start of the festive season. He planned to spend a week touring Egypt first; then come on overland to Khartoum. The evening he was due we went to Khartoum North station. If we could find him there it would save us going down to the main station. We made a hurried search of the train as it did not stop for long, but there was no sign of him so we drove on down to Khartoum where the train terminated. Although we made a thorough search we could not find him, and we even asked a British couple if they had seen anyone resembling him. We waited a day or so to see if he would turn up or a message would arrive from him.

With no further news, we went to the British Embassy and they agreed that we should send a telex to the embassy in Cairo to see if they had any news of him, thinking he may have run out of money and gone there for help. We tried to make the best of Christmas, as we were still worried as to what could have happened to Tim.

The plan had been that we would all return to England together after the festive season. As we had still heard nothing we decided to go to Cairo on our way home in the hope that we might learn something there. Fiona's ticket would not allow her to make a stop-off so we asked Wadi if he would look after her and see her onto her British Airways flight. At 3am on New

Year's Day Mike and I caught the EgyptAir flight to Cairo. As we came out of the airport two young men asked us if we wanted a hotel, and as we replied that we did they led us to a taxi and drove off to a very mediocre hotel in the outer suburbs of the city. We rested there for a while, but not liking the place, we left, saying we had changed our plans, and took a taxi back to a hotel we had seen outside the airport, the Cairo Concorde, which turned out to be ideal for our purpose and very comfortable too.

Once settled in, we took a taxi into the city and went straight to the Balkan Airline office, knowing that Tim had flown out with them and there was just a chance that he had a return reservation too. Being a public holiday, the city was very quiet. The taxi driver found the office without any problem and we were greeted by a middle-aged man, to whom we explained our problem. He said he hoped he would be able to help us but we would have to wait until the woman came in who operated the computer. We sat down and hoped she would not be too long in coming as it was really quite cold.

Eventually she turned up and sat down at the desk after the man had explained to her what we wanted. She tapped about with the keyboard and at last got that night's flight list on the screen, and after studying it for a moment or so said, 'There's no one by the name of Bennett on it.'

'Are you sure?' we asked.

'Yes, please come and look for yourselves.'

We did, and she was right: there was no name of Bennett that we could see. She then pressed another key and the flight list moved on slowly, and we continued to watch it, not really knowing what we expected to find. Then suddenly we spotted a T. M. R. Pennett.

'Look, that could be him – those are his initials, but it's not Pennett, it's Bennett.'

She then checked another list and found that a T. M. R. Bennett had flown out with them on the date we knew Tim had come out.

'Ah, yes, I remember him now. He was tall, good-looking and wore a red pullover.' So, Tim had an Egyptian admirer. He would be interested to hear the woman's comments. With any luck, he would be on the Balkan Air flight that night and we should be able to see him before he left. Feeling elated at our discovery and thanking the staff most heartily, we returned to our hotel.

The plan was that Mike was going to join the British Airways flight the following afternoon on which Fiona was booked. Because I could not get on this flight I was booked to leave Cairo by EgyptAir just before they did, and even this had a hitch. When I came to book in the next day they told me the flight was full and I would have to wait to see if there was a cancellation. I told them this was absurd and asked to see the manager. He soon assured me I was on the flight.

Tim's flight was due to leave at 2am, so just before midnight I went over to the airport in the hotel bus to see if I could find him. About half an hour later we were both back in our room. Tim was very pleased to see me and even offered to put me on an airport trolley when I complained about feeling tired. He had had a very successful tour of the pyramids, Luxor, Alexandria and Aswan. When he came to travel on to Khartoum he found the ferry he should have sailed with had sunk and not been replaced. He had sent us a telegram to advise us that he would not be able to come on to Khartoum, and thinking we were aware of the situation, went on to see some more of Egypt. The telegram, of course, had never arrived. We saw him off at the airport heading for home via Sofia and went back to the hotel for what remained of the night.

Next day we sat by the pool until it was time for me to leave to catch my flight. We reckoned that the four of us would all be in the air at the same time at one period on three different aircraft. Once I had booked in and secured my flight Mike sat and waited for the BA flight to arrive.

When he eventually boarded the plane, he heard a cry from the rear: 'Hi, Dad, I'm here.' There was Fiona with some of her friends right at the back of the plane in tourist class, all returning to their boarding schools, while Mike was up front in club class.

When Mike and Fiona arrived at Heathrow sometime after ten o'clock they dashed over to the Underground only to find the station closed: the last train had gone. They then returned to the terminal building to discover that there were no more buses that night to London, so the only alternative was a taxi, for which quite a queue had formed. After some waiting they reached the head of the queue and asked the cost to Tunbridge Wells.

The driver got out a list of fares which he consulted and then said, 'Seventy-five pounds, guv.' Muttering something about only wanting to hire the car, not buy it, Mike and Fiona stood aside and let the people behind take it while they considered what to do.

They then realised they could get a taxi to London for £20, so they took that, being pretty sure they would get some late-night train, at least to Tonbridge. When they got to Charing Cross they discovered the last train left at one o'clock, but that it only went as far as Orpington. As it was a case of Hobson's choice they took it, however before leaving, they rang home and were pleased to hear that Tim and I had arrived home safely. They then explained their position and Tim said he would drive over and pick them up, and finally arrived home at something like three o'clock in the morning. We were thankful that we had bought a new car the year before when we were on leave and it was there when we needed it.

Through Homa I became a teacher for a while. Homa taught at a private kindergarten school in the New Extension run by Linda Marshall. With a shifting expatriate population, teachers were always coming and going, which led to periodic shortages. This was such a time, and I was happy to oblige. My class was a mixture of nationalities but it was not long before I had them all singing *Old MacDonald Had a Farm* and all the other well-known children's songs.

In a block of flats beyond the Friendship Palace were families of South Koreans, employees of a well-known construction firm, Dae Woo, who asked me to help their children with their English, and it was their younger offspring that were soon getting their tongues round *Old MacDonald Had a Farm* and other similar songs. One evening I went round to the Dae Woo flats about a child and as I was coming away I saw some children playing with a goat kid. It looked so frail and hungry, so I asked one of the mothers if I could have it.

When I got back to our flat Mike said, 'What's that you've got and what are you going to do with it? You can't keep a kid in a flat.'

'Oh, Mike, it's so cute, just look at it,' I said, holding it out to him.

'But how are you going to feed it? What do they eat, anyway?'

'Milk. Look, you'll have to look after it. I'm going out to get it some milk.'

Mike said he thought our days of looking after kids had finished, both two-legged and four-legged ones.

When I went to the pharmacy to get a feeding bottle and milk the assistant asked how old the baby was. I had to tell her that there was no baby; it was for a baby goat!

The problem was when it tried to walk on the terrazzo floor it slipped and slithered all over the place, and of course it started to leave little puddles on the floor. To overcome the latter problem, when we saw it take up a certain stance, I would rush over and put an empty jam jar under it. We weaned it off the bottle onto more solid food. As it became more agile it would jump into Mike's hammock, and onto the table and beds. When it was time for us to leave we gave it to Ron Davies, one of the Ewbank's engineers, who lived in a bungalow with a large garden. Our landlord never knew about the goat!

There were a lot of goats wandering free in the suburbs of the three cities, scavenging and foraging in all the refuse tips and piles of rubbish. They would even tackle old cement bags. What amused us were the old nanny goats that wandered around with home-made bras around their udders to prevent their offspring from suckling the much-sought-after milk.

Due to the lack of time and the distances involved we did not get a chance to see anything of the Sudan. The only trip we made was when Mike Kelly from the Roads Department came out to look at the power station roads which had become prone to cracking. On the Friday of his stay he asked Mike if he would take him down to see the roads on the Rahad Scheme, with which he had been involved some years previously. As they would be away all day I decided to go along too, having made up a picnic lunch.

It was a long day as we had to go south to Wad Madani to cross the Blue Nile and the car gave trouble by overheating. Once in the scheme, surrounded by desert, we saw several images, of what we took to be mirages, of large lakes. In the settlements, we observed many of the traditional roundel houses with palm-leaf roofs, the pattern of which the Hilton in Khartoum had used round their swimming pool to provide shade from the sun. In the evening after our trip Mike Kelly invited us to dinner at his hotel, The Arak, in the centre of town. The building had been put up as an office block, but failing to find any tenants, had been converted into a hotel, of which there was said to be a shortage at the time. The Meridien Hotel was said to have had a similar beginning.

The British Council ran an excellent library in Omdurman, from which we borrowed many books. Some of them were only recently published and not ancient editions as one might expect to find in such a library. One book was the story of Karen Blixen, but one that really intrigued us was about Jordan and the ancient city of Petra, that set Mike planning a trip there. The Centre also ran a weekly film show, and among the films we saw under the African sky were *Evil Under the Sun*, *Gandhi*, *Tootsie* and *Pride and Prejudice*.

When we came to go on our annual leave in July 1984 we went via Jordan, which our tickets allowed us to do. For some reason, the woman Mike usually dealt with in the KLM office was not there and her stand-in did not know about the 'Stay on the Way' offer in Amsterdam, so it looked as though we would have to forego our visit this trip.

We did not have a very good start. We had booked to leave Khartoum on an EgyptAir flight at 3.30am, but on arrival at the airport we were told the flight was cancelled so there was nothing we could do but return to the flat, which we had closed up for our leave. After a somewhat fitful sleep we went to the Hilton for brunch and whiled away the day until it was time to leave twenty-four hours later. On these flights there were no allocated seats, so when a departure was announced there was a mad rush to the security office just outside the airport building to be the first in the queue. Once cleared there was another dash to the aircraft to secure a good seat.

Sunrise at thirty thousand feet is quite dramatic as the dark, starlit sky brightens as the great fiery ball appears over the horizon. Stepping out of the aircraft at 5.30 in the morning, at Cairo Airport, was quite a chilling experience even though it was 19°C. We had several hours in transit that were not very comfortable. The monotony was broken by a group of elderly Americans who had just 'done' Egypt and were taking the same flight as ourselves to Jordan. The leader, Hank, wearing a large yachting cap, kept his party in close order and gave them a running commentary on which gate we would leave from and his brushes with officialdom in his efforts to obtain this information. We had had similar problems as we had to retrieve our luggage from the depths of the airport even though it was labelled through to Amman.

There was strict security at the foot of the stairs leading up into the aircraft. We all had to line up for a body search and luggage identification before boarding. The plane, a Boeing 727, was only about a third full, with a large number of stewardesses, most of whom appeared to be either British or Australian. Unfortunately, we missed a sight of the Suez Canal due to cloud cover but once above we had an excellent view of the Gulf of Aqaba and the town itself; then we were descending to land at Queen Alia Airport, a very modern affair. Our visas were purchased in the airport, something we had been told about but had found hard to believe. We booked into the International Hotel.

After freshening up and some breakfast we walked into the city centre, which we found rather uninteresting with its narrow streets, except for some ancient ruins at the junction of two main roads. We then sought out the KLM office to confirm our onward flights and had no problem in getting our 'Stay on the Way' reservations. In our hotel complex we sent off some sets of Jordanian stamps to the family and one for Mike as he too was a collector; then hired a Peugeot 504 for a couple of days.

After lunch, we took the road north to visit the ruins at Jerash. It took about an hour along quite a good road, which curved and twisted its way along a series of valleys. En route we passed several establishments with hundreds of coloured clay pots lying in rows outside.

I was very keen to stop, saying, 'That's just what I need at home.'

'And how, pray, do you intend to get such a thing home?' Mike asked.

'Oh, don't you worry, I'll manage somehow.'

We drove on.

The ruins, when we arrived, were quite spectacular, lying just on the edge of the town of Jerash. There was a huge amphitheatre, and Mike climbed to the top, from where there was a good view of the site and the surrounding countryside. We then walked to the far end of the ancient city along a paved street in which the grooves made by the chariot wheels could still be seen.

After a good night's rest, we set off next morning for a visit to the

Dead Sea. It took us a good couple of hours following the road signs for Jerusalem, passing through a variety of small towns and villages. We were stopped at a number of security checkpoints but once we produced our passports we were waved on without further ado. Then we began the long, gradual descent to the valley floor, which is some thousand feet below normal sea level.

When we finally arrived at the northern end of the sea there was a faint haze over the water through which we could see a range of hills running down the far side of the sea. There were a few people in the water at the time and Mike soon joined them. The seabed was very stony and he soon lost his balance. As the water covered his face he cried out as the strong brine stung his eyes; it was really painful and there was nothing he could do to relieve the pain, and rubbing them would have made it ten times worse. When he recovered, he lay down in the water and experienced its great buoyancy and appreciated how easy it would be to lie there and read a book without any effort. After I had recorded the event with the camera we drove round to a nearby restaurant for lunch before returning to Amman.

Next day we were up at dawn to have breakfast before setting off for Petra. We decided to go by coach on an organised tour rather than drive there ourselves. We and one or two others from the hotel were picked up and set off down the main highway to Aqaba, passing the airport on the way. The countryside was of gentle, rolling hills with areas under cultivation using water pumped up from nearby streams or wells. We stopped at a cafe on the way for tea.

When we finally left the main road turning off to the right, we entered some hilly country and then made a steep descent into the town of Petra, of which we had an excellent view. The coach stopped at a souvenir shop on the far side of the town, beside which was a paddock of horses. Our guide then informed us that the tour of the ancient city of Petra would be made on horseback!

We each mounted a horse with the help of its minder and set off at a steady pace along a rough bridle path over open country. After a while we came to a narrow gorge, which we started to descend. As we went down the cliff face on either side appeared to almost close over our heads, and the ride became rough as the horses stumbled and kicked the loose stones that littered the ground. Then, turning a bend, we saw ahead of us a large doorway carved out of the rock. We had now entered a wider valley, again with steep-sided cliffs on either side. Here we stopped alongside a camel, on which most of the party had their photographs taken for a small fee, while others explored the cave-like chamber beyond the entrance.

Remounting, we proceeded down the valley, which opened out as we went. To our right, high up in the cliffs, were the ancient rock dwellings while on the left at a lower elevation were some others which we climbed up to inspect, leaving the horses once again with their minders. At the end of the valley was a cafe where we stopped for lunch. After the meal and a short rest we climbed back on our horses and returned to the souvenir shop where we bought a Bedouin *kefiyah (headscarf)* before boarding the bus for our return after a very enjoyable day. We retired early as we had to be up at 3.45am to catch our flight to Amsterdam.

Dawn had broken when we took off next morning and we had a good view of Jordan, and in the distance, Syria, as we headed for Israel and Istanbul. As we came into Istanbul Mike was very disappointed as there was heavy cloud cover and he was unable to see anything below us. He had hoped he might have better luck when we took off again, but the low clouds blocked everything out. Mike then made a silent vow that one day he would come here for a visit to see its mosques and famous Bosphorus suspension bridge.

We did not have long at home this time, having spent a few days in Jordan, and on our way back Mike had decided to take Fiona and me to Cairo to see the city and the pyramids.

A few days after our arrival back in England Tim and Mike drove up to Baker Street to meet Dinah and Natalie (her baby daughter) and bring them home to Tunbridge Wells, and a day later we went over to Bedgebury to collect Fiona, and the family was together again under one roof.

In just over a week, Fiona, Mike and I were back in the Cairo Concorde. The first thing we had to do was to go and confirm our onward flight to Khartoum. Cairo at that time was in a state of upheaval as they were busy installing a new underground railway. Having concluded our business with Sudan Airways, we visited the museum in Tahrir Square and had another look at the golden sarcophagus of King Tutankhamun, a first for me and I think Fiona as I am not sure whether she went with Mike when he took Dinah and Tim to London from Shrewsbury to see the exhibition at the British Museum.

The next day we browsed round the famous Khan el-Khalili bazaar. Sightseeing in Cairo was very easy as the hotel laid on a regular bus service to the city and bazaar, and a daily excursion to the pyramids and Sphinx. When we visited the latter, Fiona made the journey from the pyramids to the Sphinx between the humps of a camel, reminding Mike of his horse ride here some twenty years previously.

When we came to book in at the airport for our 6.10 pm flight to Khartoum we were told the flight had been delayed and we were to be put up at a hotel for the night, at which we looked forward to another night at the Concorde. When the minibus set off towards the city we knew we were bound somewhere else. The Helio Cairo Hotel was not far away but nothing like as comfortable as the hotel of our choice.

After dinner, which was quite edible, we settled down in front of the TV to watch an adaptation of one of Catherine Cookson's stories set in Australia at the time of colonisation. We were halfway through the film when a vehicle pulled up outside the hotel and the driver came in and spoke to the manager. A moment or so later he came over and told us that our plane was due shortly and we must return to the airport.

The usual formalities completed, we eventually found ourselves aboard a Sudan Airways Boeing 707. When they came to start the engines, the outer starboard one failed to fire, with the result that they had to shut the others down and investigate the fault. We remained on board; some fell asleep while others chatted with subdued voices. After a while we became conscious of a smell of aviation spirit as the engineers tinkered with the faulty engine. Then we heard the striking of a match behind us as someone in the row behind lit a cigarette.

I immediately jumped up and, turning around, shouted, 'Put that out at once. Do you want to get us all killed? Can't you smell the fumes of petrol?' My outburst brought an elderly stewardess down the aisle from the rear of the plane, who then made a desultory check of the remainder of the aircraft to ensure that no one else was being so foolish as to disobey the warning signs still displayed over all the seats.

Eventually we took off and had an uneventful flight to Khartoum. As we came to get off the plane we got into conversation with the stewardess, who turned out to be British. She told us that when we had confirmed our flight they should have warned us that the flight would be delayed, as it was known to the airline that the plane was being serviced by Lufthansa in Frankfurt and would be late.

Behind our flat, on the main road, was a large house owned by a wealthy doctor-turned-pharmacist. Mike had met him a number of times at the Habishis'. He was always asking when the power station would be finished as he wanted to open a paper factory but had been told that power would not be available until the new station was commissioned.

With him lived his married daughter, Mahah. When her first child was born we went to their home to congratulate her. When Mike, Fiona and I arrived, we were all invited into her bedroom. She was sitting up in bed adorned in a mass of gold bracelets and bangles like an empress. When she heard we were going on leave she wanted us to bring back a bedhead for her!

One evening shortly after we had returned from leave and the Habishis were on holiday in Athens, Mahah called over with a different message. It had just been announced over the radio that Wadi Habishi had died in hospital there and his body would be returning to Khartoum on the next Swissair flight. We were naturally deeply shocked at her news, as he had seemed in such good health when he left. Whether he had had some foreboding we shall never know, but just before he departed he came up and said he did not like going away leaving a lot of alcohol in the house now that sharia law was in force. He said he did not drink but over the years he had amassed quite a collection as a result of his position in the government. As we entertained quite a lot, perhaps we could make use of it? We agreed to take it but were astounded at the number of bottles he brought up. They covered the whole floor of our entrance hall. There was at least one bottle of every type of liquor we had ever heard of.

We felt it our duty to meet the Swissair flight on the evening of its arrival and attend the funeral the next morning. We were awakened by the sound of splintering wood, which we later learned occurred when the casket was removed from its packing case. The service was held in a Coptic church on the way to the Friendship Palace, the air of which was heavy with incense. Alice came with us and kept us advised as the service progressed. At the end Watiba broke down, prostrating herself on the casket in a flood of tears just before it was removed from the front of the altar. The mourners then left in a convoy for Omdurman where the interment was to take place. When the cemetery was reached only the male mourners followed the coffin to its final place of rest. Later there was a formal tribute to Wadi at the Coptic Club, which we also attended. Watiba stayed with her sisters for several weeks before returning home. I must say they were a very pleasant couple.

During her frequent visits to Khartoum, Fiona had become very friendly with Annabel Blair; she was also at a boarding school in England and became a regular visitor to the flat, often spending a night with us. Her father was a professor of English literature at the university and was also an ordained minister of the church. Annabel had a younger brother, Edmund.

One Friday afternoon after we had had the Blair family to tea we all decided to go to the Mogram funfair near the White Nile Bridge. We had never been there before, although we had heard about it from FF as he used to take Farzad there while they were staying at the Grand.

When we reached the dodgems, Mike was suddenly accosted by a Sudanese youth. 'Hello, Mr Bennett. Welcome.. It was one of the many tea boys they had had on the site. As a result, we had a number of free rides.

When Christmas came round again, the family joined us, travelling by various airlines and routes.

One morning Mike received a phone call from the embassy. 'Mr Bennett, we have your son here, would you please come and collect him?' Tim had travelled out by Balkan Air but was unable to advise us of his arrival time, and as he did not know how to get to the flat decided to make his way to the embassy, which he was sure would be able to contact us.

Before Christmas lunch, which we had at home that year, the children bringing all the essentials with them, we attended the service at the new cathedral in the New Extension. The vicar in his sermon made direct reference to little Natalie as she sat in her pram in the centre aisle.

Early in the New Year Tim decided he wanted to see something of Sudan before he left, so he took the train down to Port Sudan. We saw him off at Khartoum North on what should have been a twenty-four-hour journey. He finally arrived there after some forty hours, the engine breaking down several times en route. He came back by bus via Kassala.

Going to work one morning Mike saw a magnificent steam engine forming part of a goods train in Khartoum North station. He turned back and got Tim out of bed to go and have a look at it. He had inherited his father's interest in trains. Steam engines were still used in the south but returned to Atbara for overhaul, Atbara being the Crewe of Sudan Railways.

Dinah and Natalie stayed on after Tim returned to England. Natalie was by this time trying to walk. So that we knew where she was we made a playpen out of the settee and easy chairs until she learned how to climb out. As she went from a crawl to a walk we taught her to dance to our tapes. Dinah occupied her time teaching English to one of Dae Woo's executives and going on the Friday 'Hash'. The Hash House Harriers is an international group of non-competitive running social clubs. An event organized by a club is known as a hash or hash run which is followed by a drinking session known as the 'on on'.

At the beginning of April 1985 riots began again, which culminated in the overthrow of President Nimeiry. One morning as Mike set out for work the streets were full of armed troops and there was hardly any traffic about. It was quite eerie. He was just opening the gates to take out the car, when Watiba came out and told him not to venture out that day. He hesitated a moment; then, heeding her words, closed the gates again and spent the rest of the day at home. After a couple of hours a procession of cars passed along the main road, blowing their horns and the occupants waving flags out of the windows. In the midst of the procession was a van with a loudspeaker blaring forth in Arabic. Mahah, seeing us on the verandah, said that Nimeiry had been deposed and left the country.

Ewbank's staff had long campaigned that Khartoum be declared a hardship posting and eventually this was agreed to. The net result was that we got home leave every eight months instead of once a year. This meant we had an extra trip home to take before the job finished, and we went at the end of April for a couple of weeks. Our KLM flight took us via Vienna. The area all around the airport there looked very flat and mainly farmland, and I wondered where the famous woods were. I was surprised to see several large rabbits nibbling the grass at the edge of the hardstanding. When we returned Natalie came back with us.

I was very happy to have Natalie with us. The entrance to our flat was by way of a wide-open steel staircase onto an open verandah at the end of the building; it was a fire escape for the first floor. Along the front of the first floor the verandah was covered by the roof, whilst along the facade was an open metal screen, which also formed a gate between the two verandahs. There was also a gate at the bottom of the stairs, which was not always kept closed.

In the mornings, if the lower gate was not closed, there would be a crash on the verandah gate; Lassie had come to visit. I would collect Natalie and take her down onto the lawn with Lassie, where we would throw a stick or rubber bone for the dog to retrieve. When Lassie tired of this, we would return to the top of the staircase where I would sit and sing nursery rhymes to Natalie.

When Mike returned home in the afternoons, I would strap Natalie into the child's car seat and go off and visit Alice or Frieda. On Fridays towards dusk we would put her in her pram and walk over the Blue Nile Bridge and watch the sunset over Tuti Island.

Just after our return the NEC (National Electricity Corporation) had changed its name, and gave a dinner at the Friendship Palace to mark the completion of the project and to make a presentation to David, who was leaving at the end of the month. Mike was given an ivory carving as we were due to leave at the end of June.

One place we had always intended to visit and had never got round to it was the scene of the Dervish Dancers, who performed every Friday in Omdurman. So on our last Friday we decided to rectify this omission. It took us some time to find the place, so that when we finally arrived the ceremony had started. A large crowd had gathered, but using Natalie as an excuse we managed to gain a place at the front. To the sound of a drum and some other instrument a crowd of men in a sort of monk's habit were moving round with linked arms like the spokes of a wheel. When some small boys started their own dance on the fringe Natalie was quick to join them.

So after just one week less than four years we joined the other passengers on the British Airways TriStar *Morning Jewel Rose* and took our leave of Khartoum and Sudan. Mike celebrated the occasion by enjoying the free drinks and mildly flirting with a fellow passenger who turned out to be a journalist, and the wife of a piano tuner.

As our heavy luggage was being sent back under a diplomatic seal, we were travelling relatively lightly. We took the bus from Heathrow to Victoria and a taxi to Charing Cross and so home. When we finally arrived in the house we realised we had left Natalie's pram on the bus. This eventually turned up at the Baker Street lost property office so all was not lost.

To Mike this had been a very satisfying job. It had been hard going initially but he had things going as planned by the end. He had seen the job start on a waste piece of land and left a fully operational power station.

Tim on the train to Port Sudan

Billy the goat

Lassie

Clown on plane

9

Taff's Well, Wales

1986

We soon settled down to life in Tunbridge Wells and when I had a spare moment I would return to my toy-making and painting. Mike was working in Head Office but was expecting to go up to Tynemouth to refurbish the railway station there. This scheme fell through so Mike started working with Ben Dixon-Smith, who had had to leave Tehran shortly after we did.

Mike had several one-day visits, and some overnight visits, to South Wales and Waterford in Ireland. Then in February George Mathieson came to Mike and said that the year's maintenance period at Khartoum was coming to an end and they wanted Mike to go out there and do a final inspection. When I heard the news, I rushed to the shops to get a few little gifts for Zeinab and something for Frieda.

When Mike returned, he brought me a sackful of cotton for my toy-making. He had found Zeinab and handed over what I had sent out. He had several meals with Frieda, who was very pleased to see him. Mike also managed to meet up with Dinah, who came to Khartoum from her supplementary feeding programme with CARE in El Obeid, when she got his message to spend a couple of nights together in Room 134!

At Easter Mike went down to Sidcot for the old scholars' reunion and Tim went with him as he wanted to compare Sidcot with Leighton Park.

At Fiona's speech days, there was the awarding of prizes for the best pupils in various subjects, arts and crafts. Each year Mike asked her when she was going to get hers.

'Don't worry, Dad, I'll get one before I leave.' And she did – at her last speech day her name was read out for the best pupil in dressmaking.

Over the years, we had read a number of books by Christopher Nicole (his full name was Christopher Robin Nicole), and from the back covers I learned that he had been born in BG and had written several novels set in the colony. From Dad's memoirs, I knew he had known an Inspector Nicole when he was based at Kamakusa. I was therefore interested to know if this inspector was the father of the author. Mike looked him up in the *Author's Who Who* in the library, which gave his address as 'care of' the Jersey Yacht Club in the Channel Islands.

We wrote to him there and after a while our letter was returned, saying he was no longer there. This made us more determined to find him. We then wrote to his publishers, who replied saying they would forward a letter to him if we so wished. Off went our letter and eventually we got a reply from Spain. Yes, his father had become Director of Civil Aviation. He said he was in Spain as that was the setting for his latest book and to get the right atmosphere he felt it necessary to live in the country.

Mike's next job was to assist the construction of a dual carriageway north of Cardiff to Merthyr Tydfil. To start with he stayed in a guest house in Merthyr Tydfil, the hotel the firm used being full at the time. He then set about looking for somewhere more permanent to live. He looked at a couple in the neighbouring valleys; then as luck would have it he found a small semi-detached house on a largish estate in Taff's Well, halfway between Cardiff and Abercynon. The owner was a teacher in Zaire or Zambia, so the estate agent, Mr Toms, told Mike.

The weekend we moved in we drove into Cardiff, and bought a TV and a twin-tub washing machine at Allders. The house was small but adequate: a postage-stamp hall with a staircase leading straight upstairs, a living room and kitchen-cum-dining room with two bedrooms and a bathroom upstairs. Outside was a small open-plan lawn with a concrete driveway for the car, a wooden shed down the side path and a small back garden, most of which was on a steep incline as we were on the lower slope of the valley. From the upstairs back bedroom, we had a good view over the valley and the valleys beyond. Tim arrived that evening for the weekend and was a great help in setting up the TV and getting the place habitable.

In the other half of the semi was a young married Welsh couple with a large Rottweiler. As both were out working we saw little of them, however they were quite friendly and often cut the front lawn for us when they did their own; this was probably habitual as they no doubt had done this when the house had been empty to keep the grass under control.

Taff's Well was only a village, now bypassed by the Trunk Road. It had a small but well-stocked library which kept us in reading matter, and for the bulk of our shopping we went to a large Tesco supermarket a few miles up the valley. It had a huge car park and provided almost everything we needed including a filling station. Even on the busiest of days it never felt crowded and there was never any hint of speed or rush as in some other places. In the next valley, just outside Caerphilly there was a Carrefour supermarket, which we visited occasionally for a change. It had a cafeteria within the building which was useful.

The dreadful Aberfan disaster occurred in 1966 when thousands of tons of coal waste flowed down the hillside onto the village school that lay in its path, burying over 120 children. One of the unfortunates was the daughter of one of the secretaries, Pat, in the Merthyr office. The waste from the Merthyr colliery was taken by an overhead bucket system and dumped at the top of the valley side, and the drainage of the tip had been neglected, with the result that the water had mixed with the waste to form a slurry and, eventually unable to support itself, had flowed down the valley with devastating consequences.

As Mike went about the area he realised what an extensive system of railways there had been here when coal mining was at its peak between the two World Wars. In those days there had been four tracks through Taff's Well carrying coal twenty-four hours a day from the Rhondda Valley to the coal wharves at Cardiff. Mike found several books in the local library that gave him a good insight into the lines that had existed at the time. What really surprised him was to find that an old track ran behind the row of houses opposite where we were living.

During the summer, at weekends, we explored all the valleys and greatly improved our knowledge of the area. One could imagine how it must have looked at the time when all the coalmines were at their peak of production. Most of the valleys ran from north to south except for the Rhondda and Abercynon valleys, which ran from the west into the Taff Vale. One Saturday morning Mike heard on the radio that a fair, sponsored by Super Ted Bears, was being held in Llandrindod Wells the following day, so after an early lunch we drove up there. In a display case were teddy bears belonging to the famous, such as Queen Victoria and Margaret Thatcher. Another time we went over the mountains to Swansea and saw the famous Mumbles Head, returning along the motorway which, in parts, was still under construction.

After we had been in Wales a couple of months Natalie, now four, came to join us. During our stay we had a number of visitors; one of these was Sabine Trotti, a family friend, who was over in England. One Sunday we took her to see the narrow-gauge Mountain Railway above Merthyr Tydfil, built on the formation of an old line closed by Dr Beeching. The engine was a relic from Austria or Switzerland.

The following weekend Alison (one of my nieces) came to see us and on this occasion we took the train to Bristol and visited Clifton Zoo. It reminded me more of an ornamental garden than a zoo. When Fiona came she and Mike climbed the large hill behind the house; it was something Mike had set his mind on from the day we moved in but needed someone to make the trip with. It gave them a marvellous view up the valley almost up to Pontypridd. When Fiona and Dinah came together the bunk beds in our spare room came in very handy.

Because parking was such a problem in places like Cardiff and Pontypridd (pronounced 'Pontypreeth' and known as 'Ponty' to the locals), we usually drove down to Taff's Well and caught the train. Ponty was an unusual place at the junction of the Rhondda Valley and Taff Vale, with its narrow, winding streets. Every Saturday morning there was a market both open and closed, the latter being quite large and selling almost everything: meat, vegetables, groceries, second-hand books, ribbons and clothes. I enjoyed a good browse round and usually finished up buying oddments for my toy-making.

During our stay in Wales we managed to type some of these memoirs. Through a series of letters Mike introduced the Vincent Roth Museum in Georgetown to the museum in Australia that held the artefacts collected by my grandfather, Dr Walter Edmund Roth. Mike had been in touch with the museum in Georgetown concerning Dad's memoirs and they had expressed an interest in publishing them, but it later transpired that all they wanted was to have the whole manuscript and print only extracts from it.

One weekend we drove up to Birmingham and stayed at Tim's flat, as he wanted us to see the house he was hoping to buy, close by the BBC's Pebble Mill Studios in Sir John's Road. On the Sunday when we came to leave, Mike and Tim saw me off at Birmingham New Street as I was returning to Tunbridge Wells and Mike made his way back to South Wales.

Then one day Mike saw a notice on the office board asking for an engineer's representative for the Kilombero River crossing in Tanzania. Anyone interested should contact Alan Mitchell or Ralph Downham, the Director of the Marine Department. Mike was indeed interested – not only would it take us back to safari country, but also to the southern hemisphere. He phoned Alan but he was out of the country, so he decided to wait until he returned.

10

Ifakara, Tanzania

1987 – 1989

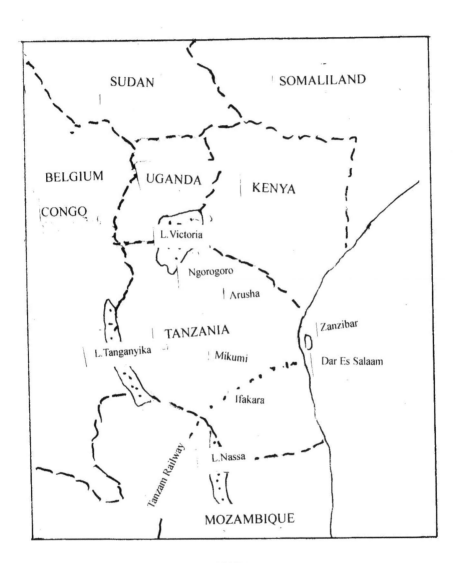

MAP 6

TANZANIA

When Mike went to London to see about his new job in Tanzania, Alan Mitchell, the project manager, told him how they had come to get this project.

It had come about in a rather curious way. Ralph Downham, the partner in charge of the Marine Department, had been at an international conference somewhere in the world, during which he had been approached by a Swiss engineer who explained his dilemma. The district of Ulanga and Kilombero in Tanzania, where they were carrying out development work, required a new ferry crossing, but as Switzerland was not a maritime nation they did not possess any qualified marine engineers and so they were looking for assistance in this field. Ralph naturally said he would be happy to oblige. The Swiss said they would also require someone to do the roadworks as well; they were doing a road rehabilitation programme in the area but were fully committed and really wanted all the work let out under one contract. Ralph commented that he was sure that the RPT Roads Department would be able to assist with this as well. Alan then explained that they had a marine engineer, Tony Lovell, out in Ifakara, at the time refurbishing the pontoon and arranging for the railway to transport the tugboat to Ifakara when it arrived in Dar es Salaam from Holland.

Mike went out in May 1987 and I followed in September with Natalie. Going through immigration took ages; then we had to wait for the luggage at the carousel.

Natalie spotted Mike and made a wild dash for the door and outside, shouting, 'Daddy, Daddy!' (a name she used to call him as a child since that is what she had heard Dinah, Tim and Fiona calling him) Mike stooped down and gave her a big hug and kiss. She was full of beans and chatted away about the journey until I came out with our loaded trolley.

We bundled everything into the Toyota, and were soon settling into the Kilimanjaro Hotel.

We spent a pleasant weekend going each day to Bahari Beach, where Natalie spent most of her time in the water. On the way to Ifakara we stayed at the Morogoro Hotel as immigration had said Natalie and I were to be registered there rather than in Dar. The hotel is on the outskirts of the town at the foot of the mountain range.

The next morning, we set out for the immigration office, then on to the land office where Mike had some information to pick up. Down in the market we bought some baskets and filled them up with fresh fruit and vegetables. The market was a lively place with a wonderful stock of produce. Thus, loaded up, we moved on to the Mikumi National Park.

Once we were well inside the park we came across a troop of baboons. When we stopped, they were somewhat hesitant, but as soon as I threw them some biscuits they came rushing over towards us. We continued to feed them with biscuits; then Mike saw one trying to get in through the window that was half open.

'Look out,' he cried, 'there's one trying to get in through the window!' I leaned over and managed to close it as the animal reluctantly removed his paw.

Next morning at the lodge there were a lot of animals to be seen. We saw antelope, buffalo, zebra and elephants. Natalie was really excited with it all. The road to Ifakara was not too bad so we had a good run through. There was quite a lot of water coming over the dramatic waterfall high up the mountainside near Kidatu, which we stopped to admire.

We arrived in Kibaoni, a small village just north of Ifakara, at midday and Mike introduced Natalie and me to Simon, his assistant. We were given a bungalow to live in in the Swiss compound until our own house was ready.

One of the first places we went to after a trip down to the river was the housing compound to see what the progress was and when we were likely to be able to move in. Steel bars were being installed on the windows and a strip light had been fitted in our kitchen as Mike had requested, but there was still a lot to be done and it would be another four or five weeks at least before it would be habitable. Mike then took us over to introduce us to the Groegges, a Swiss family, who soon invited Natalie over to watch their videos.

We had just got settled in when Mike had to return to Dar to see someone at the Ministry of Communications and Works (MOCW).

We broke the journey at the lodge in Mikumi. In the park by a waterhole close to the road we were fortunate to find about twenty elephants, who were drinking and preening themselves. At the lodge, we saw one of the hippos out of the pool and walking along the bank. There was a young couple there with two small children, with whom I was soon in conversation. It transpired that they too were living in Ifakara, behind the mission, and worked in the weaving shed. Mike did not even know it existed, although he had been to the large woodwork shops they had to see our furniture being made.

While in Morogoro next day we ran into Afzal, the contractor Benaco's site manager, who was on his way to the market. He was driving one of the new Land Rovers, which Mike was very glad to see as they had been in bond in the customs shed long enough. One of the reasons for our trip was to buy things for the house and Afzal assured us that Hassani, his office manager, would collect us at the hotel and take us shopping.

We did not enjoy our stay at the Embassy Hotel; we had to stay there as the Kilima, as we started to call the Hotel Kilimanjaro, was full. For one thing, we could not see the harbour with all its ships, which Mike always enjoyed watching and used to keep a note in his diary of all the ships in the port. Meals were slow and the background music was very much to the fore. Anyway, Hassani duly collected us and took us on a mammoth shopping expedition.

On our return, after booking into the Mikumi Lodge we went over to the park on the other side of the main road to see what the wildlife was like over there. After a long drive round the various tracks, having seen very little, we headed back to the lodge; then, just as we were passing the landing strip we saw a lion walking towards us close by the track.

Mike slowed down very gently; then stopped. 'Look at that,' he said. 'Our first lion.' He took no notice of us whatsoever and just sauntered on. We turned around and followed him as he was heading towards where we had seen a zebra and some buffalo. They had gone when we reached the spot where we had seen them a short while earlier. On our way back to the lodge we came across two elephants stripping the bark off a tree by the track and we stopped to watch them in the fading light. As we neared the lodge we almost collided with another elephant coming up the road from the car park.

When we got back to Kibaoni I asked Esther Groegges where we might get a young woman to help in the house and look after Natalie, and preferably one with some English. She suggested we tried the Folk Production Cooperative on the way to Ifakara as they taught domestic science there. Mike called on the principal, Stanford Msinga, and explained the reason for his call. He said Mike would need to see his deputy, Anna, but she was away at the time.

We eventually caught up with Anna and explained the kind of person we were looking for and she assured us she would be able to find someone that would suit us. A few days later we went back to her office where she introduced us to a young woman in her early twenties. Her name was Lucretia, and she seemed quite pleasant, but spoke no English. We again said we wanted someone who had some knowledge of English, so Anna said she would think again and bring someone round to our house in Kibaoni. A few days later she turned up with Lucretia! In the end, we decided to take her on probation and during the first few days we discovered that Anna was her aunt, which explained why she was so keen for us to take her on. Lucretia told us she was a single parent with a child of a few months. She turned out to be very willing and Natalie liked her, which was the most important thing.

A few days after we moved into our house I had the biggest shock of my life. I went into the passageway where we kept our footwear as I wanted to change into my outdoor shoes. I looked down to find my shoe and once I had located it I started to push my foot in. When I could not get my foot to go in I looked down to see what the obstruction was. I saw a small snake slithering away into the kitchen.

I screamed, 'A snake. A snake.'

Lucretia came running to see what the trouble was.

'I was just trying to put my shoe on and when my foot would not go into the shoe I looked down and saw this snake slithering away into the kitchen.'

'Snakes bad, plenty snakes here, you must be very careful.'

I looked out of the window but Mike's Land Rover was not there, so he was obviously out. When he came home for lunch I told him of my experience.

'We have to be very careful; there are a lot of snakes about. We found quite a few down by the river.'

A few days later Mike too found one in his shoe. We had taken the precaution of shaking our shoes before putting them on.

Natalie had no fear of the snakes and would often stand over one, saying, 'Granny, here's a snake.'

In October, there was a large influx of Benaco's people. With Afzal came Gatta, Lolli and his wife Wanda and son Ezio, and an old Italian, Del Pianto, who was going to be their site manager and engineer and later, their one-finger typist! He was in his seventies and walked with a limp, the result of a car accident, and used a stick for support. He had worked with Benaco on a previous job but had since hit hard times and had begged Lolli for a job. His wife had left him and he had finished up living with two Masai women and their children in his house in Kenya.

Our next trip to Dar was to pick up Alan Mitchell, who was coming out for a meeting. Just before we left Mike received a radio message that an Andreas Wyss, a Swiss engineer, was coming up before the others to have a look at the site and discuss the flooding study with him. Not only was Mike to meet Alan, but he wanted to go to the land survey office to pick up some more maps to discuss with Wyss, so there was nothing he could do but to get Simon to meet Andreas off the train and stand in for him until we got back.

As we drove to Mikumi I started with a dreadful headache and did not feel at all well. The following morning, I felt no better. We called in at Morogoro to get some money and buy some oranges for Tony. Despite our pleading the Kilima said they were fully booked; there was a major meeting in the capital and every room was taken. We finally got in at the Oyster Bay Hotel, which was in the process of a major renovation following a change in management. I was still feeling rotten when we went to dinner so I only had soup.

None of us slept very well. I woke up several times with a headache and Natalie was frequently up with an upset tummy, and each time we woke, so did Mike. As the next day was Sunday Mike decided he had to get me to a doctor. The hotel suggested we went to the Agha Khan Hospital on the waterfront.

When we eventually found the clinic, as we entered we almost collided with Afzal, who was just leaving with a youngish woman carrying a small child.

'Hello, what are you doing here? Is something wrong?' he asked.

'Well yes, Audrey has had a violent headache for the past couple of days and doesn't feel at all well. We asked at the hotel where we could find a doctor and they suggested we tried here.'

'Oh dear, I am sorry. Excuse me please one minute and I will help you.' He went out with the woman and child, returning in a couple of minutes. On his return, he went over and spoke to the receptionist and after a few words came over to us.

'I've arranged for the doctor to see you next, he's a friend of mine and I'm sure he'll be able to help you. I hope you feel better soon.'

With that he left us. True to his word, we were soon being ushered into the doctor's room. We explained the problem and he gave me a quick examination. My blood pressure was low and I had a slight temperature. He thought it could be malaria with amoebic dysentery, and prescribed an injection.

'And how are you, young lady?' he asked Natalie.

'Well, she's not too well either,' I said. 'She was up last night with an upset tummy.'

'Then I think she should have an injection as well,' he said.

'Do you think that's really necessary?' Mike queried. 'She seemed much better this morning.'

'Yes,' I said, 'I think she should have a small one.'

We then moved over to the dispensary; fortunately, we had our own needles with us, which we gave to the nurse who was in charge. While this was going on the doctor looked in and commented on the fact that we had brought our own needles.

On leaving the surgery we went to the Star and Europa supermarkets to get some mineral water and other essentials; then rested for the rest of the day.

Next morning Mike had to see Tony. When we arrived at the house where he was living we were told he was in the docks trying to extract his bus. He had bought an old London double-decker and fixed it up as a mobile workshop; he even had a door cut in the rear through which he could drive a small dinkum digger, and had shipped it out to Tanzania.

After lunch Mike went back to Dr Khan's and spoke to a very pleasant woman doctor, to whom he explained that I was still unwell. She was very sympathetic and said she would come to the hotel if she could but was unable to leave as she was on duty, but she would send a colleague back with Mike. After her colleague had given me another injection Mike ran him back to the hospital.

The next morning Mike was up at 5.30 am to go to the airport to meet Alan, only to discover that the plane would be arriving an hour later due to the clocks having been put back. When he eventually arrived, Mike told him of all our problems both business and domestic as we made our way up to see Tony, so he could fill Alan in on the progress of his work. While at the university we had a quick look over his bus, which was parked outside bearing posters depicting the need to save water.

'Very apt,' said Tony, for a place where there were no washers on the taps and no plugs for the basins or baths. This was universal as far as plugs were concerned; we always carried our own assortment wherever we went.

Before finally leaving Dar we called at the Home Butchery for our meat and fish order. This was a place we had heard about from Tony. Here we could buy lamb, beef, sausages and prawns, which they would freeze and load into our icebox where it would stay frozen until we could get it into our freezer at home. In the meantime, Alan had got a lift with Max to Ifakara, Max being the Swiss Embassy representative.

When we reached Morogoro the bank was closed so we had to stay the night at the hotel there until it opened again the next morning. On arrival, arranged for our icebox to be put in the cold room. We did not rest that night as we were troubled by mosquitoes. Next morning, we realised why – the nets over the beds were full of holes!

From the time I arrived I decided I would like to keep some chickens when we were in our own house, and the way things were going it looked as if we would be in our temporary home longer than we had originally planned. However, as the weeks passed, I decided to start collecting one or two birds as we might not be able to get them when we wanted them. This was especially so after I had bought some eggs in the Ifakara market and when I opened one to make an omelette I found a young embryo inside!

Lucretia settled into the family routine and one afternoon we took her home and met her mother and child. She lived in a bamboo-and-earth building with water being carried from a pump, and she had quite a distance to walk to reach the main road.

One morning at the beginning of December there was a knock at the door at half past six. It was Ernst Groegge.

'You will have to do something with your cock, he woke me up very early this morning.'

'All right, Ernst, we'll see what we can do. By the way, we've no water.'

'I know, the tank is dirty, we must clean.'

Henry, as we called the rooster we had acquired, would crow long before dawn; perhaps it was something to do with being in the southern hemisphere. Later the same day a Swiss engineer came over and told me they were going to spray the house without any prior warning. The previous day we had seen Esther sitting outside her house with most of her furniture, and when she said they were spraying her house we thought nothing more about it. When Mike got home and saw the mess and smell we had been left in he decided there and then that we would move to our own house, which was just habitable, and if we were in Benaco might make more effort to get it completed. One of the first things we got them to do was to construct a chicken run between the house and office.

Once we were settled in our house we decided we had a need for a houseboy to do things and go places which we could not expect of Lucretia. So Mike asked Winston, the man in charge of the ferry, if he knew of someone and he introduced us to Elias, a young man of about eighteen. The only problem was that he lived in Kivukoni on the other side of the river, so we told him to take a cottage in Kibaoni and we would pay the rent. He was a little strange at first but soon settled in and proved to be very useful. Natalie took to him and became quite a tomboy. She would often have lunch with Elias and Lucretia and share their cassava.

As we would be spending Christmas in Tanzania, Tim said he would come out and join us. Simon had asked if he could spend a week in Switzerland as he had met a Swiss woman, who worked for Swissair in Zurich, and was anxious to see her again. Tim was not arriving until Boxing Day so we had to spend Christmas Day on our own. The hotel put on their Christmas lunch for dinner on Christmas Eve, which was a disaster: the 'turkey' was pork and the pudding rhum baba. The meat was not very nice and we had to leave some.

The waiter, as he cleared away, remarked, 'The turky' was tough, no?'
'Yes,' I replied.

On Christmas Day in the afternoon there was a children's party, which was a flop. There was not enough food and drink and far too few balloons. Natalie would not sit down and watch the so-called 'entertainment' so in the end we left and went for a drive to Oyster Bay.

Next morning, we were up at the usual time as Tim's plane was due in at 9.30 and finished up being half an hour late. We waited and watched the EgyptAir plane come in and from our vantage point watched him pass through to immigration. Then we had a long wait at the exit doors. Eventually he collected his baggage, but instead of coming out of the building he was led away by some official. We later learned they had found him with some undeclared sterling, but it was all settled in the end with a reprimand.

We spent a day or two in Dar enjoying the goodies Tim had brought out with him and swimming at Bahari and Oyster Bay; then moved on to Mikumi. When we came to collect some cheese and bacon we had left in the cold room at the Kilima we discovered the cheese had been nibbled at by a rat or mouse.

The lodge was crowded and it was a good job we had reserved two rooms on our way to Dar. We took Tim into the park, and although we saw quite a lot of wildlife we were unable to find any lions for him. Our sleep was disturbed by a noisy party on the floor below. A group of aircrew from a number of airlines had come on a safari from Bahari Beach and decided to celebrate in their rooms rather than the public area.

In the end Tim and I got up and told them to 'Be quiet, we're trying to sleep. It's you British Airways girls that are making all the noise,' I shouted.

A timid 'It's not KLM,' filtered up from below.

'Then it must be British Airways,' I retorted.

Next morning, they were up at dawn with much shouting and slamming of doors to go out and see the wildlife in the park. This was not one of our best overnight stops here.

During his stay, Tim suffered from a sunburnt left arm from driving with his arm out of the window.

On New Year's Day we invited Bill, Mike's engineer, and Benaco over for drinks before lunch. It was a pleasant hour which lasted longer than planned because of a cloudburst which occurred just after our guests had arrived. We had many such storms during the year, and on one occasion Natalie sailed some plastic boats she had in the stream that formed outside our house. Later she found one boat at the far end of the compound. There were a number of thunderstorms too that were quite dramatic; one was really bad and right overhead, with the result that the site transformer on the main road was hit by lightning and we had to rely on Benaco's generator for power.

Tim went down to the site with Mike on several occasions and at that time there were a lot of hippos just downstream of the ferry, which was quite accessible now they had opened a borrow pit there. During his stay, he managed to fall foul of the law. One morning on the way to the site they called in at the local bank, which stands in its own grounds, for Tim to cash some travellers' cheques. As he came out of the building he noticed across the road a very colourful flowerbed outside a small hotel. Without thinking, and while still inside the doorway, he got out his camera and took a picture. In the meantime Mike was sitting in the Land Rover outside. After a while he saw Tim emerge together with the armed bank security guard, who led him off to a small building by the fence. Mike assumed he was asking some favour of Tim; then they came out and walked over to where Mike was parked.

'Dad, this man says he's got to take me to the police station as I shouldn't have taken a photograph while I was on the bank premises. I've offered to take the film out and expose it but he says no.'

And so they drove off to the police station where they eventually found an officer who would consider the case. The upshot was that they had to produce their passports later in the day. The officer more or less apologised, saying that if they did not appear to follow up the matter the guard would become disheartened and not bother to report anything in the future.

When we went back to Dar for Tim's return to the UK we had planned to visit Zanzibar, a place that had always captured our imagination. In the course of conversation Mike learned that Benaco's accountant, Mohamed Iddy, lived there, so he asked him the best way of getting there. It so happened that he was in Dar at the time and was able to phone Tanzania Airways for us. This proved a big disappointment as all the flights were full. Normally one of the Boeing 737s is on this route and there is no problem, but for some reason at the time we wanted to travel the Fokkers were on this service with only a quarter of the capacity, making it very difficult to get a flight. The other problem was getting back. We believed we could get there but there was no guarantee of a return flight, so we had to abandon the idea for the time being.

From the various books we had read we understood there was a regular service of dhows across the strait to the island from Bagamoyo, a small town some fifty miles up the coast beyond Bahari, so one afternoon we drove up there to see what the chances of getting across from there were like. It was an interesting trip but not fruitful; there were several other people there with the same idea and we gathered that there were no boats of any sort making the trip – in fact the beach appeared to be fenced off, which we understood was to deter illegal immigrants and smugglers.

The township had a number of old buildings and a fort dating back to the turn of the century when it was part of German East Africa, and a plaque on the ramparts in German endorsed this. It was around here that the great explorers landed when they set off into 'darkest Africa' from their base in Zanzibar.

Shortly after Tim left the first of the Tanzanian engineers, Ephrem Kirenga, arrived to work with us on the site. He was a quiet young fellow whose home was in the north somewhere near Arusha. A few weeks later the second man, Mbwale, joined us. He was about the same age as Kirenga but a bigger, well-built lad.

A month later Mike received a message that the President of Tanzania, Mwinyi, was to pay a visit to the district and would inspect the project. Madinda came down to represent MOCW. He wanted Mike to make a speech and conduct the tour of the site, but Bill and Mike persuaded him that he should make the speech in Swahili and they would be there to give him moral support and answer any technical questions that may be asked. Natalie, Lucretia, Elias and I all went down and joined the crowd and the president came over to me and said hello before passing on to where the others were standing. The president was a short man and stood listening attentively while Madinda said his piece, after which he introduced Bill and Mike, followed by Lolli, who was also there. Lolli spoke a few words to him in Swahili reminding him of a previous encounter.

It was a pleasant surprise when Mike heard that Peter Gregory was coming out to put forward to MOCW a plan for the continuation of the contract. We drove up to meet him and managed to get in a visit to Bahari Beach before returning to Ifakara. Time did not allow us to stay at Mikumi so we just drove through the park to show Peter the animals, and in doing so got lost, with the result that it was dark by the time we reached Kibaoni.

Two days after we got back Simon left for the UK, his contract having come to an end. Peter took over his desk and house and sat down to study the details of the contract. He came to us for all his meals and it was a pleasant change to have someone else to chat to.

A day or so later we had to clear up and pack prior to going on leave. Mike's contract was originally for ten to twelve months but with the delay to the works this would have to be changed, so it was decided we should go on leave now. For one thing, the job was closing down, as when the river rose no further work would be possible anyway, and Bill and Kirenga would be on site to look after things during Mike's absence.

As we had an open return ticket we decided to make the trip that had been denied us while in Khartoum. Having discovered that Ethiopian

Airlines flew to Dar, it should be possible to return via Addis Ababa and Cairo and visit Luxor and Aswan.

KLM had two very pleasant counter assistants whom we got to know quite well, and when we explained what we would like to do they said, 'No problem, just leave your tickets with us and we will deal with Ethiopian Airlines as their office is just next door.' Mrs D'Mello, at the Swiss Embassy, had kindly fixed us up with visas for both Ethiopia and Egypt.

So, on Wednesday 9th March we got up at 3.45am and drove to the airport in the Land Rover, where we left it to be picked up later by Benaco using the duplicate keys, and passed on into the airport departure hall. When Mike came to the security body search the policeman in the booth asked him to open his wallet, as it was illegal to take Tanzanian money out of the country. He allowed Mike to keep enough for our 'taxi fare' when we returned and relieved him of the rest.

As we took off in a new Boeing 767 dawn had broken and we had a good view of Dar and later Kilimanjaro, the twin peaks covered with snow. I thought we were on a non-stop flight, then when I saw water below us I realised we were over Lake Victoria and shortly afterwards landing at Entebbe Airport. As we taxied to the terminal building I saw the old airport where the famous hijack took place.

After about an hour we were on our way again. It was very clear and I had a good view of the terrain over which we were flying, some of it very rugged mountains which did not seem so very far below us. As we neared Addis the ground was flatter and had a brown, parched look about it. While waiting for our luggage at Bole Airport we checked our onward flight and were assigned to a hotel for our overnight stay, courtesy of Ethiopian Airlines, which in our case was the Hilton, a high-rise block on top of a hill on the outskirts of the city, to which we travelled in a bus, dropping others off at other hostelries on the way.

After booking in at the reception, Mike went to change some travellers' cheques and then rejoined Natalie and me. 'Right,' he said, 'let's go up to the room.'

'Right, I'm ready, where's Natalie?'

'She's with you, isn't she?' Mike queried.

'Oh my God, I thought she was with you. Where can she be? What are we going to do?'

I shouted her name and went off to ask at the reception desk, where a party of Japanese had just arrived. They and other people in the foyer started to look round to see what all the commotion was about. Once aware of the situation they joined in the search for Natalie. Mike caught up with me as we made our way to the entrance, thinking that if she was in the hotel she would be all right; if not then we could have a problem. As we neared the entrance along a glazed corridor we saw her in a grass courtyard looking into a pond.

'Natalie, what are you doing here? You know you're not to wander off on your own like this, you had us really worried,' I said in a cross but very relieved voice.

'I was only watching the frogs in this pond, Granny.'

After lunch, we hired a taxi through the government tourist office in the hotel to take us round the capital. First, we went to an old church, then drove to the far side of the city to a large covered market, finally passing back along the main street to where all the big military parades and rallies were held, and so back to the hotel. Really there was nothing of note to see apart from the Organisation of African Unity Building next to the hotel, which must be on the site of an old open market mentioned in one of Ted Allbery's books set in Ethiopia. That night we had our evening meal in our room and watched *James Bond: On Her Majesty's Secret Service* on the box.

Next morning, we rose late as Mike had not had a very good night, and after an excellent buffet breakfast wandered round the gardens and pool and then out onto the road outside, taking photographs as we went. We left at one o'clock on a familiar 727 over fairly rugged country before landing at Khartoum, which appeared rather dusty. Fortunately, we had a seat on the port side so when we took off we could see our old flat and a good view of the power station. The sky remained clear and we got a good view of the Nile and head of Lake Nasser as we flew to Cairo.

When we cleared Cairo airport we discovered our Hotel Concorde opposite was now the Mövenpick, a Swiss-based group, I believe. Before this we had been accosted by Isabelle, a representative of Royal Tours, with whom we fixed up our trip to Luxor and Aswan. Although we knew our way round the hotel, the dining area had been remodelled and made more secluded rather than the open-plan layout of before. There was a wedding or engagement reception on so the place was very busy, and we retired to watch TV in bed.

We were up at 5.45am and after breakfast we put our luggage in store, then waited for Isabelle to come and collect us, which she did just after seven o'clock. After the usual formalities, we boarded a 707 of ZAS Airlines and took off at 8.30 for Luxor. On arrival, we were taken in a bus to the Etap Hotel along with the other passengers. Whether they were part of our group or not, we never knew. After a snack, we were taken across the Nile on a ferry, where we were put in a taxi, the driver of which became our guide of sorts.

As we were getting into the car a young woman approached us. 'Excuse me, but are you going to the Valley of the Kings?'

'Yes,' I said hesitantly, 'that's where we're supposed to be going.'

'Would you mind if I came with you? I'm afraid to go in a taxi on my own. You hear such awful tales of what happens to people like me who are by themselves.'

'Why yes, of course you may.'

As we drove along we learned that our companion was a violinist with a Polish orchestra on a visit to Cairo and had come down to Luxor to see the sights. First, we went to the Valley of the Kings and followed the signs to visit the various tombs, almost missing that of King Tut until reminded of it by our friend. From here we went on to the Valley of the Queens and the impressive tomb of Hatshepsut, or Hot Ketchup, as our driver called her! After wandering round this edifice we carried on to Ramses Temple, which Mike explored on his own, we others being too tired, and finally to the Memnon figures before returning to the Etap for lunch.

Here we seemed to be part of a much larger party, which was to our advantage as we were given the same attention as the others. The meal over, we waited in the foyer for our guide, who never turned up. After a while Natalie fell asleep on one of the sofas so Mike went outside and hailed a horse and carriage and had it take him to the temples at Luxor and Karnack, around which he wandered, taking as many photos as he could for Natalie and I to see at a later date. After tea we took a taxi up to the Son et Lumière and listened to the first part, then returned to the hotel as we did not wish to miss the plane that was to take us on to Aswan.

Our guide, when he did turn up, made some feeble excuse for not coming in the afternoon, which we did not believe for one moment. On arrival at Aswan we had a longish drive in the dark to the New Cataract Hotel. By this time Natalie was quite feverish. We should have stayed here longer than one night but decided to cut short our visit, so when our new guide, who was a very pleasant fellow, came we explained our change in plan. After a phone call or two he got us a taxi and we did a whirlwind tour of the two dams, the Low and the High, before going on to the airport for a regular EgyptAir flight to Cairo.

On our arrival, we sought out Isabelle and told her just what we thought of her Luxor guides. She immediately grabbed the phone and gave them what sounded like a good talking-to, although she could of course have been shouting to a relative in downtown Cairo for all we knew.

Next day we took a taxi to a shopping centre on the way to the city centre where we found some quite interesting facades and happened to notice a shop sign reading *Natalie*. From there we went on to Tahrir Square and had a pizza lunch at the Hilton.

We were up again at 3.45 am and actually managed to get some breakfast in our room before leaving for the airport. When the minibus driver set off in the opposite direction to the airport, Mike really thought we were being abducted and imagined finishing up in some Cairo slum, only to discover we were bound for a brand-new terminal building at the opposite side of the complex.

We flew via Istanbul, where we took on some more passengers. I was in the centre section and was joined by a youngish woman dressed in a blouse and leather skirt. As we started our meal she wished me bon appétit, so I took this as a signal that she wished to talk. I learned that she was an Air France representative returning to Amsterdam and Paris after a visit to Istanbul.

'How come you are travelling KLM then?'

'Oh, I do occasionally, see what the opposition is offering, level of service, and this happens to be a convenient flight.'

'I must admit I've never travelled Air France, but when we were in the Sudan I heard the service was not very good, although in my view it really depends on the crew themselves. This is my favourite airline. Sometime

I must arrange a visit to Istanbul, it's one place I have never been to and one which I really want to see.'

'If and when you do go, stay at the Ramada. I always do, it's an old Ottoman building that has been refurbished and it's quite different. I'm sure you'll like it.'

We had a mad dash round the duty-free at Schiphol before catching our flight to Gatwick, which was delayed in the end in taking off. There was only one other passenger in business class and the captain flew with the flight deck door open the whole way so we were able to watch what happened at take-off and landing. As the engines revved up to maximum thrust we noticed that both the captain and co-pilot had their hands on the throttle controls. As we came in to land we could see the runway ahead, just like a stretch of motorway, and we seemed to rock a little due to a strong crosswind until we touched down. Fiona was there to greet us with a taxi.

Another reason for being home at Easter was that during the past year we had received a letter from a Professor Barrie Reynolds at the James Cook University in Australia saying he was planning to write a book about my grandfather, Dr W. E. Roth, and would like to meet us and look through Dad's journals. He and his wife Ena arrived after lunch on Good Friday, stayed until teatime and returned the following day and went through all the volumes of the journals, marking all the references to my grandfather, which we later photocopied and posted out to him.

While he was with us he related the trip he had made to Guyana, and some of the people he had made contact with. He had also been to Somerset House to look up old birth certificates, and down to Brighton to find out what he could about the practice Doctor Mathias Roth, Walter's father, had in the town.

All too soon it was time to return to Ifakara and the 6th April found us all at Gatwick, where we were presented with a wonderful new pair of binoculars for our safaris and wildlife hunting by Dinah, Tim and Fiona. That was after we had checked in our baggage, which was over a hundred kilos, but being three ticket holders and in business class, KLM were quite happy to accept it without any suggestion of any excess being charged, which British Airways would have done. Natalie did not appear to be at all worried at leaving her mother to go with us – which was a relief to us all.

Our flight left Gatwick at 7.30 in the evening, giving us time for a leisurely browse round Schiphol before joining our old DC 10 friend, *Edward Greig (the name of one of the KLM planes which always seemed to do the Dar es salaam route)*, for its 11 pm departure for Dar. I did not feel sleepy so I watched the in-flight movie, *Wall Street*, about which I can remember nothing, so perhaps I was more tired than I thought.

On arrival at Dar, despite a thorough search, nowhere could we find our Land Rover, so we had to resort to a minibus with all our baggage. Benaco apologised about the 'mix-up' resulting from a misunderstanding of the flight arrival time. After Mike had made a couple of business calls we collected our groceries and made our way to Ifakara.

Before going away, we had decided to put all our tape cassettes in Simon's house, which would be cooler than ours as Bill kept one of the air conditioners on as he used some of the facilities there. As soon as he saw us Bill greeted us with the news that Simon's house had been broken into and all our tapes stolen together with the refrigerator, some bedding and cushions. Fortunately, we were able to recover the cost of the tapes from the insurance company, but not the melodies. Later on, the police took Mike down to a cafe in town to try and identify a fridge there as the one from Simon's house. One thing we were glad to see was that all our hens were present and correct, Elias having been instructed and paid to feed and clean them out during our absence.

A week after our return Bill left us, his tour of duty having been completed. In fact he left on Mike's birthday; as he was driving straight through he was away early, and as it happened to be Sunday we had the day to ourselves. When Natalie woke she immediately set to and helped Mike to open his presents, which we had brought out with us. In the afternoon we went out for a walk across the new Machipi Bridge, which had been recently completed.

We passed several young children who gave us the greeting 'Shickamoo', a respectful one from the young to their elders.

One old man said, 'Hello, bwana' to Mike as he strolled past.

When I first came to Kibaoni an old man would come to the door selling pawpaws (papayas), eggs and the like, and as he approached he would call out, 'Audrey, Audrey', to which I took exception. It was only later we found out that what he was really saying was '*Ordie, Ordie?*' meaning, 'Is there anyone there? Is there anyone at home?'

But hardly a week had gone by when, one morning, Mike received a radio message saying MOCW wanted him to go to Dar as soon as possible. There were no other details so we packed up and left after lunch, planning to stay in Morogoro so we could get some money, not knowing how long we were going to be away.

In the end it turned out to be nearly six weeks. After visiting the bank we went to the Morogoro Hotel only to learn that they were fully booked; there was a large conference on in the town and all the other hotels we tried were similarly booked up, so there was no alternative but to drive on to Dar; a journey I shall not forget for a long time. There was quite a lot of traffic in the opposite direction whose lights were blinding, especially just after they had passed when there was a moment of complete darkness. To add to this, road repairs were in progress with heaps of gravel left in the road without any lights or warning – if there had not been a moon I don't think we could have made it. As in most overseas countries, when one flashed one's headlights for the oncoming vehicle to dip their lights, they would put on even more lights. In the end I drove most of the way while Mike acted as 'obstruction spotter'. Natalie was oblivious to all these hazards, sleeping peacefully between us, her head on Mike's lap and feet on mine. Fortunately, the Kilima could accommodate us.

On the 15th May Fiona arrived, having said she wished to spend her twenty-first birthday in Tanzania with us. To celebrate the occasion we spent several days at Bahari Beach, and on the day itself we went in an open boat to a small offshore island. The other passengers were some of the KLM crew Fiona had flown out with. In their off-duty garb they looked and behaved just like any other holidaymakers.

As time went by we began to run short of money, so we decided to go to Morogoro for a day and visit the bank. On the outskirts of Morogoro we saw some youths selling coconuts on the roadside, so we stopped to drink some of the refreshing liquid. When we had finished and paid, just as we were starting to move off the boy by the door suddenly grabbed

Fiona's handbag; fortunately it was hooked round her shoulder and so he was unsuccessful in his attempt to steal it.

After nearly six weeks in Dar and with no real progress being made on the future of the contract, Mike told Madinda he must return to site and supervise the work and would return at any time should his presence be needed. I too was anxious to get back to my hens as Benaco had been complaining that they were escaping from their pen and were eating the plants in a kitchen garden they had cultivated behind Afzal's house. When we were at home they would also wander into the house if the door had been left open, a thing we tried not to do, and lay eggs in the most unlikely places such as a basket of corn in the larder, and I even found one in a shoe of mine.

The real interest came when we found a hen sitting on some eggs and we looked every day to see what was happening. Elias was a mine of knowledge in the ways of nature and told us when he thought the eggs were likely to hatch.

Then one day I rushed into the house – 'Mike, Natalie, look, come here.' In my hand I had an egg, from which a scratching sound could be heard, and then the shell cracked and a small beak emerged, followed by a scrawny head. Natalie was thrilled to see the marvels of nature in her own back yard.

From hens we moved on to ducks. During a drive round Ifakara we had seen a number of ducks and I was determined to have these as well on our 'smallholding'. After a lot of negotiating, we picked up an old quacker, which Fiona christened 'Big Daddy', followed by 'Boy' and 'Girl' or some such names, and these were followed by three little ducklings which were really very cute. With these additions we decided they would need a pond, so we bought a couple of plastic bowls and set them in the ground. The problem was that the baby ducks would flop in and enjoy a swim, but because of the steep sides were unable to get out again, with the result that they nearly drowned. Twice we brought them back from near-death by drying them out with a hairdryer.

In the afternoons the women of the compound would come to our house and Elias would lift the chairs out for them to sit under the trees where at the weekends Mike would set up his hammock, and a small one for Natalie. Once a week Esther would come across with her children, Angie and Philip, who would chase the ducks and play with Natalie. Elias had made her a working model of an excavator out of old plastic cans and tins and a roller, with which they made roads in the soft ground around the house.

The other family in the compound was the Franzonis. Bruno I had met before, and it turned out that his wife, Franca, was the woman we had seen with Afzal at Dr Khan's hospital, with her young son, Jean Pierre, or 'Jampi' as he was called.

One day, coming home when such a party was in progress, I said, 'Mike, Franca was asking why we have trees round our houses and they have none?'

'They should ask Mr Bonometti (a Benaco partner) that question. He told me he needed the space for the lorries and buildings, but I stopped him doing the same here in our area.'

When the trees bore fruit later in the year we had to be careful as they came tumbling down to the ground. Elias showed us how to get the cashew nuts and prepare them for eating. He and Natalie would gather them up, light a fire, then heat the nuts in an open tray to burn off the poisonous liquid inside the outer shell. As they heated up they would burst into flame in quite a dramatic way, and once they had cooled off they could be peeled and were ready for eating.

In the afternoons Fiona would join Franca and they would sunbathe in their bikinis behind the Franzonis' house out of the prying gaze of the mechanics in the workshop nearby.

When Calum, the new director at the Swiss Tropical Institute Field Laboratory (STIFL) arrived he asked Fiona if she would be interested in working at STIFL cataloguing their research information, which she was pleased to do as it helped to pass the time. Then when his brother and sister-in-law passed through on their honeymoon, they took Fiona with them to the Ruaha National Park where there was a colony of crocodiles, and they even camped in Mikumi Park on the way back, which seemed somewhat dicey to us.

Another of Elias' hobbies was modelling, so we bought some clay from Brother Edwin at the mission and he made some very good replicas of Tanzanian houses, which he baked in the oven. This led to me falling out with Franca. During one of our absences in Dar, Elias, while minding the fowls, spent his time making these models. Franca, seeing one of them, took it from him, saying that he was not to mention it to us. Later I was in the Franzonis' house and saw the model and, after questioning Elias, he finally told me what had happened. Then there was the case of one of our hens that went missing. Again, after careful questioning of Elias we learned that the unfortunate fowl had wandered into Del Pianto's office, where he had set about it with his stick. I was naturally furious and accosted Del Pianto with the facts. We came to the conclusion that he had done this to prove himself to Franca. Franca thought it quite wrong for Natalie to eat with Elias and Lucretia as they were servants. She did not agree with me inviting village children to come into the compound to play with Natalie.

Before Fiona left Ifakara to return to England we made a trip to Mahenge; we had heard so much about the place that we felt we had to go and see it for ourselves. After crossing by ferry and passing through Kivukoni, the road continued across the plain until we came to a narrow valley and started to climb dramatically with steep hairpin bends until we reached the top, from which we could probably have seen Ifakara had it been a clear day. The township of Mahenge was on a narrow ridge, and like Ifakara, had one main street, if one could call it that. After passing through the town the road dropped down to a large, impressive building which turned out to be a convent or monastery. All around were rhododendron bushes and other plants in full bloom, making it a very colourful scene. A month or so after our visit it so happened that Mike had a visit from three members of the Mahenge Council who wished to invite him and Afzal to a reception to thank them for their efforts in improving the ferry crossing and roads in the area.

Eventually Mike's suggestion that Benaco should be given an additional works contract (AWC) was agreed to, and this then had to be set up formally. Andreas Wyss came out to organise it.

We picked Andreas up in Dar and broke our journey to Ifakara at Mikumi, Andreas saying he wanted to stay in the camp down in the park. After we had booked ourselves in at the lodge we took him down there and this gave us a chance to look at the rather primitive conditions in which the visitors lived, and we were glad to return to our own more comfortable quarters.

As we were preparing to leave the next morning we had an unexpected surprise. Natalie and I had gone ahead to finish off the packing while Mike had another cup of tea and a look over the park. As I made my way to our room I went to reception and got talking to a tall European fellow. I then saw Mike and called him over.

'Mike,' I said, 'do you know who this is?'

'No, I can't say I do.'

'It's Keith Davies from Mangla.'

'Good Lord, so it is,' Mike said, shaking his hand. 'Fancy seeing you here – what are you doing? Are you working here or on holiday?'

'I'm working here. I'm with the EEC. I've become a civil servant,' he replied, laughing.

'Tell Mike how you recognised us.'

'As I was saying to Audrey, as I sat having my breakfast I looked over to your table and became convinced that I had seen Audrey before and that you were our old neighbours at Mangla, so when I had finished I came to the reception desk here and asked if there was a Bennett family staying here. When they said there was, I knew my hunch was right, and so I was able to introduce myself.'

As we had to pick Andreas up we could not stay longer but promised to look him and Sheila up next time we were in Dar. When we did try to contact them we were told they were away on safari .

Shortly before Fiona left, Calum asked Mike if he could help him out of a problem. STIFL had been working with the government on a survey of village life. Several women in a village nearby were being monitored over a period of years on what they ate, the manual work they did, the number of children they had etc. and another survey was due to be done by a team of women who would be coming down from Dar. The problem was that there was nowhere for them to stay, and would it be possible for them to stay in one of our houses which was now standing empty? Mike said he would be quite happy to oblige.

The woman in charge was one Zohra. We had in fact met her when we went to dinner at Eric Burnier's, the local Swiss doctor. Here she had been quite docile, but when she came down on the survey she was quite different. When she started to complain about the house, the lack of essential items etc. Mike had to remind her that we were only providing the accommodation and any complaints she had she should raise with Calum, not us. Fortunately she went back to Dar and the others who came were very pleasant. Zohra did in fact return at the end of the survey, by which time she had mellowed considerably and we parted on very good terms. One girl who came was British and was working in Dar as a member of the VSO (Voluntary Service Overseas). As she had had to pay her own fare she had come by Aeroflot via Moscow, which she said had been very long and not very comfortable.

While we were still living in the Swiss compound Ernst had found a young man who specialised in carving wood. He had already made for them a Tree of Life, some figures to form a nativity scene for Christmas and several other items. The name of this man was Kiboko. He did not seem put out by his name, which was Swahili for hippopotamus, and we got him to make some typical Tanzanian chairs, which consist of two pieces of wood. The back formed one piece and the front leg, while the seat slotted through the back piece to form the other leg. Unfortunately, we lost a couple of pieces somewhere between Dar and Gatwick when we took them home.

As Mike's contract had run into a second year we were granted an extra leave, allowing us to go home for Christmas. We flew home by KLM, arriving just in time for Tim's birthday.

During our absence, in the UK, there had been an attempt to break into our house on the compound. One night after our return we were woken up by the compound siren going off. One of the armed security guards had seen someone trying to break into Afzal's house and given the alarm. Every night after this I made our house look like Fort Knox. The ironing board was wedged behind the front door and a dozen or more empty beer bottles were set below all the windows so that if an intruder should gain entry he would, it was hoped, knock some of them over and the noise would wake us up. Clearing away in the morning was a major task.

Whilst on leave at Christmas Mike had been into Head Office as usual, and had seen Gordon Matthews about where he might go to next.

Bahrain, Libya and Turkey were mentioned as possibilities, the latter seeming the most positive, and so in February Mike received a telex asking if he would confirm starting in Turkey on the 1st May. There was little else he could do but accept.

On the domestic front, the hens provided us with many eggs while the ducks were released to a new life on the pond at the mission. Natalie celebrated her fifth birthday with a party outside the house with the Groegges turning up in force.

So, on Easter Monday we said farewell to Ifakara and set off for Dar for the last time. The night before there was a terrific thunderstorm and we were without lights, but fortunately we had done all our packing beforehand. The road to Mikumi was badly flooded in places and we had to drive through the water with extreme care, never being sure just how deep it was. Near Kidatu we came to a full stop as a tree had fallen across the road and we had to wait about an hour while it was cut up and removed.

With work finally out of the way we were ready for our safari. We were determined to visit Zanzibar and the Ngorongoro Crater before we finally left and had made plans to do this on a very tight schedule. We had planned to fly to Zanzibar, but our schedule would allow us only one night on the island, so we cancelled the tickets and took the hydrofoil service recently opened by a Norwegian company. They had had a lot of teething troubles when they first started with engine failures, and we prayed it would not let us down. The *Virgin Butterfly* was a fast craft once it left the confines of the harbour and we were over in an hour and a half.

As we stepped ashore we were greeted by the smell of cloves – hence the nickname of 'Spice Island'. The reason for the strong aroma, we discovered, was the presence of a clove factory behind the quay. We took a taxi to the Bwanini Hotel, and after depositing our holdalls in our room set out to make the most of our twenty-four-hour visit. Our first call was the house used by David Livingstone before he set out to explore the 'dark continent', which is now used as a tourist office. Here we managed to arrange a tour of the island, or part of it at least, which we made in a rather overcrowded taxi after lunch as we were sharing it with a young Australian couple.

The tour was interesting in its way – an old church in the town centre, the remains of an old settlement or sultan's house, a hen farm, some old Muslim baths miles from anywhere, and an experimental farm. From the brochure I imagined the latter to be something like a garden centre in England; in practice it was a wilderness of overgrown bush and grass although we did manage to identify a coffee bush and several other fruits. Next day we explored the town on foot.

Zanzibar is a long, thin and flat island, and for centuries was a trading centre for Arabs and Persians who left their mark in the architecture of the old city before it was colonised by the Germans at the end of the 19th century, although they did not hold it for long as they traded it with the British for Heligoland in the North Sea. The old city and the newer part are divided from each other by a road. The old part is characterised by its narrow streets and the many houses and apartments with huge ornamental doors. The newer section looks more like Eastern Europe, with huge, plain-looking apartment blocks.

After lunch we left the hotel by taxi and drove to the wharf for our return journey. First, we were told to report to the immigration office; then we heard we had to go to another office for further documentation. All the while more and more people were arriving for the hydrofoil. Then we saw it skimming across the water and into the harbour.

After depositing us the previous day it had continued to Mombasa. Then there was a mad rush for the gate where it was to berth. Once it was tied up the police opened the gate and there was a surge of humanity as they all pressed forward to get aboard. Mike became separated from Natalie and me, and when the police saw what was happening they closed the gate again in an effort to control the crowd. It soon became obvious that there were more passengers than the craft could carry; return tickets had been sold on the outward trip like those for a raffle without any check on numbers. We had to get back as our flight for Arusha left at dawn the following day.

Then officials started shouting, 'Mzungus only' (foreigners only), and a policeman came over and helped Natalie and me to push our way forward to the gate. Mike followed behind us. Once we were aboard the gangplank was removed. Then some more mzungus arrived and a ladder was laid between the quay and the deck, and these people made a precarious trip across the gap until someone nearly fell through the rungs and the idea was abandoned. Then finally we were off and sailed into Dar es Salaam just before five o'clock.

Our trip to the Ngorongoro Crater, which we had been told by all the Swiss we must see before we left, was organised by Savannah Tours, based in the Kilima. The walls of their office were covered with pictures of the safari they had arranged for US President Jimmy Carter when he climbed Kilimanjaro. We were up in the morning at a quarter to four and were driven to the airport in a large Mercedes. Take-off was at a quarter to seven on a scheduled flight and landing some forty minutes later. Tanzania Airlines have the symbol of a large *twigga* (giraffe) on the tailplane of all their aircraft. As we came in to land, having seen Kilimanjaro again, we saw a large, flat plain covered with the occasional trees and bushes and, in the distance, surrounded by a ring of hills and mountains. The airport building had quite a modern look about it.

We were met by a minibus and after driving some ten minutes in the direction of Arusha came to the Hotel Tanzanite, a, small place with chalet-type bungalows set in the trees. Here we were given breakfast in a restaurant and then moved on through Arusha along a new road being built by an Italian contractor, Stirling Astaldi. In and around Arusha we saw a lot of coffee plantations, for which the area is well known. Then as we got into more open, undulating country we saw a number of Masai farmers ploughing their land, one acting as a horse while the other guided the plough. After an hour's steady driving we turned off the main road and headed north towards the Rift Valley, which was marked by a range of hills. At the foot of the range the ground was more fertile with a river and cultivated ground. Then we started to climb up the escarpment by a series of hairpin bends on a road with not a very good surface until we reached the top, on which was the Lake Manyara Hotel, where we stopped for lunch and a wonderful view over the route we had just taken and Lake Manyara itself.

We continued after the meal and a short rest, through undulating country with rich, red earth where shambas (small holdings) were much in evidence, the road generally climbing all the way. After a while the road surface started to deteriorate and became one of gravel. When we reached the entrance to the park the driver stopped to pay the entrance fee. We then continued on to the Ngorongoro Lodge, where we spent the night. As we got out of the minibus the scene was breathtaking – we were standing on the edge of a steep escarpment which dropped down three or four hundred feet to a huge bowl, in the middle of which was a lake, part of which was covered by hundreds of pink flamingos. The plain, which extended over a large area, looked to be completely flat and covered with grass, but very few trees. Having deposited our holdalls we went up to the verandah of the hotel for tea and to continue taking in the view. Although we combed the area with our binoculars we could only see a few elephants and the flamingos, but then we were too far away to see anything else.

After a restful night, we were up at a quarter to seven and after breakfast climbed into a very old and battered Land Rover, which incidentally we complained about on our return to Dar, for our tour of the crater. To get there we descended a very rough, stony track, in fact it was more like a stream bed, until we reached the floor of the bowl. Here we made our first stop amid several other Land Rovers and safari vehicles to watch a small herd of elephants. Apart from a few bare patches the area was covered with grass which varied in height according to where we were in the crater. Having seen enough here, we asked the driver to move on. Whenever he saw another vehicle he recognised he stopped and spoke to the driver and they exchanged information on where the various animals were to be seen.

We had quite a long drive with several false stops and reverses before we came to our next sighting but it was worth waiting for, as there, sitting upright in the short grass, was a lion with a magnificent mane. He was quite disinterested in our presence and we almost felt we could get out and walk round him without any problem. Then, looking further, we saw another lion quite close by. The lions I referred to in Mikumi were in fact females, and when Fiona was with us we came across a lioness with three cubs, whom we sat and watched, hoping they would move or play with each other.

As we moved round Mike would get up periodically and look out through the observation hole in the roof, but the track being rough in places, he found this uncomfortable as his camera and binoculars were in danger of being damaged. We then drove over to the lake to take a closer look at the flocks of flamingos gathered there. Our guide-cum-driver allowed us to get out and take some photos of ourselves 'on safari'. Then we moved on, during which time we saw a hyena, a jackal and a small flock of ostrich, but no giraffe.

As we continued we asked the driver, 'Is it possible to see any rhino?' He acknowledged that with any luck we would find one, and sure enough, having gone over to the far side of the crater, there in the longer grass we saw a large black rhino and with it was a baby. We were very lucky as while we watched they were moving away and it was not possible to follow them. As we moved to the foot of the escarpment through a belt of trees we came across some more elephants before starting the climb back out of the crater.

After lunch at the lodge we packed up and drove back to the Lake Manyara Hotel, where we stayed the night. Our room had a magnificent view over the Rift Valley and the large pink patches of the flocks of flamingos gathered there. The pink colouring apparently comes from some salts in the water in which they live. During the afternoon, there was a dramatic thunderstorm with a huge rainbow stretching right across the plain, and we spent the time sitting on the verandah absorbing the breathtaking scene.

Next morning when we reached the foot of the escarpment we left the main road and entered the Lake Manyara Park and visited first a small but very informative museum. From there we drove through a small forest, beyond which was a hippo pool teeming with the beasts, most of whom were out of the water on the opposite bank. There were hippos of all sizes; some of those in the water would open their mouths to reveal huge, ugly-looking teeth.

After we had watched them we drove back to Arusha where we had a break for shopping. Apart from buying a couple of holdalls in which to take some of our possessions home, I spent much of my time selecting batik scenes in a shop we discovered close by where we had stopped. Our shopping spree over, we drove on to the Hotel Tanzanite, for lunch and our overnight stop.

That afternoon we heard there was a small zoo next door, so we went to see it. There were a number of animals and birds on display but the star of the show was a chimp called Millar. He had us well entertained as he had a teapot and mug, and was pretending to pour tea out of the pot into the mug and then picking it up and drinking from it like any human. During the night, we were under a relentless attack from some very persistent mosquitoes.

On the flight back we had a good view of Zanzibar and Dar as we came in to land. Back in the Kilima, we had to finalise our packing after buying a selection of Makonde carvings and then pay KLM for our excess baggage. Hassani drove us to the airport for our flight home with *Edward Greig* and so it was time to say, 'Tanzania, *kwaheri*' (Tanzania, goodbye).

For Mike, it was a successful tour. Although we had a rough time early on, the job had finished the way Mike thought it should and we had been able to visit places denied us when we were in Khartoum. Natalie talked of her friends there, Elias and Lucretia, for many years after.

There was a sequel to this in that shortly after we had left the Kilombero rose to a record level and flooded the road on the north bank, washing it away in several places. The fact that it was not all lost, Mike put down to the constant supervision that had been given to the construction.

Monkey – on roaf to Ifakara

Tumwe – dugout canoe on River Kilombero

Burning cashew nuts with Elias and Natalie

Lioness in Mikumi Park

11

Düzce and Bolu, Turkey

1989 – 1994

Black Sea

Kilyos Zonguldak

Istanbul Duzce Bolu Trabzon

Troy

Kutahya Ankara

Pammukkale TURKEY

Izmir Afyon Cappadocia

Konya

Bodrum

Antalya Side IRAQ

SYRIA

MAP 7

TURKEY

'The 1st of May is in the Devil's pay', so they say. Perhaps not a very auspicious day to set out on a new job in 1989, but Mike had committed himself to that date while still in Ifakara so had to abide by it.

We flew from Heathrow on the afternoon flight by British Airways, stopping at Istanbul before our final destination, Ankara, where we were met by David, the project manager.

We made our way to the company flat which was located over the Ankara office, which we shared with our consultant partner Yuksel Rendel.

The Turkish government, in planning to build a new motorway between the Bulgarian border and Iraq, decided to go to international tender for both contractor and consultant, with the result that American, British and Italian firms became involved in this huge project, which, at the present time, is only engaged in the stretch from Edirne on the Bulgarian border to Ankara. Yuksel Rendel secured the consultant role for the supervision of the centre stretch of some 110 kilometres between Istanbul and Ankara. The client, KGM (Karayolları Genel Müdürlüğü) General Directorate of Highways, had decreed that both contractor and consultant must be joint ventures between local and foreign firms; thus we were the junior partner with Yuksel Rendel the consultancy arm to a major Turkish contractor.

After a quick phone call home, we retired to bed. Next day Mike and I moved to a nearby hotel. Three days after our arrival David took us to Düzce, the bulk of our luggage having gone on ahead in a van belonging to Astaldi, the Italian contractor. The road as far as Gerede was a dual carriageway, first along a plateau and then into quite mountainous country; the most dramatic part was just beyond Bolu when we dropped some 500 metres down the steep escarpment onto the plain of Düzce. We passed through the centre of the town, which lies to the south of the main highway, the infamous E5, or Londra Asfalti, as the locals call it. The town seemed to be a bustling, thriving community; then once over the Asarsuyu River we were in a small suburban area with fields beyond. The site office was about one kilometre from the town centre and consisted of a long, low, prefabricated type of building.

Mike's office was a small one and looked even smaller with all our bags stacked up in one corner. It was now 12.30 pm so we proceeded along the corridor to the far end where the canteen was situated and consisted of two rooms, one for junior staff and the other for senior management. Here we met some of the other staff and expatriates. There was Iain, a young, fiery Scot in his mid-thirties; Richard, a fellow in his fifties, on his first job abroad and in charge of the computer; and Mark, whose contract expired at the end of the month.

After lunch we met James, a thin fellow with curly hair, who had just returned from lunch at home with his wife Mary. Collecting our overnight bag, we drove back to town and looked at the two buildings in which the firm had flats. The first, on the outskirts of town, was where James lived on the first floor, while immediately above him was the flat occupied by Iain and Mark. The other flat was very near the town centre and we were to occupy the flat at the top on the fourth floor, which we duly inspected after a long climb up the stairs. The flat was long and narrow in layout with the lounge and kitchen at the front facing west and the bedrooms at the back.

The inspection over, we drove to the Seven Hotel on the main street where they left me and returned to the site.

When Mike returned to the hotel he found me in a rather depressed mood, having spent my time walking the streets of Düzce around the hotel and wondering whether I would ever come to terms with the place. After Mike told me of his afternoon's activities we decided we would move to our flat the next day even though David had said we could stay put for a few days while we settled in.

We met up again at 7.30 pm in the first-floor restaurant only to find it deserted, which David found rather extraordinary as he had said it was quite a busy little place. We were redirected to the roof restaurant. Here was quite a different scene: a largish room packed full of men, with not a woman to be seen. The reason for the state of the two restaurants was, we discovered, that we were in the holy month of Ramazan (Ramadan), when most of the citizens would be fasting at home until sunset.

The meal over, and as we sat drinking small glasses of tea or Turkish coffee we were joined by James and his wife Mary, a strawberry blonde with a pair of large glasses balanced on her nose. During this period of idle chatter, we discovered that James and Mary had just moved out of our flat to the one they were now occupying at Bektaş due to the loss of a ring.

Mary had employed the wife of the *Kapici* (caretaker) to clean for her. While the girl was in one of the bedrooms Mary had done some washing, removing from her finger a ring with a jade stone, and put it on a ledge above the sink. She had not replaced the ring when she finished but had gone to hang out the laundry and then forgotten about the ring until much later. When she went to put it on she could not find it, so asked the girl if she had seen it. The girl denied all knowledge of the ring, carried on with her work and when finished went home. When James got home from work and heard the story of the ring he went immediately to the police and reported the loss. Next day the ring was recovered from a jeweller and the thief identified as the *Kapici*. Our landlord, Sadi Erisen, had no alternative but to fire the couple. Mary later identified the *Kapici* as a waiter at the Seven Hotel.

Next morning after breakfast Mike went to the site with David, who organised a van to take our luggage to the flat, and with him came Ilhan, the interpreter, to instruct the driver and help us buy some bottled gas, without which we could not cook. When we arrived at the end of our street we found it was closed off by an open market so we had to carry our cases from the nearest dropping-off point.

We had just arrived in time for Şeker Bayram, or Eid ul-Fitr, as we knew it, so we had four days in which to settle ourselves in. James, Mary, Iain and Richard took off in the site car for Cappadocia. One of the first things we noticed was the volume of the calls by the muezzin at the various mosques around us. From our observations, they no longer climbed to the tops of their minarets on every occasion but resorted to a loudspeaker or cassette tape.

Our apartment block was relatively new and contained twelve flats, or apartments as they called them. Eight were served by one staircase and the other four by a separate entrance, thus in our case there were two flats per floor. On the ground floor were the Vardars, or the Akcakocas as we called them in the early days when we could not remember their name, only because they had a flat in the nearby Black Sea town of that name. He was a gunsmith, while she was a socialite, always out and about in the latest fashion. Their neighbour was a widow, the mother of the tenant in the flat below ours. Above her was Richard, who like Iain had come out just a month before us and was waiting for his wife to join him. His neighbour was our landlord, Sadi Erisen.

Above them were Khorhan Uzmay, his wife Nehal and young son Evrim. Khorhan worked for Astaldi, and we saw little of him or his family during the first six months of our stay in Düzce. When he and his family eventually moved to Bolu, three other families were to move into that apartment during the time we were in Düzce. At the top our neighbours were Ivo and his common-law and heavily pregnant wife, Nella. Ivo was a foreman with Astaldi and had met Nella while working in Peru. Their daughter, Silvie, was born shortly after we arrived.

After Bayram, Mike's work started in earnest. At about twenty past seven Mike and Richard would wait outside the flat for the site car to come along from Bektaş and pick them up, except on Mondays and Thursdays when there was a market and they would walk up to the first intersection which was free of stalls. They had an hour for lunch at 12.30 and finished at 5.30.pm. On the first morning, however, Mike found Iain waiting with Richard and wondered why he was at our flat and not coming along in the car from Bektaş. As Mike spent most of his time out on site with him he asked him one day if he was sharing a flat with Richard and not Mark.

'Yes, I was sharing with Mark but then he brought his girlfriend Caroline along to stay in the flat and things became impossible.'

'Why, in what way?'

'It wasn't too bad to start with but she's a very moody creature – one minute she's talking to you and the next she's completely ignoring you.'

'Is she on holiday out here or what?'

'She was teaching in Istanbul but Mark found it a drag going there every weekend or waiting for her to come here, so he got her to change her school and come to Düzce.'

'But that's crazy, she's no right to be in the flat anyway. Does David know about it?'

'I think so but he won't do much about it now that Mark's leaving. Anyway, that's the reason I moved out.'

The so-called 'bachelor' flat had a telephone and a TV and video to try and keep the occupants entertained at home rather than them seeking it outside and so possibly offending the locals, who were very wary of us '*Yabancis*'(foreigners). The phone was free, in one sense of the word, for all to use if one put one's name and call destination, time and length in a book provided, and James would calculate what each owed at the end of the month. David would bring videos, English ones, from Ankara whenever he came over as the only programmes that anyone could watch and understand were football matches. We used the phone on very limited occasions as it was such a palaver to get a car to go over to Bektaş and then interrupt the occupants, so we used the PTT (post office) instead.

During the first few days James gave Mike a hand-drawn map of Düzce showing the location of the good shops and other places we would need to visit. Mary started to visit me once a week as though this was our first tour abroad, the first time bringing a potted plant as a welcoming gift. On the first such call I asked if there was an easy chair spare for me to use; the flat, when we arrived, had a cane two-seater and another two-seater that was broken and dangerous to use. Mary said there wasn't, although we discovered she had a reclining chair on her balcony for her cat.

When I asked if there was a spare mirror, I was told, 'You can only have a mirror if you give something in exchange as I'm making an inventory of all the furniture for David.'

One day while out I decided to pay a call on Mary, who was very surprised to see me on her doorstep and made out that she was just going out, but not before I had a chance to see that her flat was filled with some very comfortable pieces of furniture.

Our contracts stated that everybody would be entitled to a set of cane furniture in the living room, but instead of the company buying it the early arrivals were told to go out and buy their own furniture, with the result that they bought what they fancied and not what was authorised. It was about the same time as I paid a visit to Mary that James invited us to a Sunday lunch but the invitation was not followed up; this was, we were sure, because Mary did not want us in her flat to see all the furniture that she was not really entitled to. Having thus summed up Mary, we had little more to do with her from that day on.

We had only been in Turkey about a month when it was decided Natalie should come out to us while Dinah moved up to Durham. Fiona was to bring her out, arriving at 2.30 in the morning. This meant we had to find a hotel in Istanbul.

It was not until the next morning that I finally got us in at the Eyfel, a small hotel in the old city, and incidentally right opposite the Ramada, the one recommended to me by the Air France representative on a flight from Athens to Schiphol. The great attraction to Istanbul at that time was a large international conference which made huge demands on hotel accommodation. When we turned up at the Eyfel our problems were not over, as through some booking error we had only one double room instead of two. What were we to do?

'Look, we've tried everywhere to find two double rooms and you assured us when we phoned that you could accommodate us. We have two family members arriving in the middle of the night and must have beds for them.'

'We're very sorry about this. We accept that we offered you two double rooms but one of our staff subsequently let one of them by mistake. We do have another room, a double, but it is used as a cleaners' room in which they keep their service trolley and other pieces of equipment. You are welcome to this room, which we will let you have at a reduced rate.'

We readily accepted and used the hotel as our base ever after. In fact, they told us we never needed to book, as 'they would always find a room for us'; the cleaners?

They did in fact have another hotel in the same street, the Pisa, which they sometimes referred us to. I preferred the breakfast there to that at the Eyfel as they had a large self-service buffet as opposed to the waiter service at the Eyfel. The staff at the Eyfel were a happy crowd and we got to know them quite well, and to the extent that they even confided in us about their love lives. One was hoping to marry a South African, another an American, whom they had met in the hotel. The hotel catered for coach parties, mainly from the recently liberated Central European countries, and appeared to do reasonably well throughout the year.

Before going up to Düzce Fiona was anxious to try and find out what had happened to her old school friend Gunesh, from Bedgebury, so we took a taxi along the coast road to Yeşilköy, where, after some difficulty, we found the correct flat. Her parents were in the middle of lunch so we did not go in. Her father said Gunesh was now married and living in Cyprus and as he was flying out there the following day Fiona was welcome to go along with him, but of course such a trip was not possible. Instead he gave Fiona her address so she could write to her friend. This she did, but received no reply. Many years later, they met up again through Facebook!

It was while we were trying to book a hotel in Istanbul, by phone from the post office, that we met Tulay. She had come to make a call to her mother in Izmir and while waiting heard us speaking in English and asked if she could help. She was an English teacher at a local school, as was her husband. They lived in a flat, as do most people in Turkey, with a daughter, Udzel, who was nine years old. She invited us to tea the following day, which we drank out of small glasses with sugar and without milk, as in other Middle Eastern countries. With her was a fellow teacher, somewhat younger than Tulay, called Moket, who was from the south-east of Turkey. The flat, like many others, had no central heating, even though the winters could be bitterly cold; instead they relied on a stove in the hall to heat all the other rooms by radiation.

I went to see Tulay on a few occasions with minor problems and queries, and met her mother, whom I liked very much. Whenever we had met Tulay she was always complaining about how poorly off they were and how expensive everything was.

When we went out to Turkey we worked on the basis that we might be there for only one year. All the posts were on a 'man-month' basis and when our time ran out David would apply to KGM for extensions. So, in the summer Dinah and Tim decided they would come out with Natalie and see something of Turkey. One of the places Mike most wanted to see was the Sumela Monastery near Trabzon, or Trebizond as it was called formerly. The universal means of public transport in Turkey is the coach, hundreds of them traversing the country every day between the major towns and cities. Mike did not fancy some twelve hours on a coach, but then he happened to read that his favourite form of transport, a boat, was possible. During the summer, Turkish Maritime Lines made regular sailings from Istanbul to Trabzon. So together with Ilhan, Mike went to the Bektaş flat and got him to phone for some reservations and even wrote to confirm them, but received no reply. When we eventually got to their offices one could see why: the place was in glorious chaos with queues a mile long extending well outside the building.

Just before the family came out at the end of July there was another public holiday, the Kurban Bayram or Sacrifice Festival, when an animal, usually a sheep, is slaughtered to celebrate the return of the pilgrims from Mecca. All those who have made such a trip can give themselves the title 'hajji', one who had made the hajj.

As we had the use of the site car over the holiday, we decided to head for Çanakkale on the Dardanelles, as we had discovered from our guidebook that not so far from here was the village of Truva, the site of the ancient city of Troy, which one always associates with Helen, the face that launched a thousand ships, and of course the Trojan Horse. So after lunch on the Wednesday we joined the throng of traffic on the E5 to Adapazarı, where we turned south up the Sakarya Valley and found the traffic to be less heavy. Running alongside the road and river for most of the way was the Istanbul -Ankara Railway Line.

After about fifty kilometres we turned off to the right along a secondary road to İznik, famous for its tiles in former times and a capital city in Lycian times. Along the road the local farmers were selling delicious-looking peaches at wayside stalls, freshly picked in the nearby orchards. These farms were quite enterprising: in order to keep their crops watered they laid a system of small-bore plastic pipes across the fields over quite considerable distances to a stream in the valley bottom, out of which they pumped the water.

Skirting round the northern shore of Lake İznik, we joined the stream of traffic from Istanbul heading for Izmir and the south. It was too early to stop at Bursa so we continued along the bypass and westwards, the heavy traffic leaving us west of Bursa when it turned south. When we came to look for somewhere to stay the hotels in the small towns we passed through did not look very inviting and in the end we finished up in a nice new hotel on the front at the port of Bandırma on the Sea of Marmara.

We dined that night at an outdoor restaurant where the manager spoke German, settling for a fish supper for which we were heavily overcharged, to which Mike objected without avail in his somewhat rusty German. German, we discovered, was the second language for tradesmen and the like, although English is probably almost as common. German is used by those who have worked in or visited Germany or Austria.

As we crossed the undulating countryside we came across fields of sunflowers, which, as they turned to follow the sun were a sea of colour, like a Van Gogh masterpiece. So startling was the scene that we stopped for me to photograph the landscape as well as the head of an individual flower.

On the northern end of the Dardanelles we could see the town of Gelibolu (Gallipoli) on the opposite shore. On reaching Çanakkale we made for the Truva Hotel, recommended by our book, but unfortunately, they were full so we had to settle for the Anafartalar by the ferry crossing. In some ways this was better as Mike could sit and watch the three ferries run a non-stop shuttle service over to the town of Eceabat on the European side.

In the afternoon we set out for Truva. Once clear of the town we entered some large pine forests, which reminded us of the Mediterranean coast of France. After about half an hour or so we came to the village of Truva, which gave one a constant reminder of the German, Schliemann, who first discovered the remains of the city of Troy. There was Schliemann's house, Schliemann's Carpet Shop, Schliemann's Leather Store, Schliemann's Curios and the like. Just beyond the village was a toll gate through which we passed into a large open car park, while rising out of a clump of pine trees was a huge timber horse. Having parked the car in the shade of a tree we had a closer look at this amazing structure and discovered that, like the ancient Greeks, we too could climb into the beast. After ascending a couple of rather difficult stairs the view from the top was quite rewarding. Looking out to the west we could see the end of the Gallipoli Peninsula and the large obelisk erected to commemorate the dead from the fierce battles fought there in the First World War, who on the Allies' side were mainly from Australia and New Zealand, battling to scale the steep cliffs. Here Winston Churchill met his Waterloo against that champion of the Turks, Mustafa Kemal, later to be known the world over as Atatürk. Every city, town, village, office and business complex has a statue and picture of this charismatic leader. While I browsed through racks of postcards and books on Turkey and Troy Mike had a quick walk through the ruins, which were still under excavation.

Before leaving Çanakkale the next morning we took a trip in a small tug-like boat over to the pretty little village of Kilitbahir, where we explored a very impressive-looking castle, or at least Mike explored it while I conversed with an elderly German couple bent on the same exercise. We headed home by the same route as we had come and spent the night on the Bursa bypass at the Almera Hotel, a modern, well-furnished place which was soon invaded by several coach parties. We took dinner in the rooftop restaurant and, for a change, did not settle for fish.

Bursa is a fascinating city perched on a hillside at the foot of Mount Uludağ. We drove right through the town centre and up to the ski lift terminus before making a detailed tour of the city's sights. Having completed a quick look at the main attractions we continued on our way by a different route, which included a long descent down a steep scarp slope into İznik where we had a fish lunch at a lakeside restaurant. Before the meal Mike had a swim in the lake.

Prior to setting off for home we had a look around the town at its ancient ruins and local museum. I noticed, on the top of some old towers and a minaret storks could be seen starting to build their nests, having recently arrived in the country.

It was about a week later that Dinah, Tim and Natalie came out for a visit. As Mike and I had had a weekend in Istanbul at the beginning of July for Mike to go to the American Admiral Bristol Hospital for a check-up we used this opportunity to get to know the city a little better. The hospital being in the new city, the Golden Horn dividing the old from the new, we explored Taksim Square and Cumhuriyet Caddesi, which seems to consist of nothing but airline offices, and the recently opened McDonald's before walking down the elegant İstiklal Caddesi with its fashionable shops, and which now boasts a tram that runs along its length. The flower market and arcades, or *pasaji*, were particularly interesting. Just past the Four Seasons Restaurant we caught the tube to the Galata Bridge. This is said to be the smallest underground railway in the world, being only some seven hundred metres long.

Probably the most visited place in Istanbul, after the Blue and Aya Sofia Mosques, is the covered bazaar. This is a vast complex of arcades with rows of shops on either side, all protected from the elements by a series of roofs. The crowds that pack it in the holiday season make it almost impossible to move around. The bazaar has sections specialising in particular wares and there are touts everywhere offering the visitor the best and cheapest goods, be they carpets, watches, leather goods or the like. Dinah bought some Turkish fez hats while Tim and Mike settled for a leather belt each at a giveaway price just before closing time. During subsequent visits Mike bought some meerschaum pipes and always had difficulty finding the area where these were sold, and had to remember to turn right at the Haji Carpet Shop and left at the Caykaneh (tea shop).

Strolling back to the Eyfel and Pisa Hotels, we womenfolk being in the former and Tim and Mike in the latter, I spotted a toyshop and was in before the others could say, '*yok*' (No)!. Here we met Fedra. Fedra was an Iranian who spoke very good English with a North Country accent, having been educated at a school in Cheshire. While talking to her we got on the subject of food and remarked how much we missed Iranian food, at which Fedra asked if we had tried the Iranian restaurant, the Persepolis, in the side street opposite, which was owned by her uncle. So we decided to try it that evening and thoroughly enjoyed a *chelo* kebab, as we used to know it, with sumac spread on top. When we next saw Fedra we told her of our visit to her uncle's restaurant and how much we had enjoyed our meal, but that we had missed the raw egg on the rice.

'Oh, you should have asked for it – they do serve it but most customers do not know about the egg.'

To get to Düzce we took a taxi to the Anadolu bus station near Topkapı, where we boarded a bus bound for Düzce. Later on as we became more knowledgeable we would take the Kamil Koç bus bound for Ankara as this was quicker and more comfortable. It depends, however, on what one calls comfortable – in summer the air conditioning or ventilation system can be too cold and draughty, while in winter one's feet are subjected to blasts of hot air from the below-seat heating ducts. The worst irritation is the almost non-stop music transmitted by the radio or cassette player, with which the driver is constantly fiddling. The better coaches have a TV screen at the front for the passengers' entertainment. Water is freely available on request and more recently hot drinks and biscuits are served, especially now that double-deckers are being introduced, equipped with tables and a toilet.

Passing over the Bosphorus Bridge makes one feel well above it all; the ships passing below looking almost like toys. The bridge is also well known for its suicides, although no one, so hell-bent, is said to have survived the fall. Proceeding eastward, the coach invariably calls in at Harem, the ferry terminal on the Asian side and adjacent to the docks and the Florence Nightingale Hospital.

Dinah's week in Turkey was soon up and Tim and Mike accompanied her back to Istanbul, and as her flight was departing after midnight Tim escorted her up to the airport. The following morning Tim and Mike got the ferry over to Haydarpaşa station as they had decided to make a trip to Ankara by train, returning to Düzce by bus.

When Tim left for home Natalie and I travelled with him; I was going to stay in England until Natalie returned to school. I had left the fridge and freezer filled to overflowing with prepared food so Mike was well provided for.

When I returned, Mike met me in Istanbul as two days later we were due to sail to Trabzon – Mike had booked the tickets while Tim was out with us. To help while away the time before we sailed we took a trip on a new tramway that had opened only a few days before not far from the hotel, and part of which we had noticed from the coach on our way into the city. It was all very modern and clean, and so we saw another facet of Istanbul.

I had brought a whole host of things back with me for the flat, and as this was too much for us to take on the boat we arranged with the hotel for us to leave it in their security room and we would retrieve it in due course.

We found our boat, *Istanbul*, at one of the quays just east of the Galata Bridge below the Topkapi Palace. We arrived at three o'clock expecting to sail at five, but by the time they had completed the loading of all the cars and coaches it was seven o'clock when we finally got away. This was a pity as it meant we passed along the upper Bosphorus in darkness. As we arrived on board we were conducted down to our two-berth cabin, which was somewhere amidships, just above the waterline. It was small but adequate for a couple of nights. Mike took the top berth, saying that climbing the ladder would be good exercise. The only oddity of the boat came when I went into the shower cubicle and toilet to check them for cleanliness and disinfect the bowl and basin with Dettol, as I usually do on such trips. As I opened the door I came face-to-face with a man entering from the far side! To save space, adjoining cabins shared the toilet facilities. The mental note was to lock *both* doors before stripping!

Sitting on the deck awaiting our departure, we got into conversation with a Turkish woman who was married to an Australian and living 'down under'. She was back in Turkey, alone, on a visit to the land of her birth, and was on a trip to see old faces and places. It was an enjoyable trip as there were frequent stops, calling at Sinop, with its NATO warning dishes high on the clifftops; Samsun; Ordu; Giresun and finally Trabzon, where we arrived in rain at about five o'clock in the afternoon. The last day at sea had been wet and the sea somewhat rougher than previously. While at Sinop we sat on deck in warm sunshine, and we only went ashore at Giresun for a short stroll.

As soon as we had settled in our hotel in the main square we went out to a nearby travel agent we had seen from the taxi to book a day's sightseeing tour to the Sumela Monastery and Trabzon itself for the following day, and from there to the Turkish Airline office where we managed to get a flight back for two days hence to Istanbul via Ankara, the direct flight being fully booked.

We took our evening meal in the hotel and, as in most better-class hotels and as on the boat, we were serenaded by a male singer who accompanied himself on a Japanese organ, or whatever they are called. Watching him operate was like seeing an airline pilot checking the controls before take-off as he leaned forward to switch on and off various synthesised instruments. Some melodies were quite pleasant while others were not quite so, and it was always these that seemed to last longer than the others.

We were a little disappointed the next morning to see that it was still wet, with a fine drizzle falling. There were some twelve to fifteen of us of different nationalities, a couple of whom were in our hotel, in the small bus that was to take us on the tour. We set off up a valley, down which a dirty, swollen river was flowing, but shortly afterwards we had to turn off onto a narrow secondary road halfway up the valley side because of some landslide that had partially blocked the main road. At a place called Maçka we turned east to reach our destination.

As we alighted from the bus all eyes turned to look up the mountainside to catch our first glimpse of the monastery, which was just visible in the swirl of mist and drizzle that hung in the valley.

'Wow,' I said, 'it's going to be some climb to get up there', and it was. At the foot of the slope, after crossing a small, fast-flowing stream, was the usual souvenir shop and restaurant where some of our party stopped for a drink. People who had arrived on the scene earlier than us were already making their way back to the coaches, cars and taxis.

The path zigzagged its way up the steep slope, and through the foliage and mist we caught occasional glimpses of the monastery.

'Hell, we don't seem to get any nearer,' I panted as we paused for another rest. 'You go on ahead, Mike, I don't know if I'll be able to make it.'

An elderly woman passing remarked, 'I know it's very hard and I'm worried about my husband as he has a heart condition.' Eventually she and I made it to the top. After paying our entrance fee and declaring our nationality we then proceeded down some steps into the monastery, which consists of a series of rooms on the outer face with others cut into the rock on the cliff face. There were several lovely wall paintings depicting the life of Christ but most of these had been badly damaged and defaced.

Monks first inhabited some caves in this mountainside in the 4th century, when an icon of the Virgin Mary painted by St. Luke was brought to the area. Later Byzantine emperors added buildings to form the complex, the remains of which we see today. The monastery was finally abandoned in 1923 with the exchange of populations after Turkey gained its independence from Greece.

Talking to our guide, I asked how the monks had got their water?

'They had to walk down to the stream and carry it up on their backs,' I was told. Yet as we left I saw what looked like the remains of a substantial aqueduct. I don't think the monks were so ignorant as to walk down the mountainside when gravity could bring the water to their doorstep.

After lunch at a nearby restaurant we returned to Trabzon and continued our tour. First we were taken to a mosque, which we entered after removing our shoes. The floor was covered with carpets and by the opposite wall was a narrow staircase leading up to what we would call a pulpit. Near the entrance was a small table on which there was a cassette player, which the muezzin used to call the faithful to prayer.

Moving on to the outskirts of the city we came to the Aya Sofia Church, a remarkable example of late Byzantine art. Built in 1245 by Emperor Manuel Comnenus, it fell into a bad state of repair as the Greek population dwindled and finally left in 1922; fortunately the building was rehabilitated by a group of archaeologists in the 1950s. Like Sumela, the church was rich in frescoes depicting the story of Jesus Christ, and a number of these have survived the ravages of time to enable them to be restored to their former glory.

Back in the coach, we drove up to the top of the slope at the back of the city to visit Atatürk's summer residence, presented to him by the grateful citizens. The house, built to an Italian style of architecture, was set in beautifully kept gardens laid out with rose beds round an ornamental fishpond and bordered by tall pines. The interior was very austere, the lounge with a large, old-fashioned radio; however, the rooms were full of photographs and trinkets, and one picture showed Atatürk with King Edward VIII when he was Prince of Wales on a visit to Turkey.

On our return to Düzce Mike found another engineer had arrived, Behnam, or Ben as we all called him. He was sharing the bachelor flat with Jack, who had replaced Mark. Ben came to work with Mike and he more or less replaced Iain, who moved up to Yeniçağa. Ben, an Iranian, was in fact married to an English woman, Heather, who lived in Manchester. He had been sent to England when he was eighteen or nineteen, initially to London to learn the language; then moved to Manchester to enter university.

This did not worry Mike unduly as Ben was a pleasant fellow quite prepared to do what he was told, and got on well with our Turkish colleagues when he discovered that Turkish bore quite a strong resemblance to Farsi. When he left in 1992 he was quite fluent in Turkish. Because of his ability to chat to the Turks he became a mine of information as to what was going on.

When James heard about the Hash House Harriers he decided to set up a group in Düzce. He would draw up facetious notices about the hash and sent copies to all and sundry, and persuaded David to give two cases of beer on behalf of RPT to the 'on-on' afterwards. James' English was not the best, so his notices were, to us at any rate, usually doubly comical and equally confusing to the Turks and Italians.

Our problems regarding the telephone were resolved in rather a strange way. I was in a shop asking for something when a man came in and said, 'What is someone doing speaking English in Düzce?'

'I'm speaking English because I am English.'

'And what is an English person doing in Düzce? Are you on holiday?'

'Well, I'm here because my husband is working on the new motorway.'

'Oh, he's with Astaldi then, so he's Italian?'

'No he isn't, he's English.'

'How do you like Düzce?'

'It's all right but it's not easy getting some things.'

'I'm sure I could find whatever you want. What is it you would like most?'

'What I would like most I don't think you could get for me: a telephone.'

'A telephone you would like? All right then, come with me.'

Our newfound acquaintance, Ilhan, was true to his word and the next day we were phoning home from the flat to tell the family the good news and give them our number. Ilhan then started calling on us in the flat at odd hours, and even brought his wife and children round. There was some method behind this: he was looking for a job. Could Mike get him a job as a driver with Yuksel Rendel or Astaldi? Then he turned up to invite us to a wedding reception in a hall in the gardens adjacent to the Atatürk Memorial. We were interested to see such an event, and so accepted.

When we got there, we felt a bit out of place, being somewhat overdressed compared to the other guests. The reception had a slow start but once the dancing started things livened up, in fact they livened up a little too much as a fight broke out at the far end of the hall and there was a mad panic as people tried to run from the immediate scene of the conflict.

'Come on, Mike and Audrey, let's get out of here.'

'Don't panic, it's no good running over there; there's no door. Just wait a moment and we'll make our way out in an orderly fashion,' Mike said.

That was enough of Ilhan for us; he came to see us a few days later to apologise for the fracas and then told us that he was going to Adapazarı to open a shop and asked for first refusal on our phone when we left. It seems one buys a telephone line in Turkey and is then free to sell it when it is no longer required. Some buy them as a hedge against inflation.

The only problem we had with the phone came after about six months. Mike started to get strange calls from a woman who would ask, 'Are you Christopher Michaer?' (That was the name the PTT had registered Mike as and included in the phone book.) When Mike replied in the affirmative, not knowing who it was, she would say, 'I love you, do you love me?' Mike replied that he did not know who she was and he did not love her, and rang off.

After about a quarter of an hour the phone would ring again. When Mike answered, he heard heavy breathing and children giggling in the background; then the throaty voice would come on again.

'Hello, Christopher Michaer, I love you, do you love me?' Mike put down the receiver without a further word.

I had to answer the phone at the weekends as it was then that the children were likely to call. In the end I got a whistle to blow down the phone once I was sure who was calling. I even got Nella to speak to them in Turkish, but the lady retorted, 'You're not Turkish and you're not Christopher's wife.'

Eventually the calls stopped. As first I thought it might have been Ilhan's wife as she spoke a little English and the giggles could have been her boys; the reason for my suspicions was that very few people had our number, unless whoever it was just browsed through the phone book and picked out names at random. Later we learned that Turkish people also received such calls.

When we were alone after the visits from the family I settled down to my toy-making again. I asked Mike to enlarge some patterns and when I came to make them up they were somewhat larger than I expected! I looked forward to the market in the street below, where I could browse through the stalls picking up the odd ribbon or button for my toys.

I had a friendly butcher who always seemed to know what I wanted, even though we each spoke in our own language. It was the same at the place where I got a bag of cotton to use as filling, so there was always something to do.

As our turn for the car at weekends came, we would go for a short drive around Düzce or venture further afield. One such trip we made was to Amasra, a pretty little fishing village on the Black Sea. We set off after work on Saturday along the E5 to just beyond Bolu, where there was a new restaurant adjacent to a flour mill, The Filiz, that specialised in spaghetti dishes; some said it had an Italian chef. It was very clean with some well-laid-out gardens surrounding the building.

After a late lunch, we continued to Caydurt, where we turned off to the north onto a secondary road and through some quite mountainous scenery. We even came across a coalmine in the middle of nowhere, until we struck a better road near Mengen, where the best chefs in Turkey are said to come from. From here the road took a gentle climb and finished in a tunnel hewn out of the rock, leaving a very rough and wet face, and the road surface felt as if it were part of the wall, the way the car bumped and lurched about as we crawled along. There followed a long run down a valley to the plain beyond. After crossing a wide river, we were stopped by some policemen who were stopping all cars passing along this stretch.

While waiting our turn for questioning we got out our passports and as soon as we moved up to the policeman we waved them at him and said, 'British', to which we got a 'Hos Geldiniz' (Hello) and were waved on.

We were now running alongside the Ankara-Zonguldak railway line until the road veered off to the north-east. Just after bypassing Bartın we began a dramatic climb over a mountain range, where, on reaching the summit, we saw the Black Sea hundreds of metres below. Then we began our descent down an equally spectacular road with hairpin bends, blind corners and sheer drops at the edge of the road. As we descended we saw the coalmine that offered employment to many of the inhabitants, and then the little township with its harbour and breakwaters – a very pleasant scene.

There were no hotels as such, just pensions and rooms. We settled for a place that called itself a pension but was in fact just a set of rooms as no meals were served. We had a fish supper at a restaurant by the harbour. The next morning we woke at a normal hour and prepared to set out to find somewhere to have breakfast.

Everywhere was very quiet with not a soul about; we had found a real 'sleepy hollow' until a young fellow guest happened to see Mike's watch and said, 'Excuse me, sir, but your watch is wrong – we put the clocks back an hour last night so now it's only seven o'clock.' We had breakfast at a nearby cafe.

We came to Amasra again the following year and stayed in rooms over a restaurant. The night turned very cold so we had to get the proprietor to light the wood stove in the bedroom.

At the end of October Jim Hyde (RPT) came out on a routine visit – he and Gordon used to rotate such visits – and invited us all to a meal at the Seven Hotel. After we had eaten Jim tapped the table with a spoon and said he wished to make an announcement.

'About this time twenty-five years ago, Mike here joined RPT at Ferrybridge Power Station.'

'Fawley,' Mike muttered.

'Sorry, Mike, yes, Fawley, and since that time he has worked on many projects in different parts of the world and, as a token of our appreciation of his loyalty and continuous service, we wish to mark the occasion with a presentation. Mike, in this envelope are some photos of various decanters and glasses. When you have made your choice let me know which you would like and we will arrange for them to be presented to you next time you are home on leave.'

We eventually chose a whisky decanter, which Mike received some two years later.

It was about this time that Mike got an occasional sensation, for want of a better word, in his chest, which he passed off as indigestion. I, however, saw something more sinister in this.

'It's your heart; you must see a doctor. Look how your father died at fifty-two.'

'Yes, dear,' said Mike, 'but his case was quite different: he was overweight and would never see a doctor. No, it's just indigestion, I tell you.'

'No, it's not. You must see a doctor about it.'

So Mike saw Dr Omer Erturk, a very pleasant man with a good command of English who sent Mike to have an X-ray of his chest at a local laboratory, and because of its rather dusty and musty atmosphere and the general disorganisation, I was sure they had overexposed Mike to the deadly X-rays, even though the apparatus was of modern Japanese design.

Somehow from there Mike finished up seeing a female heart specialist at the Admiral Bristol Hospital in Istanbul. Here he was put on a treadmill, and after what seemed like a ten-mile jog was diagnosed as having a slight case of ischaemia, or heart flutter. The doctor recommended he had a thorium injection test and was subjected to a body scan to locate the source of the trouble. Mike made an appointment there and then and paid for the test. Here one paid before the treatment, not after. When we got back to Düzce and slept on it Mike decided to cancel the test and get a refund. If something such as this was necessary then he would prefer for it to be done on home ground, and that is how he became a patient of Dr Maw in Tunbridge Wells.

I soon developed a rapport with Dr Maw as his wife, who acted as his secretary, who both knew Turkey very well. Mike's visits resulted in another treadmill test at the Kent and Sussex and X-rays at the Nuffield, while Dr Edwards and the practice nurse continued to monitor his cholesterol.

Due to lack of work during the winter months and the general frustrations of the job, Head Office announced that everyone would be given a free ticket home for Christmas. This came as a very welcome break as during the first week of December the temperature dropped from 0°C to –22°C in as many days. The summer had been pleasant enough and Mike went to work in short-sleeved shirts but not shorts; this would have been frowned upon.

Winter began in mid October and that was when the heating in flats and offices had to be turned on. During our first winter the central heating in both our flat and the office was quite inadequate and we had to have an electric radiator to supplement the heat source, with the result that in the following spring the radiator size in both places was increased by fifty per cent.

Through enquiries we found we could get home via Schiphol and Gatwick by either Turkish or KLM Airlines, and for the first such trip we chose the former as KLM were fully booked, and found it very comfortable. As we had several hours to kill before our onward flight we took a train into Amsterdam from the airport complex and had a good insight into suburban Holland as the train, although fast, made frequent stops. We even had time to walk down the main shopping street, where we saw a working model of a town occupied by teddy bears in the window of a large store.

While living in Turkey, reading the *Turkish Daily News*, an English-language newspaper produced in Ankara, and listening to the BBC World Service, we were able to get a better understanding of life in Turkey and keep abreast of what was going on in the outside world, where great events were taking place. The Berlin Wall had been breached and barriers in the whole of Central Europe were collapsing.

Atatürk's reforms in the early Twentieth Century were far-reaching: the language was overhauled using the Roman script in place of Arabic, a civil law code was introduced, the wearing of purdah-style clothing by women was frowned upon and the fez was replaced by the cap. The population as a whole was told to take a first or forename and one that meant something, so one meets people called Cheese, Sea, Moonday, Mirage etc.

A word here on Turkish pronunciation would not be amiss. 'C' is pronounced 'J'; hence 'Doozjay' and 'Kapyjay'. 'Mustafa Taş' is in reality 'Mustafa Tash', because in the alphabet there is a letter 'S' with a vertical tail, giving it a 'sh' sound; likewise, there is a 'C' with a tail giving a 'ch' sound. A 'G' with a bar over it is silent and some 'O's and 'U's have umlauts as well. There is also a 'J' which is pronounced like the 'G' in the French *gendarme*. There is a famous seaside resort called Side, so most British tourists go home to announce they spent their holiday 'inside', when what they should be saying is 'sea-day'.

Turkey has long been called the gateway to the east, and no doubt will retain this label for some time to come. Politicians strive for the day when they will be permitted to join the Common Market, which they see as a panacea for all their ills, but with raging inflation and the fact that they are a Muslim country it may be many years yet before this comes about.

The country is very divided on what path it should follow: there are those who are Westward-looking and thinking while others are still steeped in the traditional Islamic ways of life, especially around Düzce and Bolu where the muezzin are some of the loudest. Many women and young girls wear a headscarf almost all their waking hours. Girls of poorer parents are educated in special Koranic schools where education is free, and even those in state schools are well drilled that Mohammed was the only true prophet, even though the Koran accepts Christ as a prophet of equal standing. It is said that the more fundamentalist institutions are funded by Iran and Saudi Arabia, and the terrorists operating in the country are also funded by the former. The Turks are a very sensitive people – they objected very much to the fact that there was a well-known bird with the same name as their country and wanted to change the latter to Türkiye, but had to drop the idea when they discovered that Western typewriters could not produce such a word and that the pronunciation would remain the same. Like all Muslims they are generally very kind, hospitable and helpful, and one must bear all these points in mind when in social intercourse with them.

During our Easter leave in 1990 we finalised the arrangements for a contractor to build our utility room at our home in Tunbridge Wells, and, shortly after our return to Düzce, having stocked up the fridge with enough food to last Mike for a month, I returned home to act as clerk of works.

The change in the weather meant James could start organising his hash runs again, which improved as they progressed, with contractors Balfour Beatty at Hendek being invited to take part, and they in turn reciprocated. On such occasions, they all had to leave work early so the Hashers could get to Hendek, or wherever, and complete the run before it was too dark to see.

Iain had once asked Hatice, a shop owner who went on the Hash, if she could use her influence in getting the car he had brought down from Germany into the country as he was having problems with the Customs and Excise Department. This she willingly did. When it was time for Iain to leave she and Derya gave him gifts and even laid on a farewell party for him. Derya, with whom we became very friendly, worked for Astaldi and when people had problems in the town they would go to her because she had such a good command of English.

Hatice and Derya became very disillusioned about the type of expatriates they were meeting in Düzce. Much later we explained to them that civil engineers were sometimes not very good ambassadors for their country.

Most days, Ben would spend time in Mike's office discussing everything under the sun, and current events would be included in their conversations. When the Rasht earthquake occurred in Iran, Ben, by listening to the Iranian news in Farsi, could give Mike many more details that he could glean from the BBC World Service or *Turkish Daily News*. It was rather ironic that we had seen more of Iran than Ben had. Shortly after he married he worked for a Dutch consultant on the development of the port of Bandar Abbas. He was not very happy there as he found it too hot in summer; he even complained of the heat in Düzce whereas Heather was quite happy in Iran as there was a bus to take her and her friends to the beach every day, something not available to her in Düzce.

For the Kurban Bayram, as we had the use of a car again we decided to head for Cappadocia, spending a couple of nights in the Ankara flat whilst we 'did' the capital.

As the government had decreed that all heavy lorries were to cease running on all major roads during Bayram we had an easy run to Ankara. The following morning, we spent ages trying to find the Atatürk Mausoleum. We religiously followed the signposts but then they were no more and there were few people around to ask the way. Eventually we found it by following the crowd of other visitors, most of whom were Turkish families. The actual mausoleum is not at all pretentious, but the approach and courtyard outside are on a grandiose scale. A small museum housing the cars used by Atatürk was quite interesting to see, along with the other curios therein.

From there we went up to the Museum of Anatolian Cultures on the hill next to the Citadel. This is a small but well-laid-out museum with display cases and labelling in English as well as Turkish.

Once Ankara was behind us we turned off the Konya road and headed across to Avanos and Ürgüp, the principal towns of Cappadocia. It was shortly after this that we saw a tortoise ambling across the road.

'Mike, Mike, please stop, I want to lift it off the road before it gets run over.' We stopped and I lifted it to safety, and in gratitude it relieved itself on my foot, much to my disgust!

We had expected to see quite a flow of traffic as we neared Cappadocia as it is listed as one of the 'musts' to all who visit Turkey, but there was very little about even when we reached Ürgüp. We drove around the town several times before deciding on the Turban Hotel as our base. The rooms are set apart from the hotel complex in a series of small two-storey buildings scattered around paved areas and flower beds all set at different elevations. The reception, dining room, bars and other facilities are located in a single-storey building on the edge of the complex alongside a pool.

On entering the dining room we were asked the usual question, 'Which group?'

'We're a small group, just the two of us.'

'Oh, yes, sir, please come this way', and we were led to a small table by a window instead of joining a group on the long tables set for twenty or thirty people.

The Cappadocian landscape is really remarkable and it is almost impossible to find words to describe it. Its formation was started some thirty million years ago by three active volcanoes, Erciyes Dağı to the east and Hasan and Melendez Dağı in the south, which poured forth their volcanic ash over the land lying below their slopes, which was then covered with a harder layer of volcanic material. Years of erosion carved away at the softer material below, leaving columns of harder ash upstanding with the tops still capped with the harder rock. These are known as 'fairy chimneys' but to many they look more like phallic symbols.

The area became a sanctuary for the early Christians fleeing from Arab persecution further east and, because of the soft nature of the ground, they were able to excavate homes for themselves in the soft rock. Just to the south of this area there are the remains of whole underground cities where they lived completely hidden from their enemies. Near Göreme there are numerous churches carved out of the hillsides with names like the Church of the Apple, the Church With the Buckle, the Church of the Sandal, with a cast of a footprint of Jesus brought from Jerusalem, and the Church of the Snake, all of which contain frescoes depicting the life of Christ in various states of disrepair. One of the more amazing sights is a huge crag in the village of Ortahisar, out of which houses have been carved and which is said to be the only rock with sash windows!

When we left Ürgüp we drove round the southern perimeter and realised that this amazing landscape occupies a relatively small area. To the east we saw Mount Erciyes still capped with snow, as were the twin peaks of Hasan and Melendez.

We continued eastwards over the flat plains of rich farmland to the city of Konya, where we did not like the hotel recommended by our guidebook, for once, and settled for one around the corner. Finding somewhere to eat was not easy. Eventually we found a restaurant but it was not licenced; however, this was understandable as Konya is one of the major religious centres in Turkey.

On our return to the hotel we discovered there was a live football match between England and Germany about to be shown on TV, so we sat down to watch and it was soon obvious who the Turks favoured as we were the only ones cheering our team. With us in the lounge-cum-reception area, apart from three or four Turks, was a young woman in her mid-twenties. As we got into conversation I discovered she was from Norway and lived in Ankara with her Turkish partner. As she appeared to be alone I asked in a diplomatic way where her boyfriend was.

'He's gone to visit his family in a nearby village but he can't take me with him.' Even she supported Germany, saying Britain was full of football hooligans.

Konya was formerly known as Iconium. Based on the legend, it was here that Perseus produced the Medusa's head from his bag and fixed it to a pillar like an icon, hence the name. This place had been the Seljuk capital from the 11th century to the 13th. In the latter millennium, it was the home of Celaleddin Rumi Mevlana, who founded the Mevlevi Dervishes. The tombs of Mevlana, his son and other followers, which we visited, are covered with richly embroidered cloths with the turbans of the deceased on top – an impressive sight. The Mevlevi Order was banned by Atatürk as being a suspected secret society. Unfortunately, we were unable to see the Whirling Dervishes in their conical turbans and flowing white gowns, as they are said to only perform once a year on the 17th December, the anniversary of the death of their founder.

Natalie decided she liked Turkey and asked if she could spend her summer holidays with us, and we were very happy to have her. To give her a seaside holiday we had to find somewhere that was easily accessible by bus. Some English travel brochures we had listed both Kilyos and Şile on the Black Sea as locations they sent tourists to; Kilyos was on the west side of the Bosphorus while Şile was to the east. We decided on Kilyos.

At Kilyos we stayed at the Turban Hotel, which was right on the beach. The accommodation was in single-storey buildings nearer the sea with multi-storey blocks behind, the whole set among pine trees. The restaurant was at the eastern end and operated on a cafeteria basis with the choice of eating inside or out. Every meal involved a walk through the conifers, and after breakfast we would use the back entrance to go into the village for the paper as we were anxious to keep abreast of the news following the Iraqi invasion of Kuwait, and to buy other sundry items.

We had a day's outing to Sarıyer, a town on the Bosphorus, on the way passing through a new estate of houses that had collapsed due to an earth tremor.

After about six or seven months in Turkey we were confined to the flat one Sunday for National Census Day, and for some reason foreigners were to be included in the survey. To avoid complete confusion Khorhan Uzmay came with the woman enumerator doing our block to act as interpreter. After she had asked the usual questions – how old are you, where were you born, father's name, mother's name, how many children etc. – she departed and Khorhan made an apology for more or less ignoring us since our arrival and said they wanted to know us better. We were invited to join them for meals and, with them, were invited to the landlord's flat. Then in October we were invited to spend a weekend in their flat in Istanbul. In the same building were Nehal's married sister and her parents. Her father and Khorhan's were both vets and trained together in Ankara, both of them now living in retirement.

It was during this weekend that Mike asked Khorhan as we were driving around the city (their flat is in fact on the Asian side) to call at Sirkeci station to enquire about trains to England. Having seen how quickly winter fell in Turkey we decided we would start our Christmas break at the beginning of December and so try and miss the worst of the winter. So as not to spend too long in England for tax reasons, the thought struck Mike that we could follow the route of the old Orient Express, which is what we did, with some rather major diversions.

When Fiona heard of our plans she said she wanted to come too and flew out at the beginning of December to join us. Prior to this we had to spend a frustrating day in Istanbul trying to find the Bulgarian Embassy to get our transit visas, which we just managed to do before they closed at noon for the day. As the train did not set off until early evening we had a day to kill, part of which we spent on an enlightening tour of Topkapi Palace, a place we had not yet visited. The harem section was particularly interesting, but with two guides speaking at once in English and Turkish it was not always easy to understand what one was looking at.

We left the Eyfel Hotel with far too much luggage for such a trip, and in plenty of time as we still had to buy our tickets, which Mike paid for in an assortment of currencies. Fiona had already purchased hers in England. While waiting for the train to be shunted into the platform we were accosted by a rather grubby Norwegian who smelt of liquor, and who claimed to be penniless and thus unable to return to the land of his birth. Having just bought our European Domino tickets after a bit of a struggle Mike felt in a generous mood and gave him a contribution towards his ticket home and, although he protested otherwise, we felt sure it would be used to pay for his liquid supper.

The train eventually arrived and we found our compartment near the head of the train. The *Intercontinental* train is confined to one platform, but the old Edwardian splendour of the station can still just be detected in the now drab dining, waiting and restrooms, used originally by the Orient Express. We had finally stowed away all our luggage and were settling down for the starting whistle when two young Australians, Sharon and David, came in with their large rucksacks and claimed two more of the seats. They were a pleasant couple who originally hailed from Carlisle.

There was no restaurant car so we ate and drank what we had brought with us. By the time we departed it was dark, so it was a case of sitting, reading, sleeping or talking. The train rumbled on at a steady pace, reaching the border about midnight. Here it was pouring with rain and we spent about an hour with very little happening apart from the usual officials hustling up and down the platform. In the end, we gave up waiting to move on and retired to our bunks, three deep on either side of the compartment. We had already fallen into an uneasy slumber when there was a bang on the door and a call for passports.

It was a pretty uncomfortable night; at times the train felt as though it had square wheels, then there were flashes of torches as people groped their way down the corridor to the not-so-clean toilet. When we finally managed to see something out of the window we saw everywhere was covered with snow. We eventually arrived in Sofia at ten o'clock, over two hours later than the scheduled time. While still at the station Mike changed DM30 into the local currency, the leva, then we took a taxi to the Sheraton Hotel where a hot shower helped to restore our spirits. We then set out to find somewhere to eat. There was thick snow and slush everywhere, making it very difficult to walk. We saw one or two cafes with queues outside which looked as though they catered for the workers and students, so we returned to the hotel for a very good lunch and were entertained by a charming young lady at a grand piano.

After our meal and our experiences of the morning we took a taxi to the Alexander Nevsky Cathedral. It was very dark inside, making it very difficult to appreciate the interior. Most visitors were purchasing and lighting candles so I followed the tradition.

We walked part of the way back to the hotel, looking for some dolls as souvenirs. The shops at that time had very little to display or sell, making window-shopping all the more difficult.

Next morning, we were back at the station to catch the equivalent of the train by which we had arrived. It left some twenty minutes late at 9 am. We were lucky in that we had a compartment to ourselves, however to start with it was freezing cold but once we got underway it was soon too warm for comfort. It was an interesting day; the scenery varied between flat farmland and narrow gorges with fast-flowing rivers. At the border with Yugoslavia the customs officers were very polite and perfunctory about their business, all of them having a second look at Fiona. We also had a visit from two smartly dressed young women, one of whom held a tray in front of her like an usherette in a cinema, which acted as a counter as they were offering to change money.

We arrived in Belgrade at 5 pm local time. Like most continental stations this one had a hotel reservations office, where they recommended the Toplice Hotel. Reaching it involved driving through the city centre, which appeared to consist more of the old stone-faced type of building rather than the usual modern glass-and-concrete monstrosities of present-day architecture.

During the night, there was a further fall of snow but this had stopped by the time we set out to find a travel agency, from where we had to get our seat reservations as the guidebook advised us. After going around in circles for a while we learned that the agency had moved, so we decided to leave that for a while and went up to the Citadel, where, from a commanding height, we overlooked the confluence of the Sava and Danube Rivers. I had to confess I was not aware that Belgrade was on the Danube.

As we started our return to the city centre we found ourselves in an outdoor military museum, which had some very interesting exhibits including some midget tanks. After a stroll through several pedestrian precincts we found the agency and bought our tickets. As time was getting short we settled for lunch in a nearby restaurant.

As we were travelling second class we drifted into the appropriate waiting room at the station, which was full of people and heavy with cigarette smoke. It was only when Mike went out to check whether our train had arrived that he found the first-class waiting room, but by this time it was too late to move. In our below-station surroundings we were kept amused by an old gypsy-type woman who appeared to have had too much to drink and a puppy which looked as though it was trying to suckle at her bosom while she argued with a male of similar appearance.

Our train was eventually shunted in and there was a mad rush for the seats even though they were reserved. This time the compartment was full, and even fuller with all our luggage.

There was one young fellow with whom we got into conversation, but he was very hesitant to talk. He said he was from Kosovo but could not say much as 'He – nodding his head towards an elderly man asleep in the opposite corner – 'is a Serb.' The young man had a cousin with him and as far as we could make out was bribing the ticket collector as his relative had no ticket or papers, and kept vanishing from the compartment.

At Novi Sad, on the frontier, the 'Serb' got out and our friend became a bit more talkative. He was travelling on to Czechoslovakia to try and start an import-export business. We eventually arrived in Budapest at 11.30pm. The hotel reservations office was virtually closed, although outside were a couple of women who looked like madams, who offered us rooms. Without bothering to enquire further what they had to offer we took a taxi to the Ramada Hotel and relaxed in luxury for what remained of the night.

As a result, we were up late, which got us into a disagreement with the staff in the restaurant. The brochure said breakfast was served from 7–11am, whereas the waitresses and the manager maintained the times were 7–10.30am. The fact that they were setting out tables for some conference or 'Come to Hungary' week did not help matters. Despite this we enjoyed a good breakfast.

As the Ramada is located out of the city centre on St. Margaret's Island in the middle of the Danube we decided to find something a little cheaper and nearer to the station. After some searching we found the Metropole not far from the main railway station and on the road leading down to the river. We had an excellent lunch in the Weinstube of the Grand Hotel nearby; then stayed in our room for the rest of the afternoon and evening; our 'around the continent in eight days' experience was beginning to take its toll.

On enquiring about a sightseeing tour of the city we found our hotel could fix us up, and so ten o'clock the next morning found us boarding a coach for a trip round Budapest. The city is really two cities divided by the Danube. Buda on the north side is the older of the two and has most of the historical buildings, while Pest is more the commercial centre even though it has the Parliament Building. The coach was equipped with headphones in a language of one's choice, which kept us informed of what we were or should be looking at.

Apart from the first night, which was 'Hobson's Choice', the idea was that we travelled by day so as to see something of the country through which we were passing and then slept one or two nights in a capital city. This meant some very early starts and late arrivals.

The morning we left Budapest our call was for 5.30 am to give us just enough time to get to the station. The train was the best we had travelled on to date: clean, modern and appeared to be of the InterCity type, which indeed it was as its final destination was somewhere in Germany. We managed to get a compartment to ourselves and settled down to the three- to four-hour run to Vienna. Just before the train was about to set off a small, youngish-looking woman came in and asked if there was a spare seat, to which we said yes there was, somewhere under our coats and cases. She kept us in conversation throughout the journey which, when I had time to look out of the window, was through flat farmland covered in thick snow.

Our companion was Polish by birth – why do we always connect with Poles, remembering our friend at Luxor? – and married to Douglas, a professor of maths at Oxford. She spent her time working with children, and in order to do this shuttled between Oxford and Budapest. She was presently off to Vienna for the weekend to see a god-daughter again after many years. As a result of her conversation we were in Vienna long before we thought we were due in, time having passed in a flash.

After changing some money, and while deciding which taxi rank to patronise, I spied the Austrotel across the square – we need look no further. The young receptionist soon had us booked on a coach tour from outside the opera house, which gave us just enough time to have a very belated breakfast – in fact it was brunch.

Our rubbernecking started in the city centre where preparations for Christmas were well underway, then we moved on to pass by Beethoven's apartment, the lower part of which is occupied by McDonald's. We then passed over a stretch of water, thanks to which, if poor old Strauss were alive today, he would have to change the title of his waltz to the *Dirty Danube* as there was certainly nothing blue about it. Then towering over us was the famous Ferris wheel that featured in the film *The Third Man*. Back over the Dirty Danube, we climbed up the snow-clad slopes of the Vienna Woods, where we stopped for a very expensive cup of coffee laced with Irish whisky.

Suitably refreshed, we re-joined the coach and to the strains of Strauss we drove through the woods where children were playing and tobogganing down the slopes among the trees to the Schönbrunn Palace. By this time the shades of night were falling fast so we had a stroll through the extensive grounds, which seemed to be filled with Japanese.

We dined in a side cafe of the hotel rather than the main restaurant. Feeling tired after our exertions we decided to relax in our room with the TV. After fiddling with the controls we found something rather erotic, so we switched off the set. The real shock of the night was when we saw a note on top of the TV informing us that the channel we had just found carried a supplementary charge.

'Oh, my God,' I said, 'that means the hotel knows what we've been watching.'

'It does indeed,' echoed Fiona and Mike. 'What will they think?'

'What does it matter anyway? Hundreds must watch it during their stay,' Mike said. 'I shall be paying the bill and you can wait outside if it worries you so much.'

We caught the 9.30am for Prague from the Franz Josef station, giving us a leisurely start to one of the most delightful journeys we had yet made. Being Sunday, the station, a very modern-looking building, was virtually empty, as was our train until some fellow travellers joined us at Tabor. The scenery was like a living Christmas card: dense pine forests, the branches covered with thick snow and frost. Small villages, with some dwarf-like houses; children skiing and skating, with ice hockey very popular once we were over the border. One thing that interested me was the style of the church architecture: now we were travelling through an area where the tower was in the form of a spire or steeple, whereas before it had been of the 'onion' style, as I call it.

Arriving in Prague at three o'clock we had great difficulty finding a hotel, as all those we visited claimed to be full. We eventually found one and went back to the station to collect Fiona and our luggage. The room we took was large and cold, partially due to the fact that the central heating was not very effective and one of the windows was cracked. It served us well as it was central and close to the station; had we not been birds of passage we would have looked for somewhere else.

We found everything very cheap. Our evening meal in the Ambassador

Hotel, almost opposite ours, was £5 or the equivalent. We had to spend the best part of the following morning queuing at the Čedok Travel Agency to book our seat reservations for our journey to Berlin. After a while we had to take it in turns to stand in the queue while the others sat for a while. There were the usual arguments, queue-jumpers, misguided travellers and the like. Our tickets finally secured, we wandered down to Wenceslas Square and browsed round the shops and stalls there before going up to the Intercontinental Hotel for lunch in the coffee shop. It was from here that our afternoon tour of the city started. This was quite interesting as far as it went, but as most of the talk was in German we had little idea of what we were seeing. As the president was in residence the palace apartments were not open, and the tour finished up in a synagogue and the cemetery outside, which, because of lack of space, had to extend upwards instead of outwards.

Our train to Berlin left at 7.10am, which meant another early start, so early that we had breakfast on the train. Before leaving Prague we were shunted from platform to platform in the customary continental way before we set off along a river heading for the border, where we were anxious to see whether our tickets would be valid in East Germany, as we had not specified the two Germanys when booking. The ticket collector accepted them without a word except for the odd 'Danke schön'.

At Dresden an old man joined us, with whom Mike carried on a rather laboured conversation, his German no longer as good as it used to be. He pointed out the camps and airbases occupied by the Russians along the way, and spoke of their reluctance to leave for an uncertain future in their own country while here their wives had been able to get a job to supplement their income.

As we neared Berlin we were delayed by track works, but once past this obstacle we were in East Berlin, where we had to get off as the train was going on to Rostock. As we needed to get to the western sector of the city we took the S-Bahn, on which we travelled free as there appeared to be nowhere to buy tickets and no one to collect them at the far end.

At the hotel reservations office, we were very lucky, so we were told, to get a hotel, The Hermitage, halfway down Kurfürstendamm. We rested that afternoon; then went to a nearby Chinese restaurant for dinner, where they allowed us to order far too much by not saying how large the portions were. Afterwards we did some window-shopping on the Ku'damm but there was so much snow and slush underfoot we returned to the hotel, where Mike attempted to phone Bernhard but after several attempts concluded he had the wrong number or an old one.

Next morning after breakfast Mike asked the receptionist to give him Bernhard's number and was soon connected, but had difficulty in convincing him that he was not talking to his Italian friend Michelangelo as he could not believe that we could possibly be in Berlin. When the penny finally dropped, he was round like a shot and was overjoyed to see us again, and to meet Fiona for the first time. First, he took us on a sightseeing tour of East Berlin – so easy now there was no more wall or restrictions – before going back to Schöneberg and Gisela. After a look at the extensions to their flat, we went to an Argentinean restaurant for lunch and then on to the station to try and get some sleeper reservations for the following night, without success, so we wandered round the Europa-Center and had a meal there before going back to the flat to see a video of the Berlin Wall and share a bottle of wine.

Bernhard explained that he and Gisela had retired several years before but were just as busy with trips abroad; they were very friendly with the vice-director of the Berlin Zoo and accompanied him and his wife on wildlife expeditions. After, as we walked to the car, Gisela gave us a traditional send-off with some handbell-ringing.

We spent the following morning with Bernhard in the KDW department store (the Harrods of Berlin); then later, wandering through the Christmas market, a series of stalls near the Kaiser Wilhelm Gedächtniskirke, which we also visited for a few moments of reflection. We parted at the station, where we caught the 12.05 to Hanover, giving Mike a chance to see the countryside he had passed through in the dark in 1954.

As we had some three quarters of an hour to wait for our connection, Mike said he would take Fiona to see the Cafe Vaterland and Am Kröpke, only to discover Bahnhofstrasse, as he knew it, was now one vast shopping precinct, and by this time it was too dark to identify much at Am Kröpke. Our train to Cologne was a slow-stopping one, but it was warm and comfortable and with a compartment to ourselves we were not inconvenienced.

On our arrival, we made our way to the Commerz Hotel, recommended to us by Bernhard. Here we had rather a cold night due to a poor central heating system. Passing through the station concourse under the tracks we found a working 00 gauge model railway, on which Mike spent several Marks to keep the trains rolling. Our late evening meal was taken at, yes, McDonald's. On our way back to the hotel we looked at the illuminated cathedral, which at that time of night was closed.

So dawned Friday 14th December and we prepared for the last stage of our journey. Despite the poor heating, it was a pleasant hotel, and fortified by a very good breakfast we set off for the station to catch the 9.08am to Ostend. The train was quite full, so we occupied a compartment reserved for old age pensioners on the understanding we would vacate it if necessary. We were lucky as there were no OAPs on our route that day.

Just beyond Liege the locomotive broke down, with the result that we missed the hovercraft which would have got us home at a reasonable hour and had to wait until six o'clock for the normal ferry, which got us to Dover at 8.45pm. Here we had a nail-biting wait, as to get to the station for the last train at 9.30 we had to take a bus, which only left when everybody had cleared customs. We were on the point of taking a taxi when the driver finally appeared and we were on our way. We got into the house just before midnight after a very enjoyable two weeks' journey through Europe.

Just before Christmas Mike went up to Head Office to receive his twenty-five-year presentation whisky decanter from David Hookway, which the mail office packed up for him to get it home safely.

The year of 1991 could also be called 'the year of the holidays' as we certainly had more than the traditional one. As Easter was early we arrived back in time to enjoy Şeker Bayram. We planned to go down to Antalya, so drove down to Afyon where we had a good lunch at the Ali Baba restaurant. As it was late afternoon by the time we had finished we decided to stay in the town, which is dominated by a huge black rock towering up some 225 metres and capped by a large stone fortress. The town's official name is Afyonkarahisar or Opium Black Fortress, now poppies were replaced by sunflowers in the surrounding plain. The fortress is said to date back to Hittite times, the oldest known civilisation in Anatolia.

The next day, Mike's birthday, was highlighted by a two-hour visit to a carpet factory at Muratkoy, where a crowd of young women laid out endless carpets while we made our choice. From there we moved on to Pamukkale, the Cotton Castle, where a whole hillside is covered in a white, carboniferous deposit in the form of waterfalls, stalagmites, stalactites and grottoes, emanating from the hot springs in the ancient city of Hierapolis on top of the plateau.

After a night in Denizli we made a detour to take in Aphrodisias below the slopes of Babadağ (Father Mountain), an ancient city dedicated to the goddess of love, Aphrodite, which has only been excavated in depth in the last thirty years and is well worth a visit. Back on the main Denizli-Aydın road we stopped at a restaurant for lunch, where the owners had installed a large shower to enable patrons to remove the worst of the dirt and dust from their vehicles. Later we saw several of these along this stretch of road. We also made another detour to see the ancient city of Hyssa, founded in the 3rd century BC by Antiochus I.

On our way north the next day we stopped in Didyma to see the famous temple, said to be one of the oldest oracles in Asia Minor, particularly noted for its carved head of Medusa.

Skirting round the back of Kuşadası, the centre for the British tourists, we made our way to Selçuk to see the ancient city of Ephesus, one of the best preserved and most visited of all ancient remains in Turkey. As we walked round we could see extensive restoration work underway by the Austrians. The site is dominated by two large amphitheatres and the much-photographed Library of Celsus. Ephesus, like Troy, was close to the sea in ancient times, whereas today both are several kilometres inland.

Some eight kilometres south-east of Selçuk is the House of the Blessed Virgin Mary on top of a ridge of hills, to which she came with St. John. Her tomb, is said to be about a mile from the house. This and the house were discovered about a hundred years ago in a rather strange way. A German woman, Catherine Emmerich, who had never visited the area and had been an invalid for many years, had a series of visions, such that she was able to give detailed directions as to where the house was to be found. This would appear to be further evidence that the early Christians were driven out of the Holy Land and found their way into Anatolia. The disciple is buried close to Ephesus.

From here we moved on to Izmir, where we spent a couple of days. Mike understood that in the holiday season steam trains ran between here and Selçuk but despite many visits to the station we did not see any. During a trip across the bay we saw the *MV Istanbul*, on which we had travelled to Trabzon. A year later this vessel caught fire off Tekirdağ in the Sea of Marmara while on a cruise to Izmir, with rather embarrassing results. A traveller on board filmed the evacuation of the ship, the footage of which he gave or sold to the various TV channels. This showed many of the passengers covering their faces as though to ward off the glare from the flames. The story was that many of the passengers, mainly males, were not where they were supposed to be, having told their wives they were going to a conference in Antalya, but were instead on this illicit cruise with their lady friends.

On our way home we stopped at Sart to see the remains of Sardis, the ancient capital of Lydia, located on the royal road of the Persian empire. In the mid 6th century BC, Sardis was said to be the richest city in the world and was also the home of Croesus. Its wealth came in the form of gold washed down from the Taurus Mountains which was collected from the river by means of sheepskins; perhaps the origin of the legend of the Golden Fleece.

Just before stopping for the night at Kütahya we turned off to see the Temple of Zeus at Aizanoi, which is the best-preserved ancient temple in Turkey. It really is an amazing sight; this wonderful structure set in the middle of a field on the edge of an isolated rural village. While Mike was walking round the ruins, I was busy photographing some ducks and their young I had found nearby and having a long conversation with their owner.

At the weekends during the summer we would pack the car after lunch and set off to explore more of the Black Sea coast. On the coast north of Karasu the map showed there to be an area of scenic beauty, so we decided to spend a Saturday night there. When we arrived all we could find on the beach were some cheap and dirty-looking chalets; there was nothing in the village behind so we headed eastwards to the newly opened Akcakoca Hotel.

The hotel has some sea-facing rooms, while those with a southern aspect overlooked the hills behind. We asked for one overlooking the sea, but the room we were given was right at the western end and overlooked the town more than the sea, so after I had a few words with the manager we were moved to 'a room with a view'.

The hotel was quite full and after the evening buffet supper while we were still in the restaurant two young girls came up to us and started to ask us whether we were English, where we came from etc. Having given them some satisfactory answers I related my chat with the manager about our room and when I had finished the more confident of the two said they had come with a party from Istanbul, and like us had had words with the manager about their accommodation.

Next morning was warm and sunny and we settled round the pool like most of the other guests and were soon joined by our two friends from the previous evening and some of their party. Just before lunch a middle-aged man in a swimsuit came up and asked if we were Mr and Mrs Bennett. He explained that he was one of the directors and was very sorry to hear about the problem with our room and was there anything he could do to make amends? We said no, the problem had been resolved and we were very happy where we were. Our friends had had a word with him at the disco the previous night. We all posed for photos and parted the best of friends, and when we returned to our room we found a large bowl of fruit waiting for us. The manager was replaced by a very pleasant fellow who stayed for as long as we were in Düzce.

At the end of July Tim and Natalie came out for a ten-day break, or at least Tim did; Natalie was staying longer. We met them at Istanbul Airport and rented a car from Avis there. Next day we drove westwards to Gelibolu (Gallipoli), where we crossed the Dardanelles by ferry to Çanakkale. Here we stayed at the Truva Hotel, the place Mike and I had been unable to get into on our visit in 1989.

We had a pleasant evening meal by a pool inhabited by a number of terrapins, the waiter complaining that the new hotel down the road was taking all their customers away. The meal over, we walked along the promenade, past the new Akol Hotel, to where a fair of sorts was being held. After Natalie had had a stick of candyfloss we returned to the Truva.

We all had a very restless night as we were plagued by mosquitoes even though Tim managed to score several bloody hits.

Next morning after a somewhat belated breakfast, feeling very battered and bitten we drove off to Truva (Troy). Natalie amused herself climbing up and down the gigantic wooden horse which dominates the scene while Tim did the ruins. Mike sat in the hot sun watching the moving scenery while I 'did' the various gift shops and settled for a handful of postcards.

Back in the car, we drove eastwards heading for the Aegean, stopping for lunch at a very pleasant cafe run by the Forestry Department in the middle of a pine forest. We hit the coast close by a small town called Altınoluk and then pressed on to Edremit, and searched for a hotel. Finding none to our taste, we returned to just outside Altınoluk where we had seen the Gunes Hotel, where we stayed for a few days. It had a lovely pool and the sea was very clear.

We met up with an Austrian family – he was a mining engineer who had come on a package holiday from where they hoped to visit Bergama, Izmir and Ephesus, not realising that they were going to be put down miles from anywhere with no possibility of hiring a car. Admittedly there were buses, but they would have taken the best part of a day to get to the places they wanted to see. One evening we all invaded the junior disco and had a jolly good West Indian-style 'jump-up', with us calling the tunes.

When we came to leave one of the families we had befriended asked to drive along with us. Up in the hills we stopped at an al fresco cafe for tea and cakes before we finally parted. Dreading the Truva mosquitoes we decided to stay at the Akol, from the tenth floor of which we had a superb view over the Dardanelles. On our way back to Istanbul we stopped for an excellent fish lunch in Tekirdağ at a cafe we had found on our outward journey.

As we had paid for our trip home by rail in 1990 out of our own pocket, RPT said Mike could either claim the fares or have another trip home, so we settled for the latter at the end of August and took Natalie back with us at the same time.

It was shortly after our return that Yusuf, the *Kapici* (caretaker), said he had a friend who was an English teacher, who wished very much to meet us. So, after some hesitation we told him to bring him round. And so it was, one evening just as we were getting ready for bed, that there was a knock at the door and there stood Yusuf and his friend Halil. Halil was in his late forties or early fifties with a shock of grey hair. He was very polite and spoke almost in a whisper, making it very difficult to hear what he was saying. After some hints from us about the time he took his leave, saying that he wished to come again with his wife and daughter.

As we had exchanged telephone numbers we decided to invite them round for an evening snack so we would know when they were coming rather than be got out of bed by another late-night visit. His wife was quite young-looking and his daughter, Ceydam, had the most beautiful features. Ceydam spoke very little English so her father had to act as interpreter, and as with most conversations in Turkey we got onto the subject of Islam and Christianity. Always an interesting topic.

In November Mike saw me off at the bus station as I set off home for Alison's wedding. The fridge was packed with precooked food so Mike had little to do but warm it up when he got home and prepare some potatoes and veg to go with it. I kept him in touch with events through daily phone calls until I returned some two weeks later.

This year we decided the children could do all the preparations for Christmas, with the result that we arrived home with only a few days to spare.

Shortly after our return to Turkey there were some heavy falls of snow and Mike had to ask Yusuf to dig the car out of the drift in which it was buried before he could go to work. When he did eventually get there he spent most of his time on drafting his memoirs.

In February Ben's contract finally came to an end and he and Heather packed up and departed for Iran, taking their three cats with them in specially made boxes. Ben was planning to build houses on land he owned on the shores of the Caspian for his siblings and himself.

I had become quite friendly with Heather; she would come to the apartment one afternoon every week and we would discuss the latest news, she would tell me what she had heard from Ben and, if I had not heard it already from Mike, I would ask him about it when he came home.

The day after they left Mike went over to their flat to check that everything was in order and to collect the TV for safekeeping. With Ben's departure Mike was the only expat left in Düzce.

Mike discovered through Mehmet that a draughtswoman, Noor, had a terrapin and during a weekend visit to Ankara he was going to buy her another one, so Mike asked him if he would buy two for me, which he said he would be quite happy to do. As the Monday was market day Mike phoned me to meet him before lunch at the bridge as he had something for me. I was, as one might imagine, amazed and delighted with my new pets.

When David and Tony made one of their rare visits to Düzce Mike reminded them that it had been agreed that we were still due a three-seater settee and some replacement dining chairs. We needed the settee to relax on while watching TV. So, on getting the nod we went down to Kelebek, a local furniture manufacturer, to order same, having been there before when we first arrived to buy a couple of what they called 'television chairs'. Our visits usually caused a bit of a disruption as only one or two of the staff spoke any English, so they had to be summoned while we sipped the obligatory cups of hot tea.

There were three people we met who spoke some English: the manager, Alattin; the production engineer, Mustafa; and the quality control man, Harkan. So when the Bennetts arrived a call went out for one or all of these people to come down to the reception area. They were very keen to show us over the factory, so we made a date for just that, which we found very interesting. Then they said they wished to improve their English – would we teach them? We said yes, we would be happy to. So once a week a car would come to the flat and take us to the factory for an hour's chat.

Out of this, we discovered that Mustafa lived in the street behind ours and he was then very keen to come and visit us. To show their gratitude to their 'instructors' they took us out to dinner one evening at a restaurant on the Bolu Mountain, which was very enjoyable. When we finally selected a covering for the settee and dining chairs they agreed to re-cover our two TV chairs to match. We, or rather RPT, got a good discount on our purchase.

As this could well be our last year in Turkey (we hated the long, cold winters), the family decided to take what could be their last chance to come out. Tim, Dinah and Natalie managed to get on a BA flight together, leaving Fiona to follow some hours later on a THY (Turkish Airlines) flight. As they could not all fit in the car, Mike, Tim and I drove back with all the luggage and the others followed on the bus.

What really made their visit so memorable was when Tim produced a video camera out of his bag. Great fun was had by all as we learned how to operate it and then to try and catch each other doing something funny.

As the Kelebek crowd had heard so much about the family they were very anxious to meet them, so we invited them round to supper, asking Derya to come along as well. Mustafa's wife, Wilden, also came, and when Natalie had her party before her final departure, Wilden assisted with the cooking and preparation of the table and balloons. The next day we went down to the Akcakoca Hotel for a few days, terrapins and all. After the others returned home Natalie stayed on until the end of August when I took her back.

In mid August Nehal and Khorhan decided to have Evrim's *sunnet* or circumcision. Khorhan was now back with Astaldi and living in Bolu. We were invited and put up at the hotel where the dinner party was being held. Khorhan had invited all the senior people from Astaldi, Yuksel Rendel and KGM. We filmed the proceedings with the camcorder until the battery ran out. The following day we joined a family party at Khorhan's for lunch. Here we saw a video made by his brother-in-law of the actual *sunnet*, which had been performed in a clinic.

As mentioned earlier, Mike had no idea how much longer he would stay in Turkey and so time was running out for us to visit the south-west coastal area, which we were determined to see. So, at the beginning of October we loaded up the car, including the terrapins and camera, and set off, making Kütahya our first stopping point.

We spent three nights in Antalya, using it as a base to explore the historic sites at Perge and Aspendos. The Roman theatre at the latter place is really impressive for being so well preserved. After our tour of the building we went on to Side for lunch, this being the furthest we went eastwards.

In the evenings, we had a cup of tea in the bar after our meal and it was here we met Peggy and Jack, who were on holiday from Israel. From

Antalya we moved on westwards. To start with the road was well graded and quite wide and had obviously been improved to cope with the tourist traffic, but it later reverted to a narrow, twisting lane perched right on the edge of the sea. There were some magnificent views and Mike was glad we were out of the tourist season and the traffic was very light. We had lunch in Kaş and fell in love with the place – because of its inaccessibility it has not, as yet, been ruined by huge hotels and motels.

Before reaching here we had a bit of excitement just beyond Demre where we had a look at the church where St. Nicholas, the patron saint of sailors, was bishop before he became better known as Father Christmas. Proceeding along the narrow road we came to a hold-up in the traffic. The road on the way up to the plateau was being improved by bulldozers pushing surplus rock down the scarp face onto the old road. This meant the road was closed for short periods when these operations were in progress. When we finally set off in a single-line convoy we came face-to-face with someone coming down the other way who had obviously ignored the red light. Fortunately, the offending vehicle met up with the car in front of us. After much horn-blowing and light-flashing the culprit reversed into a lay-by and we continued the perilous climb to the top.

We were lucky with all the hotels we stayed at except Fethiye. Here we couldn't find anywhere in the town itself and finished up at Calis, just to the north, where we were pestered by mosquitoes, despite liberal spraying by me. The following day was one of the most pleasant and relaxing. We left Calish as soon as we could and drove to Dalyan. Here we took a ferryboat (after wisely turning down a very expensive offer of an exclusive trip to the turtle beach in our own boat) down the waterway to the beach where the turtles lay their eggs in the sand. Just outside Dalyan we saw the famous carved tombs in a cliff face. When we arrived, there were no signs of any turtles and even less of any eggs, so after a quick look round at the beach we caught a boat back and had lunch at a waterside cafe.

Whilst waiting for our meal we were entertained by a kitten that insisted on climbing in and out of the camera bag. This also happened in exactly the same way at Side and our hotel in Bodrum. At Side further amusement was caused by the cafe owner's two puppies that had us all laughing at their antics.

After Bodrum we started the homeward journey as we retraced our tracks back to the main road at Yatağan. Our next stop was at Pammukkale as we wanted to see the ancient Roman city of Hierapolis, which we had missed on our previous visit. We spent the night at the hotel right on the edge of the cliffs, and Mike had a dip in a thermal pool which was situated right outside our room. The water was indeed very warm and not suitable for energetic swimming. On our way home, we called at a carpet factory which appeared to be full of German tourists.

Although Mike had always said he would never move up to Bolu there was now little choice and he was not ready to go back to England at this stage.

Nehal found us an excellent flat on the third floor in Mutlu Sokak, Happiness Street, right opposite a mosque.

We moved on a Saturday at the end of November, giving us the Sunday to settle in. The weather forecast was not good and it had been agreed that we would abort the operation if it was pouring with rain. The day dawned dull but dry. The lorry and men duly arrived at the appointed hour but said they could not move until they got some money for diesel from James. By the time James arrived, making all sorts of excuses as to why he was late, it had started to rain, but as we had just begun the loading we just had to carry on.

The lorry was away by lunchtime, covered with a heavy tarpaulin which we hoped would protect our belongings – the essential items were in the car, although we did not have a lot of spare room as Derya was with us as a translator. We arrived in Bolu at about the same time as the lorry and on the doorstep to greet us was Mehmet, our official interpreter. The removal men were very happy to find that this flat had a lift, something that we were glad of too, with the result that the moving up of the furniture and effects was soon completed.

In the block at street level were several shops, which proved very useful later on, one of which was a cafe frequented by students from the university. Dying of thirst, we all went in, having paid off the men, for a cup of tea. By the time we left the young manager had ordered two bottles of gas for us on his mobile phone, having been asked about gas supplies by Mehmet.

Back upstairs, we started to straighten things out and it was not long before our neighbours across the landing made themselves known. They were the Chelilebash family and they owned a kebab cafe on the main thoroughfare leading into Bolu from the E5. Mehmet knew the cafe as he often took a meal there but had never spoken to them. He was very interested when he learned that they came from Adana. They had two attractive daughters, Vuzlat and Beste, aged seventeen and fifteen. They also had a son, Umut, who was about seven years old.

We all had dinner with Nehal and Korhan at their flat, which was only a few minutes' walk away; then spent the night at a hotel, which was very busy with what looked like a football team and a netball team. We were up early so we could make full use of Derya's services before we put her on a bus back to Düzce.

We had not been in the flat very long when there was a knock at the door. When we opened it we found Beste with another girl about her age. She was Aycan, from the flat below ours. They had come to help us. Before we knew where we were the whole of Aycan's family, the Goltepes, were up to introduce themselves. With them they had Muge, the youngest member of the family; she was some ten months old. The biggest surprise came when the father offered us the use of a spare telephone he had until we got our own transferred from Düzce. Strange how we came by our telephones in Turkey.

Mike had a couple of half-days off from the office to get us settled in and, with the help of Nehal as Korhan was away at the time, to buy a TV set and VCR. It did not take us long to feel really at home in Bolu with all the kind help we had from our newfound friends and neighbours.

Two weeks later we were catching the bus to Istanbul for our Christmas and New Year break back in England. From Bolu the journey took an extra hour and we were not looking forward to the return journey, so we were very pleased when Korhan and Nehal offered to meet us at the airport on our return.

In fact, we did not go direct to Bolu but stayed the night in their flat in Istanbul, and the following morning went with them to christen their new car. We drove to the Eyüp district of the city where they bought a sheep and the meat, when cooked, was served to the poor at the adjacent mosque.

After lunch with Nehal's family we drove back to Bolu, a fairly quick journey, as the completed motorway had been opened to the public at a big ceremony just after Christmas.

Mike's relations with Tony were better than those he had had with David. When the family was out in 1992, the weekend we spent down at Akcakoca we invited Tony and his wife, Helen, to join us for lunch, which they did, and from a remark he made they would have stayed the night in the area had the hotel not been fully booked.

After we first moved in we did not see quite so much of Aycan and Beste once they had got to know us, but their mothers became frequent visitors. There would be a knock at the door and on the doorstep would be Murel with some dish she wanted me to try. We would retire to the kitchen where the dish would be tried and praised; then we would have a chat in our limited way. When things got really difficult and our sign language was to no avail one of the girls would be summoned to help out if at all possible. Vuzlat was a much better interpreter than Beste and she understood more than she let on. In the case of Aycan's mother, Muhadder, she would often send Aycan to ask if she could come up for a visit, and when she did come she always had Muge with her. Before she learned to walk Muge would move round on her bottom sitting in an upright position, the first time I had seen a baby move about in this way.

On the first day of Bayram, Murel (someone who shared our landing at the flat) and family, including Suleyman, came over to pay their respects as is the custom. After them came the Goltepes, the children showing off their new clothes which they all acquire at this time of year. Another family from the apartment also called during the day bearing gifts. During a lull in our visitors we heard the banging of a drum and a pipe being played. Going onto the small balcony, we saw the two musicians who had woken us during the nights of Ramazan (Ramadan)to remind us to take food before sunrise.

It was on the Wednesday of the holiday week that Murel invited us over for an evening meal as they had some relatives staying with them from Adana.

The following evening, 25th March, Fiona rang to tell us that

Antony had phoned her to say that Mike's mother had died that evening. It came as a shock to both of us, although it was something we knew we were going to hear one day and we had wondered whether we would be in Africa, Turkey or perhaps at home. Mike managed to get in touch with Antony the following day and to make the necessary arrangements.

It so happened that we were booked to go home for our annual leave on Friday 3rd April, the day of the funeral, and we already had the tickets. Being Bayram everywhere was closed, so Tim managed to get our tickets changed to 31st March so we would be back in time for the funeral on the Friday.

The service on the Friday afternoon went well. The vicar gave a brief precis of Da's life, which he had obtained from Antony. After the service, Mike thanked Mr Hall and his wife, the next-door neighbours, for coming, and the librarian and the representative from Age Concern who had also come along. Da's long-time friend Hildegard Bates said she could not attend a cremation as it reminded her too much of the Nazis' persecution of the Jews in the 1930s. Mike phoned her to thank her for her support and friendship over the years and her floral contribution.

On 19th May every year Turkey celebrates Atatürk's Youth and Sports Day with parades by children throughout the land. Murel was keen to go as Beste was in the display at the sports stadium, and she asked us if we would like to go too. We went along with Mrs Soylemez, who owned a chemist's shop and whose daughter, Selen, was also taking part. She lived in the same apartment block as us. Mike recorded quite a lot of the parade on the camcorder.

On the following Sunday, we were invited to a wedding. Zeynep (one of the secretaries at Mikes' office) had a sister, who worked for Astaldi, was to marry another employee and the wedding was to take place in the Kızılay Hall in Düzce as that was where the bride's parents were living. It was strange going to this particular place as we could see and hear such occasions from our old flat. Now we were looking at our old abode from the rooftop of this building. Mike's colleagues from Bolu turned up, they had even laid on a bus, and of course a large number of Astaldi people were there too. Derya's sister, Oya, was there and Mike had a couple of dances with her.

One Saturday in early July Umut, next door, was having his *sunnet*. In Turkey, this is a big day for all young boys, the day when they are considered to become men. The boy is dressed up in a red cape with a crown on his head and a wand-like stick in his hand. Before the operation, he has to be taken to see something beautiful, so we all bundled into different cars and, with horns blowing, a recognised custom, we set off for Kolkoy reservoir, which is a very attractive setting close to Bolu, and several other similar parties were there at the same time. Here on the shore we stopped for some music and cakes that I had made the night before; then returned to Bolu and the clinic.

Umut went off for an injection and while he was waiting for it to take effect Mike and I went for a walk outside as the waiting room was somewhat stifling with humanity and cigarette smoke. When we returned Umut was just setting off for the surgery. Several people thought Mike was going to follow with the camera. There was no way he could do this, so he offered the camera to a relative with some quick instructions on what to do.

Back home, we had a snack in our own flat – next door was full to capacity anyway – then went over for a service conducted by the local imam from the mosque. The room was full with family and friends, and dominating the scene was a specially decorated bed for Umut to rest on.

The service over, we returned home where Mike sat back and watched Steffi Graf beat Janna Novotná at Wimbledon, where at the presentation afterwards, the defeated Janna had a cry on the shoulder of the Duchess of Kent. We all reassembled in the evening for a grand dinner with much drinking and dancing. Because of the number of people invited, one family spent the night in our lounge. We gave them a key so we never saw them come or go.

A month or so later one Sunday afternoon we had a bit of a scare. I had gone next door for something and sometime later went back and asked Mike to go over with me as Umut had done something to their TV and they could not get it to work. Mike had a quick look at it and got it going again.

When we came to leave, we discovered, to our horror, that we were locked out of our flat. I did not have my key and Mike did not have his because I knew he was staying in the flat until I returned. What to do? The *Kapici* was called and consulted; fortunately, he had worked in Germany some years previously and so spoke the language, therefore Mike was able to communicate with him to a certain extent. I used the phone to speak to Nehal about finding a locksmith but as Korhan was out she could not help. Then the *Kapici* came back with some spare balcony-door keys. If someone could get onto our balcony, which was adjacent to our neighbours', then we might get in that way. The *Kapici* was starting to climb over but Mike said we could not risk him going over.

I turned to Mike and said, 'Mike, you're not going. I'll go.' And go I did, swinging my leg over the rail across the gap and onto our balcony!

One day shortly before we were due to leave Turkey Mrs Soylemez called and asked me to come over to her mother's house at the end of the road to meet her elder daughter, Selmin. Selmin came to see us on one or two occasions after this, later we met her younger sister Selen, who was rather shy and would not come into the flat on the odd occasion when she brought something for me.

One Saturday they told us they were going on a picnic the following day with their neighbour and invited us to join them.

In Turkey, they say all the best cooks come from Bolu, and in this I think they refer to Bolu as a province as Mengen is the town that boasts of its cooks. It was to this small town that we went first as the chefs' school there was having its annual exhibition. We had seen part of it on the TV news the previous evening when they showed a continuous barbecue made of U-shaped concrete units to hold the charcoal; the whole thing must have been about fifty metres long.

As Mike was coming up to retirement he told Tony that he did not wish to stay in Turkey for another winter and wrote to Jim Hyde in Head Office to confirm this, saying he needed to do some urgent work on the house before the onset of winter, and this was accepted. Mike also discussed it with Gordon Matthews when he came out in July; he tried to persuade him to stay on, but Mike was adamant and said he wanted to leave no later than mid September.

When it was near time for us to leave Tony said they would like us to have a farewell dinner as had been done for others in the past, and although he knew we did not like such occasions, what did we think about it? We said we would like that very much, and we had a very enjoyable evening. Mike's colleagues from Bolu invited us to a dinner at the Köroğlu Hotel and said we could invite anyone we wanted. We felt we would stick to just the locals, but in the end they invited all the expats. Although we were invited guests all the others had to pay for the evening, so knowing that their incomes were pretty low we paid for our share as well.

Our neighbours were sorry to see us leave and brought various gifts for me and the family, even though they had never met them. On our last evening, the Soylemez family invited us to dinner at the Köroğlu Hotel. Köroğlu means 'son of the blind man' and refers to a real bandit who lived and roamed the forests in the 16th century, a sort of Turkish Robin Hood. His father had been a groom with the local baron, and when asked to select a horse given as a gift by a wealthy neighbour, the poor groom selected a crippled colt, for which he was punished by having his eyes put out, and thus his son became a bandit to seek revenge for the ill treatment of his father.

After the meal we agreed we would walk part of the way home. After passing the town's largest mosque we came by a hall where a wedding reception was being held. We had just stopped for a moment to listen to the music when the girls said, 'Come on, we can go in if you like.'

'But we don't know anyone here, we can't just barge in like that.'

'Oh yes we can, anyone can go in, they don't mind.'

So, in we went and had a dance or two, congratulated the happy couple, then, after taking some film, we continued home.

They served us with breakfast in their flat before Korhan and Nehal came to take us to Istanbul. All the neighbours were out on their balconies waving and calling goodbye as we loaded the car and drove off. And so ended our sojourn in Turkey of some four and a half years.

Mike said it was the worst job he had worked on, mainly due to the office set up and to some of the other British ex-patriate staff, whose ethics and values, neither he nor I shared. However, we were both glad we had been able to see so much of Turkey and things greatly improved

with our move to Bolu. One thing for which we were most thankful –
we had made so many nice friends including Derya and her family back
in Düzce, Selmin, Selen, and Korhan, Nehal and their family, who have
visited us in England since our return and who phone us regularly.

Wooden horse –Truva

Pammukkale

Flat friends with Derya

Mike with Nehal and Khorhan

Carpet sellers

Goreme – Cappadocia

Some of my toys

Selen and Selmin

12

Going Back to Guyana

We always said that when Mike retired we would take the family back to British Guiana (now known as Guyana) so that we could introduce Dinah and Tim to the land of their birth.

We decided to go out there for Christmas 1995 with New Year being celebrated on Tobago. But first Mike and I would go out there on a reconnaissance mission as one of the places we wished to visit was the Kaieteur Falls and so we needed to know how this could be achieved.

Sunday 19th March saw us leaving Tunbridge Wells for Heathrow. We took a BWIA flight to Trinidad on their plane, *Sunset Barbados*. After a flight of eight and three quarter hours we arrived at St. Lucia for a short stop. It was very hot and humid. On our way to Piarco, we had a glimpse of Tobago over to our left, where we arrived at 8.45 pm local time (4.45 pm in England).

Here we transferred to *Sunjet Dominica*, an MD-83 of BWIA, for the forty-minute flight to Timehri Airport, passing through a thunderstorm on the way. We were met by Deodat, a taxi driver, who soon had us on our way to Georgetown and the Tower Hotel. We were given a poolside room, 103, in the hotel annexe. We got into bed at 1am.

We were up early next morning and, putting on the TV, were just in time to catch the news, which appeared to be all about a breach on the sea wall at Buxton. There were some dramatic pictures of threatening waves beating against the wall with scenes of flooding behind. We had breakfast in the adjacent Main Street cafe where we got into conversation with a man called Abrams, a contractor who used to work for the PWD (Public Works Department), which prolonged the meal somewhat.

For our first port of call we walked up Main Street to the old PMA (Petroleum Marketing Agency) office to see my old friend, Gem Eytle at her Frandec Travel Agency. Gem and I had a long chat about old times while Mike watched the traffic outside through the open window. From here we walked up to the Walter Roth Museum of Anthropology and into the office of its director, Denis Williams. He was a little unsure who we were until Mike reminded him that we had exchanged correspondence in the past about the possible publication of Dad's journals. Shortly after this his partner, Jenny Wishart, joined us. As they were going out we arranged to come back the following day for a longer chat.

We moved up Main Street towards Kingston, passing the Park Hotel where Mike stayed when he first arrived in 1958. Nearby was the British High Commission, which of course was new to us. The Transport and Harbours Department Building looked much the same as it did in the old days. We crossed the old railway line; looking down Lamaha Street we could see the outline of the old railway station building. We then turned into Barrack Street and onto Duke Street, where we saw the huge new American Embassy that is now located on this road.

On our way back to the hotel we had a look through the gates of Government House, or State House as it is now known. Looking down Middle Street we saw the guest house where we first met, looking much the same as it did then. I stopped to sample the wares at a handcart selling coconut water, something that would never have been tolerated forty years ago.

Tuesday morning found us in a taxi going up to the television studios at D'Urban Park for an interview for Channel 10 with a young presenter, Caroline Beresford. This was something Gem Eytle had arranged, as far as I can remember. Caroline gave an introductory opening, saying we had come back after nearly thirty-five years, and proceeded to ask us about our impressions and the possible publication of Dad's memoirs. The interview over, Caroline then said she would like to meet us at the National Museum the following day to make a video about the museum and Dad's work there.

After leaving the studios we stood outside at the roadside to get a taxi back to town. The first one to come along was a minibus, which looked rather full so we declined. We waited, hoping our wait would not be too long. Then along came a jackass cart (dray cart), so Mike jokingly made a hitch-hiking gesture with his thumb and much to our surprise the driver stopped, so we hopped aboard! We rather enjoyed the ride. Getting off at the junction with Vlissingen Road we made our way to Castellani House, now an art museum. In our day, it was the home of the Director of Agriculture and subsequently, I believe, the residence of Forbes Burnham.

After a brief look around we made our way along a path to the Botanic Gardens and zoo. Running the refreshment stall at the entrance was Muriel Northe's granddaughter, with whom I had a long chat. Muriel was my Nanny and now, a lifelong friend. Moving over to the office, we found George Lee in charge. He was the younger brother of Stanley, who used to run the zoo in our day.

On Wednesday morning, we went out to video St. George's Cathedral, as the morning before the sun was shining directly into the camera, so we decided to wait until there was a cloudy sky. While Mike was filming, I got into conversation with a blind man, one Boysie. He told me a long story, which resulted in me saying I would arrange for a collapsible walking stick to be sent out to him but was a bit doubtful of getting him a blind man's watch. As we walked down the High Street, or rather Avenue of the Republic as it is now known, we noticed that Lopes Bedstead House was no more, just an empty site. Horis Lopes was a great friend of my father.

When we got to the National Museum we hung about waiting for Caroline; then we got a message saying there had been a mix-up and she would not be able to come but could we make it on Friday instead?

For lunch, we went to the Del Casa Restaurant in Middle Street, after which we called in to a travel agent to get hotel and safari details for our visit in December with the family.

Back at the hotel, we got a call from Jenny Wishart to say that Peter Pritchard, a conservationist, was to give a lecture that evening on the turtles of Guyana at eight o'clock in the Hibiscus Room and we should go along.

After lunch in the poolside cafe we were interviewed by Ann Benjamin for one of the newspapers. During this time, Mike was amused by a cat that befriended us and a kiskadee that was flying around the room.

After Ann had left us we took a taxi to Regent Road to look at the old family house. First we stopped off to see a house where the dentist, Dr Carter, used to live. We then crossed Albert Street and saw Gordon's corner shop where I used to buy sweets as a child. My old home, 149 Regent Road, was no more, having been replaced by a two- or three-storey concrete structure, now being used as a shipping office. The Ince house next door was still there, but in a poor state of repair, as too was the genip tree in the back garden.

We went down the side of number 149 to see the houses behind and I got into conversation with one of the tenants and had a 'bit of old time story'. From there we went next door to see the Too Chungs, who were very pleased to see us. After a chat we went across the road to look up Gloria Smith, my old piano teacher. Back at the hotel, we went into the bar to see our interview with Caroline on the television there. For dinner that night we had pepperpot and black-eyed pea soup.

On our way to the Pritchard lecture we met Alan Humphrey, owner of the hotel, who said the meeting was private but when he heard who we were he allowed us in.

We had quite a long chat with Pritchard after the meeting. He said Schomburgk's Travels should be reprinted and that Margaret Chan-a-Sue had a copy. Richard Schomburgk's Travels in British Guiana was translated into English from German by my grandfather Walter Roth.

Thursday morning we spent at the Walter Roth Museum. While we were waiting for Denis and Jenny to arrive, we were entertained by their young daughter, Kibileri. We had met her elder sister, who was painting a frieze in the hallway at our hotel. Mike had a look at a large-scale map of Guyana and was able to confirm that the mission Harold Smith, 'Colonel' Lopes and he had visited was at Kurukabaru and the people there were Patamonas. From Denis we discovered that Moray House, which featured in Dad's memoirs as the home of the McTurk family, was situated at the corner of Camp and Church Streets and was now owned by David de Caires. We had a thorough look round the museum, filming as we went.

Leaving the museum, we walked round to Christ Church where we were married and found it much as it was back then. There was some scaffolding up the front so presumably some preservation work was in progress. The clock was still working. As we walked back we noticed that the Promenade Gardens had been closed off. Looking across the Parade Ground to our old flat on Carmichael Street, we found it was no more.

We had lunch in the Cazabon Room at the hotel, after which we took a taxi for a drive along the East Coast Road. We started off along Main Street, seeing the Pegasus Hotel and the Amerindian structure Umana Yana for the first time. Then, after passing the bandstand along the sea wall, which was covered in graffiti, when we reached Kitty we did not turn right as expected but continued straight on along a new road, Clive Lloyd Drive, a one-way road, which beyond Kitty turned into a dual carriageway. Scandal Point was no more and the Carib Hotel we used to visit on a Saturday night looked to be closed up.

On the right, we passed a large open-air cinema that was not there in our day. On the left, there were small industrial buildings, which gave the area an untidy look. Reaching Triumph, we turned off to look at our old house. The PWD appeared to have moved out. We walked down to the sea wall, which was quite new in this area, and it looked as though the beach of our day had been eroded. Mike said he saw what looked like parallel groynes, which may have been erected to encourage accretion to take place. Opposite our old house, new houses had been built, and down towards the sea wall looked as though it was being used as a tip area.

Back in the taxi, we made our way to Buxton. Passing through Annandale Mike noticed that the footbridge he had put in for the schoolchildren so they did not have to walk on the busy road was still in use. When we got to Strathspey the land to the left was flooded due to the recent breach and a temporary roadway had been made for access to the site. As we moved on through Coldingen, to our right, a whole new housing development was underway. We went as far as Enmore (it still had its cinema), and then turned back. Beterverwagting Police Station was much as we remembered it, and the chimney of the old Chateau Margot estate was still standing.

After Kitty, we went down Vlissingen Road, and as we drove round we were very conscious of the changes in the old traditional houses. Some had been pulled down and replaced with concrete-and-glass structures of not too high a standard, and the old remaining timber houses looked dilapidated and in need of repair and a good coat of paint. We had also noticed how many of the drainage trenches were full of rubbish, which obviously hindered the flow of water when the *kokers* were opened.

Turning off at the cricket ground into Regent Road, we turned left into New Garden Street and right into Charlotte Street to look at the old Bank House. I wanted to get out and take a photo of the building but the driver advised against this, as the place was now the Ministry of Foreign Affairs. We moved further down the road; and, turning into Oronoque Street, I showed Mike where the Zitmans had lived before turning back into Regent Road. Passing through Bourda, we were conscious of the great increase in the volume of traffic compared to our day. Reaching Camp Street, we turned right, passing the Ursuline Convent, as we knew it, so that Mike could take a photograph of Moray House. We returned to the hotel via Murray Street, which had changed its name to Quamina Street.

At 5.30 pm we went to the Heritage Society AGM where we met Dorothy King, my old ballet teacher, Crystabel Dean and Lucille Campbell. Jo Singh was presiding at the top table. I got my friends to pose for the camcorder. The meeting itself reflected the state of the society: poor attendances, people failing to pay their subscriptions etc.

Friday morning was spent at the National Museum with Caroline Beresford and her camera crew. They took quite a long time to set up their camera and the extra lighting they needed. We saw the McTurk table that we had borrowed to cut our wedding cake on all those years ago! The session over, we went to the Pegasus Hotel where we had lunch by the pool with Elaine MacPherson. From there we returned to her house for tea and, while there, Lawrence Thompson turned up and joined us for a cup (Elaine and Lawrence both old friends of ours).

Fiona rang us during the evening to say that Henrietta, the canary, had laid an egg!

The next day, Saturday, we went to the Frandec Agency to confirm our flight to Barbados and pay the airport tax of $1,500. We posted some cards and had a wander through the Booker Stores as we knew it and bumped into Lawrence Thompson, with whom we had a chat.

Then it was back to the zoo for another TV interview, this time for Capitol News. From here we made our way to New Market Street for a lovely lunch with Gem and Holly Eytle. After the meal, Mike and I went outside to film the house as this building was almost an exact replica of 149 Regent Road.

After a short rest back at the hotel, we took a taxi to Werk-en-Rust to have tea with the Bhattacharyas, the doctor who had brought both Dinah and Tim into the world. Both had aged; the doctor looked quite distinguished with his white hair while his wife appeared quite matronly. After tea and cakes and a chat about old times we took our leave and returned to the Tower Hotel.

That evening the hotel was having what it called a 'beach party' in the poolside cafe. A small trimaran yacht had been placed in the pool to create the atmosphere of the seashore. We invited Denis, Jenny and Kibileri, together with Elaine MacPherson, to join us. It was a pleasant evening with a steel band playing until one o'clock in the morning!

Dawn and Mickey McTurk had invited us to lunch at La Bonne Intention (LBI). A taxi was to pick us up and take us there. Imagine our surprise when we came to get into the taxi to find Diane McTurk sitting on the back seat! Having seen the film of her and her giant otters at Karanambo it was our great desire to meet her and now we had the chance to see her and talk to her.

Once we were settled at LBI we sat down to a long chat with Diane, most of which I filmed for later reference. Diane said the camera crew had made the film of the otters over several visits. They had even tried to create a pool near the ranch in which to take the underwater shots but it had not proved to be a great success.

When I asked her about Noonie McTurk, Dad's friend, whom he had hoped one day to marry, Diane did not really know her. I had thought that the problem might have been because the McTurks were Catholics, which Diane said they were not, and Dad at that time was not, but it seems Michael McTurk was opposed to the union as he felt that Dad would not be in a position to support a wife. The outcome of this meeting was our decision to spend Christmas with Diane at The Karanambo Ranch, when we came out with the rest of the family.

Mike then had a chance to ask Diane about her family, as some aspects of the history still puzzled us. To understand the following one needs to have read Volumes I and II of Dad's journals. The first thing Mike asked her about was the house at Kalacoon at the mouth of the Mazaruni River. Diane said the house was the official residence of her father, Michael McTurk, as a magistrate and Protector of the Amerindians. When he retired McTurk wanted to buy the house and estate but his wish was not granted. It will be remembered that my grandfather, Dr Walter Roth, took over from McTurk as protector of the Amerindians on the Pomeroon when he arrived with Dad in 1907. McTurk was the son of Dr McTurk, who went out to British Guiana in the 1800s. He married a woman from Liverpool and raised a family out in the colony. Sadly, his wife died. Then, back in England, he met and married another lady and took her back with him and started a second family. One of the children in the second family was Edward 'Tiny' McTurk. The Kalacoon estate was eventually sold and turned into a quarry.

Michael McTurk was a close friend of H. P. C. (Henry Prideaux Colin) Melville. Melville took over a cattle ranch at Dadanawa from a Dutchman who had imported the animals from Brazil in the 1880s. This became known as the Rupununi Development Co. Ltd. His son, John, went to school in Georgetown and during this time lived with the McTurks at Moray House.

Mike then asked Diane how the family came to live at Karanambo. Her father, 'Tiny', after returning home from the First World War where he had served with the Royal Flying Corps and the Royal Navy Volunteer Reserve, said that all he wanted to do was to marry his sweetheart, Connie Gordon, and settle down far away from the 'madding crowd'. Tiny was in fact born at Kalacoon in 1898. He joined a company dealing in balata and looked up his old friend, John Melville, who had his own ranch at Wichabai on the Rupununi River. Tiny was then commissioned by his employer to find an estate on the Rupununi River somewhere between Wichabai and Apoteri, which is located at the confluence of the Rupununi and Essequibo Rivers. The estate he found was Karanambo. The Caribs, who had decided to give up warring and move south, had abandoned it. Karanambo is said to mean 'left by the Caribs'. After Tiny left the scene Diane's brother, Mickey, ran the estate; then when his family needed schooling he decided to move back to Georgetown and Diane took over the running of the estate.

After saying farewell to the McTurks we went back to the hotel, collected our cases and took a taxi to the airport. Our flight by *Sunjet Anquilla* left at 7.15pm for the forty-five-minute flight to Piarco. We had a wait of just over an hour before our onward flight to Bridgetown, where we arrived at 9.45 Collecting our cases, we were soon in a taxi bound for the Sea Breeze Hotel.

Waiting for me in our room was a most beautiful bowl of flowers from the children. The day was Mothering Sunday. The room was very nice, overlooking the pool and beach with its own kitchen. The next day we noticed a nasty smell in the room and complained to the manager. They carried out a search and thoroughly cleaned the room but could not ascertain where the smell was coming from. Then we happened to go back to one of our cases and discovered that this was the culprit! It was a very fishy smell by this time.

As we had been nowhere near any fish we decided the contamination must have occurred on the flight over from Guyana. We went to the BWIA office in Bridgetown and complained. It turned out that a shipment of prawns had been placed on top of our case and contaminated it. We flew home on the Thursday 30th March after a very enjoyable trip.

On 8th April Henrietta's chicks hatched out, which resulted in Mike building an outdoor aviary for them. In May Mike and I drove over to see the Tilleys in Spain. We crossed over from Newhaven and spent the first night in the small town of Sées and the second night at Cahors. During a visit to Barcelona Mike had his wallet stolen while on the Underground, which was a real nuisance. From Spain, we drove east to Divonne where we were lucky enough to find Villa Beaujeu, my great-grandparents' retirement home, which we found very interesting. As the place was deserted we were free to wander at will.

At the end of June we booked our flights to Guyana. The plan was to spend a few days in Georgetown; then fly to Karanambo for Christmas, calling on Kaieteur and the Orinduik Falls on the way there. We would then return to Georgetown before flying on to Tobago for the New Year.

Because Diane was difficult to contact we liaised with her friend, Wendela Jackson. Wendela had been a parliamentary researcher in London.

August proved to be a very hot month, weather-wise, and Fiona bought her first house on Poona Road, Tunbridge Wells, which was to keep Mike quite busy over the next few months.

Then Wendela asked for a deposit for our trip to enable her to book a plane and make other reservations. We also made a booking at the Crown Point Hotel, located near the airport on Tobago.

In October, we had a visit from Bernhard and Gisela, Mike's German friends, which made a welcome change. We went to the hop farm at Paddock Wood and London Zoo. In November Mike bought a Micra as a runabout for me.

Sunday 17th December found us all meeting up at Heathrow Airport on the start of our epic trip back to Guyana. We were the first to arrive; then came Dinah and Natalie. There was no sign of Tim, and we started to get really worried as to whether he would make it in time. We were due to take off at 11.55am but were delayed for an hour, during which Tim finally arrived.

We had an uneventful flight aboard *Sunjet Trinidad* via St. Lucia as before; then after a short wait at Piarco we were aboard *Sunjet Guyana* for the fifty-minute flight to Timehri Airport, where we arrived at just after two o'clock local time. Problem – Fiona's case was not among the baggage on the carousel, so we had to go and report it missing. A waiting taxi soon had us installed at the Tower Hotel. After a mix-up over the rooms we were ready for an early night.

When we got up there was a message from Wendela to say she would be sending her friend Annette round to the hotel to collect some more money for the trip and fill us in on the latest travel details. At eleven o'clock Annette arrived and over a coffee we heard the plans to date. It appeared that Diane was inviting two girls from the British High Commission and two young men from the American Embassy to make up the Christmas party. As the girls would be travelling with us the visit to Orinduik Falls had been cancelled, as we needed to carry extra fuel for the plane. She then told us that it had been announced that Peter Pritchard and the Santiago Zoo were going to take over the running of the local zoo.

In reply to an earlier query, flights to Mabaruma were made on Mondays and Fridays unless a private plane was chartered. She also offered to find out about the hire of a minibus for us to go down to Rosignol.

We then all assembled in the reception area and set off for a walk round town with Annette. First, we went round the corner to Fitt's hairdressing salon, where I had a chat with Noreen Fitt. From here we went up Carmichael Street, pointing out to the family where we used to live before we left BG; then into Main Street to the Walter Roth Museum. Here we found extensive repairs going on and the place, more or less, closed to visitors. Denis Williams and Jenny Wishart were not there. After some coconut water from a cart in Main Street we returned to the hotel for a Bank's beer and fish and chips beside the pool.

On Tuesday morning Wendela phoned to suggest that we took sweets and cigarettes for gratuities for the staff at Karanambo, and any wine we might want as there would be none up there. We also had a message to say Fiona's case had arrived at Timehri Airport so Tim and Mike took a taxi to go and collect it. They were back in time for a poolside lunch, after which Dinah, Tim, Fiona and Natalie had fun in the pool playing around with a lilo they had found there. My friend Roslyn came for afternoon tea.

Tim and Mike then went to the Lands and Mines Department now located up in D'Urban Park to buy some large-scale maps of Guyana. Back at the hotel we collected the others for a visit to the zoo and Botanic Gardens. What interested me the most was the large mausoleum erected to house the body of the late president, Linden Forbes Sampson Burnham. We then had a fascinating time watching a group of manatees we found in a nearby pond.

The afternoon and evening turned wet so we were confined to the hotel. In the evening Dawn, Mickey and Michelle McTurk came to the hotel for dinner. Before the meal we met up with Alan Humphrey.

Thursday morning was somewhat chaotic due to the power being off while they changed over a transformer. Wendela rang to say she had managed to arrange for a minibus to pick us up at nine o'clock and take us down to Rosignol.

We started off by going up Water Street, driving very slowly to avoid the many waterlogged potholes, so Mike could show the family his old office at PWD that was still standing, much as he knew it then, along the sea wall to Triumph, where we all got out and went up to the house where Dinah had spent the early months of her life. The present occupants, Leo Ramotar and his wife, were pleased to see us and we had quite a long chat. The tennis court had gone and the layout of the garden had been changed. He had been a district commissioner but had been out of the country for some of the time we were there so we had never met before.

From here we drove down to West Coast Berbice along a fine asphalt road – what a change from the old burnt-earth surface of our time! As we crossed the new Abary Bridge we noticed that one of the spans of the old bridge had finally fallen into the water. The day warming up, the rest of the party soon dropped off into a doze as we approached Rosignol. After looking at the bridge Mike had built to give access to a government compound we drove down to Blairmont, where I had a chat in the local dialect with two hucksters ('small time' traders) sitting in the shade of the *stelling (Dutch for wharf)* building. Natalie was intrigued by the large crabs in the mangrove swamp alongside the causeway leading to the *stelling*.

We then drove to the ferry terminal at Rosignol and watched the boat come in. On our way back to Georgetown we called in at the Letter T estate, which was deserted. We also looked in at the orphanage at Plaisance to see Sister Noel Menezes, and Tim gave the boys a football to play with.

Back at the hotel, I had a rest so the others went to the Caribbean Rose for lunch only to find it closed, so they repaired to the Palm Court for a roti and curry lunch.

Mike managed to contact Steve Naraine, his old colleague from public works. Steve said he was going over to West Coast Demerara next Wednesday to look over some sea defence works that were going on there, and would pick Tim and Mike up at one o'clock at the hotel. That evening we had Muriel Northe and Elaine MacPherson to supper.

We were up early on Friday morning as we were off to Karanambo. After breakfast, I managed to get hold of Wanda Willems, who invited us to Kaow Island, saying she would send one of Bell's boats to pick us up at Parika. We then went to the Guiana Stores to buy some rum.

Having packed up, we boarded a minibus and drove up Main Street to the British High Commission to pick up Lynn and Elaine and then went on to Ogle airfield. Here each of us was weighed and then our luggage was also checked for weight. The outcome of this was that some of our luggage would have to be taken up by another plane, as we were overweight.

We made our way across the tarmac to a small twin-engine Britten-Norman plane belonging to Air Services Ltd., which we boarded. The sky was overcast and as we took off just after half past eleven it started to rain.

We had a good view of the coastal strip as we headed north out over the shoreline before swinging round to the left and heading to the south. To the right, we could see the city and the pontoon river bridge spanning the Demerara River. We crossed the Demerara and headed for the Essequibo River, which we crossed half an hour after take-off. Cruising along at 110 miles per hour through rain and broken cloud some half an hour later, we were flying up the Potaro and then ahead, we saw the Kaieteur Falls. Then we were circling round to land at the nearby airstrip.

We all disembarked and were met by a couple of guides or wardens and wandered down past the old guest house until we came to the falls. We all rushed to the edge to wonder at this magnificent sight, sheet and sheets of water dropping over the edge and falling into the chasm below. A rainbow was developing as the sun shone through the clouds above and birds, swifts or swallows, were swooping round and behind the falling cascades of water. Tim spent ages hanging over the precipice filming the water as it sped over the edge to the bottom of the fall.

While this was going on a picnic lunch was being laid out on a rocky outcrop close by. The repast over, some of us tried to walk downstream to get a better view of the fall but were unable to get as far as Mike had done in 1960.

Then it was time to go back to the plane and head south for Karanambo. After take-off we had one more glimpse of the mighty Kaieteur and then it was out of sight. At first we flew over what looked like a forest-covered mountainous region until we hit the plains of Rupununi, after which the land was sparsely covered with trees. As we approached our destination we saw the landing strip and the thatched encampment of Karanambo.

Once out of the plane we were greeted by Diane McTurk, to whom we introduced the family. The pilot, in the meantime, had taken our luggage out of the plane and stacked it at the edge of the runway. Saying farewell, he boarded the plane and took off. We stood watching the plane until it became a speck in the sky. Diane led us to the little *benabs* where we were to sleep during our stay. Mike and I had one hut; Dinah, Tim, Fiona and Natalie shared another. The *benabs*, made of wattle with a palm-thatch roof, were simple yet adequate. They had open fronts, in which hung a hammock with two chairs. Going inside, there were twin beds covered by a mosquito net. Behind the bedroom was a bathroom with a washbasin, toilet and shower. I later discovered that we were not the only inhabitants; we were sharing with two bats in the roof, the *benab* having no ceiling.

We were up at six o'clock the next morning, Saturday, for a wander round and a walk down to the Rupununi River. All our meals were taken in the main building, which had a large dining room with several hammocks hanging along one side. Two sides of the room were open to the elements. Behind one wall was the kitchen, and behind the other, Diane's private quarters.

After breakfast, the two Americans arrived with the rest of our luggage. Mike was laid up with an upset stomach and a temperature. In the afternoon, several abortive attempts were made to get the Land Rover going for a trip round the farm to be made. They eventually got away. Mike told me to go along as he was feeling a little better. There was also a boat trip which set off upriver but had to return when there was a violent thunderstorm. It rained during the night, rain falling on our mosquito net, which we had to cover with a plastic sheet the next morning.

After a good night's rest Mike felt a lot better. He reckons he caught a chill on his stomach from the aircraft fan blowing on his sweat-covered front. After breakfast the whole party except for the Bennetts and Lynn from the High Commission set off in the Land Rover for a trip to Lethem, the nearest town to the ranch. The only trouble was, without the battery from the Land Rover nobody could use the radio transmitter should there be an emergency.

For lunch, chicken pie was served; Mike had to make do with boiled potatoes! In the afternoon, we all went down the river in the motor launch, passing a number of caiman as we went, until we were driven back by another rainstorm. On the way we passed a family of Amerindians paddling along in their canoe.

We dined alone at eight o'clock, as the Lethem party did not arrive back until gone ten o'clock. The night sky was clear and filled with stars.

Monday was Christmas Day. We were up at 5.30 as we wanted to see and hear the dawn chorus, which we had missed. We walked down to the river where all was peace and quiet with nothing to see.

Breakfast was a drawn-out affair with people arriving all the time. There was a loud cry from the children's hut when they discovered giant toads had invaded it! We then wandered round the camp until midday when a bell was rung to summon all the camp children and their parents to come for the present-giving ceremony. We visitors either lay in the hammocks or sat on the low walls. The room had been nicely decorated and the tree was surrounded by parcels and presents.

The children then gave us a carol concert with old favourites like *Jingle Bells*, *Joy to the World*, *Silent Night*, *O Come, All Ye Faithful* and *The Twelve Days of Christmas*. It was amazing how well they sang and knew so many verses to each carol. There was one break in the carols when it was discovered that it was Cecil's birthday, to which he was given a rendition of *Happy Birthday*. Cecil was one of Diane's employees. The proceedings were livened by Diane and me doing a dance together. Many of the gifts for the children were toys we had brought out with us for the occasion. This was followed by a football match with two teams of locals and visitors. For lunch we had a traditional pepperpot!

Diane's unexpected Christmas present was the arrival of one of her giant otters, Tugga, wandering into the camp area from the river! He made for one of the outhouses where he had stayed before and in which Diane had installed a pool. We all watched as he devoured a whole fish.

In the afternoon, we made up a boat party and went off upriver. We stopped after some twenty minutes and got out and wandered through some thick scrub until we came to a large pond covered in Victoria

Regia lilies. On the way back, Diane pointed out a large jabiru stork at the top of a dead tree. Diane runs courses for ornithologists and artists to come and study the flora and fauna of the area.

Back in the boat, and just before we set off, the wind had dropped and the water surface was quite calm. In the distance we saw one or two caiman, one of which gradually came closer and closer to the boat; then, just when we thought it had gone, it shot up almost alongside the boat, to the screams of some of the women in the party!

For Christmas dinner we had roast chicken, which Mike was asked to carve, served with wine provided by the two American boys.

I was up early on Boxing Day, as I wanted to go down to the river to see the parrots and macaws in the trees. Just as I was coming back along another path I saw Diane going down to the river followed by Tugga at her heels. Arriving at the riverbank, I sat down at the top and watched Diane, who by now had waded into the water and was calling the other otters by name: "Wally, Wally, Wally', 'Tugga, Tugga, Tugga', Nonny, Noony-No, Anonymous, Footloose and Fancy-Free. Despite her constant calls no more otters appeared on the scene. Then Mike, who had wandered down to see where I had got to, joined me. We left Diane with her otters and went back for breakfast.

Another boat trip was organised. This time we went downriver for some distance, where we disembarked and walked through a small forest until we came to a stretch of water, on the banks of which was an aluminium boat. Our boat hand fixed up an outboard motor and we cruised along with Diane pointing out various birds as they took off at our approach.

We were up at six o'clock on the Wednesday morning for breakfast at seven, as we had to get down to the main airstrip to get the plane back to Georgetown. The luggage having gone on ahead, as soon as breakfast was over we all piled into the Land Rover and were driven through the bush to the airstrip. The plane, a Twin Otter, belonged to the government airline and was part of a regular service, calling in at Karanambo as and when required.

As we took off we had quite a good view of the ranch and surrounding countryside. Karanambo is three hundred feet above sea level whereas

Kaieteur is 1,400 feet above sea level. We were flying at seven thousand feet. One surprise was that the pilot was a woman.

Back at the Tower Hotel there was a mix-up over the rooms. The ones allocated to us had damp walls and were unaired. We complained and were assigned some better ones. We then went down for a second breakfast.

At one o'clock Steve Naraine turned up and took Tim and Mike over to West Coast Demerara to look at some sea defence works under construction. To get there they had to cross over the pontoon bridge. As they crossed Steve said that they had problems with corrosion on some of the pontoons, and how on one occasion a section of the bridge broke loose and was swept upstream on an incoming tide! On the way back to town Mike asked Steve about some of the people he used to work with and what had happened to them.

That evening we were invited to dinner at LBI (La Bonne Intention, a plantation), the other guests being Marjorie Tingakee Kirkpatrick and old Mrs Kirkpatrick. Mr Kirkpatrick in our day was Director of Telecommunications.

On Thursday after breakfast we were picked up by Marjorie, her driver and young nephew, and we walked round to Quamina Street to see Bunny King but she was not at home. The house next door was once the home of Wanda Willems, and beyond that was the Bishops High School, to which we next moved. We were then taken on a guided tour while Marjorie and I reminisced about old times. The place seemed to be in need of a good coat of paint; there was some graffiti on the walls, and phrases like *Katy loves William*. The netball area was underwater. The music room was devoted to teaching steel band music.

From here we drove over to the Public Buildings where Frank Naraine took us on a guided tour. We saw the Council Chamber where all the debates were held and the retiring room where Dad would go and smoke his Rupununi tobacco. We then went up onto the roof for a panoramic view of the city, passing through the domed annexe where the archives were once housed and where my grandfather did his research.

From here we moved over to the famous Stabroek Market. Here

Marjorie had provided us with an armed guard as thieving was rife; a change from the old days when one could wander round at will, feeling perfectly safe. The tour over, we returned to the hotel for lunch.

In the afternoon Marjorie, Mike and I went to the University of Guyana as I was interested to see what old books they had on the country which, according to Jacques Willems, were some of Dad's collection which he had asked to be given to the university. From there we went to the orphanage to see Sister Noel Menezes.

That evening we joined the McTurks as guests at the home of the Kirkpatricks at D'Urban Park.

Not a lot happened on the Friday. After breakfast Marjorie arrived and took us out shopping; Mike sat in the foyer reading a Dervla Murphy book he had brought with him for such occasions. Natalie finally appeared at ten o'clock and during her breakfast, Adam the American from Karanambo came in and joined us.

After lunch Jenny Wishart and Kibileri turned up, followed by Maureen Blaquiere, which led to photo opportunities at the poolside.

After they left Mike and I went to Quamina Street where, this time, we found Bunny King at home. So we could identify her father in Dad's journals Mike asked her what his first names were: Walter Naplaton King. Leaving Bunny, we went across the road to the Frandec Agency to pay our airport tax and say farewell to Gem Eytle. She asked if we would mind copying out of Dad's journals what he had written about Jim Eytle and sending it to Lester Eytle, a one-time mayor of Lewisham, who, she felt sure, would be interested. Mike did this on our return but nothing more was heard.

I believe we left Guyana on the Saturday for Tobago with a short stopover at Piarco. We were not at all impressed with the Crown Point Hotel on Tobago, so the next morning Tim and I took a taxi and went off in search of another hotel. After a couple of hours we were back to say we had found a lovely place, the Turtle Beach Hotel, on the coast a little further north. While making enquiries at another hotel nearby we ran into the Dixon family, whom we had known in Khartoum!

We moved to the new hotel right away and soon settled in. During the next day or so I phoned William St. Aubyn in Trinidad as it was our intention to call in and see them on our way home. We asked him to arrange for a minibus to meet us at Piarco and take us on to his home.

Our New Year's Day celebration was somewhat overshadowed by Fiona's accident. Surfing outside the room before dinner, a large wave swept over her, bringing with it a thick branch which struck her on the nose. This resulted in a taxi-dash across the island to a local hospital for treatment. They were back in time to celebrate her return and the New Year with a bottle of champagne!

On the Wednesday, we tried to hire a car for the day but could only get one on the following day, so we hired two taxis and went out to the Buccoo Reef, which we found very disappointing. Compared to when we came here in 1959 on our honeymoon there were hardly any fish to be seen. The heavy tourist industry had obviously driven them away. We were back at the hotel in time for a barbecue lunch on the beach.

The following day we hired a jeep, so Mike, Tim, Fiona and I drove up to Plymouth and Scarborough, stopping here to get a new battery for my watch and then back to the hotel to pick up Dinah and Natalie, who had been having a lie-in. With the other two on board we drove up to Speyside for a fish lunch at Jemma's Seafood Kitchen. On our return journey we called in at the Bacolet Beach Hotel where we had spent part of our honeymoon. I should say we called in on what had been the Bacolet Beach Hotel. It had been hit by a hurricane a few years after we had left. Someone had tried to re-establish it with breezeblock chalets but it all had a very unfinished look about it. From here we went and had a look at Fort Bennett!

Friday was spent on the beach, it being our last day on the island. Saturday morning we packed up, made our way to the local airport and flew to Piarco, where a minibus was waiting to take us to the St. Aubyns' at Diego Martin. First, we did a tour of Port of Spain, passing the Queens Park Hotel, where Mike stayed overnight on his way to BG in 1958, and then a stop at the cricket ground to walk on the hallowed turf. I believe we even stopped at a supermarket to purchase something before going up to Diego Martin.

Arriving at St. John's Road we were greeted first by two large, barking dogs and then by Bill, Dot and Lilian. Lilian had been Dad's secretary for many, many years. We had a very pleasant curry lunch, after which

Bill gave us some old books on BG that had once belonged to his father, Douglas, who had been in charge of the offshore prison. Douglas had been a master shot and attended Bisley.

After a cup of tea and cakes it was time to bid them farewell and make our way to the airport for our return flight to England. And so ended a wonderful fortnight in Guyana and the West Indies.

Karanambo - Rupununi

Rupununi River - is there room for me?

Kangaroo kiss?

With Buster and Cilla

Mike with Rocky

Sophie

Mcgregor

Mike and Audrey

Hugh (my Brother-in-Law) and Betty

Fiona and Maude

A Visit to Buckingham Palace
L to R Fiona, Natalie, Dinah and Tim

A visit to Buckingham Palace
L to R. Fiona, Mike, Dinah, Richard, Natalie, Me and Tim

Epilogue

During a visit to the neighbouring town of Crowborough (where I like to shop at Waitrose), I saw an advert posted by someone wanting to sell an African Grey parrot. I discussed it with Mike and we agreed that I should give the woman a ring. When I went to collect the bird, I found it was being kept in the bathroom of a small bungalow. And so Rocky came to join us. Not having kept a bird for many years, I joined the Parrot Society as I would need to know where I could find an avian vet.

It was some months later that I had a call from the same society to ask if I would be interested in taking on a blue-and-yellow macaw. Mike was very enthusiastic as he loves macaws. It transpired that the bird was at a gay pub in East London. When we went to collect Buster, he was living in a large room above the pub, which he shared with Priscilla, a Miele Amazon. The pub was run by an American and his partner, who would bring the birds down to the smoke-ridden bar in the evenings to entertain the customers. They would be fed on French fries, and that was all I could get Buster to eat when he first arrived at our house.

As we were collecting Buster there was a woman who was taking Priscilla (or Cilla). I said to her, 'If you ever want to give the bird up, please give me first refusal as I don't think the birds should be split up.' Two or three months later the woman phoned to say she could not keep the bird as her neighbours were complaining about the noise. So Cilla came to be reunited with Buster. We paid for both birds.

One day we received a letter from a Judit Brody, a Hungarian woman who had been a teacher and had also worked at the Science Museum Library. Her grandson suffered from curvature of the spine and when she came to research the disability she came across the name of my great-grandfather, Dr Mathias Roth, who was an expert in this field, as too was his son, Dr Bernard Roth. Judit had written to the Walter Roth Museum in Guyana to see if she could make contact with a member of the Roth family. They gave her our name and address. She came to see us and as a result we learned more about my family.

Mike was interested to meet Judit as he had been doing quite a lot of research into my family history. When he was working in Aberdeen he would take one of Dad's journals back with him as he found them to be really interesting. There were eleven volumes in all, each of three hundred pages – quite some reading matter! Mike eventually got them typed up and published. When Dad died, we received many letters asking for information about his work and that of his father.

Every morning we would open the bird cages in the utility room and Rocky would fly into the lounge and perch on top of the door and start to chew the wood! Chased off here, he would fly and settle on Mike's head. Then one summer's day the outside door was open and Rocky took a chance to fly out. It all happened so quickly that I did not know what was happening. With all the trees at the back he was out of sight in a flash.

We put up flyers all around the district asking anyone who saw Rocky to call us. We had it announced on the local radio station and in the local press, and we even offered a reward. We would receive calls saying, 'We think your parrot is on the roof of the house opposite' but when we got there the bird, probably a pigeon, had already flown. Rocky was sadly missed as he was learning to talk and was a real character; even Buster would call his name for many years after his disappearance.

Mike was spending a lot of his time up in London at the various offices ordering copies of birth, marriage and death certificates and the wills of our two families, and typing it all up when the copies arrived in the post. We were contacted by Russell McDougall, an associate professor in English at the University of New England, New South Wales, Australia, who had got our name and address from Judit Brody, who also had some connection with Australia. Russell was interested in the works of my great-uncle, Henry Ling Roth, and came to visit us when he was over here to do some research at Durham University.

It was shortly after Rocky flew off that I decided to join the Roman Catholic church. I had attended some of their services in Georgetown before I was married and liked the atmosphere and ceremony of the church.

I had mentioned to my mother at the time that I liked the church and she had said, 'If that is how you feel then you should follow your heart and join.' I know that Dad had joined shortly after he arrived in British Guiana but this had not influenced me in any way. Mike and the family were quite happy with the idea and it made quite a difference to our lives. The church was very active in organising pilgrimages and outings to London and other places of interest. My sponsor when I joined was Mary McKeon, with whom I am still very friendly.

One such pilgrimage that we attended was to the Passion Play at Oberammergau which is only held every ten years – we were there in the year 2000. We also went on pilgrimages to France, Rome twice, and Spain. Mike often remarked that we would probably never have seen these places had I not joined the church. While in Spain I fell in love with the great walled city of Ávila; quite what attracted me to it I can't really say.

Sir David Attenborough came to Tunbridge Wells on a book-signing exercise so Mike and I went along, taking a copy of his *Zoo Quest to Guiana* with us for him to sign. We had a long chat about his visit to Georgetown with Charles Lagus.

When Fiona was on her gap year she and her friend Annabel went to India.

Tim came in one day and said, 'Mum, don't you think it would be fun to go out to India and see what Fiona and her friend are up to?' So we did just that, while Mike stayed at home to look after the birds. Having met up with Fiona, we went on to Amritsar to see the holy Sikh city and then up to Simla to escape the heat. While there, we were amazed at the number of monkeys climbing around that had a limb or two missing. When we returned home I wrote to David Attenborough to ask him if they had been born this way. He replied saying, *Oh, no, they lose their limbs through fighting, accidents etc.*

Then in 2003 we received a letter from Russell McDougall saying that he and Iain Davidson were going to hold a seminar at Coffs Harbour in February the following year on 'The Roth family, Anthropology, and Colonial Administration', and invited us to attend. This was exciting news; we had often said we would like to visit Australia, especially as my father was born out there, but it was a long journey to get there. Now we had the incentive.

The plan was that Mike and Tim would fly to Singapore and sail from there to Brisbane, from where they would take the train to Coffs Harbour. I would fly out and join them there, leaving Dinah or Fiona to 'bird-sit'. All was booked, but then Mike happened to go to the doctor and was diagnosed with prostate cancer and advised not to travel until his medication had been set up. This was a great blow as Mike had offered to give a paper on Dad's life and work in British Guiana.

Mike was devastated to learn that he had cancer and very upset at not being able to go to Australia. Tim and Dinah rallied to the cause, saying they would go to Coffs Harbour and give Mike's paper. They did the round trip all within one week. Tim would take the camcorder and film as much of the seminar as would be allowed. When they came back they said they had met relatives they never knew they had! I knew my Great-Uncle Reuter had gone to Australia where he married and had four children, three girls and a boy. The boy, sadly, died in his early teens. Dad had met them all before he left Australia but had lost contact with them.

Two months later Tim said he was going to take us out to Australia to see Coffs Harbour and meet some of the newfound relatives. Mike and I were very happy at the prospect of going 'down under'.

First we flew to Dubai and then on to Singapore. As the following day was Mike's birthday Tim had booked us in at the famous Raffles Hotel. When we finally arrived, we were all pretty tired after the long journey. My work was not finished, as once Mike and Tim were asleep I stayed up to blow up balloons and put up a '*Happy Birthday*' poster. I was woken up next morning by shouts of surprise from Mike as he entered the bathroom and saw my night's work. As he moved into the front room he found birthday cards from the family on the floor by the door.

We spent the day at the Jurong Bird Park. It was a very pleasant day with a bird show for children at lunchtime with parrots performing various tricks, and a larger show in the afternoon in a canopy-covered area. Here macaws like Buster were flying around and through hoops; there was a cycle race between two parrots, then a singing yellow-headed Amazon was brought on and the presenter asked who, in the audience, had a birthday today. Several people answered including Mike and they were asked how old they were. The bird then sang *Happy Birthday*!

Back at the hotel after a refreshing shower we had tea, but with a difference. As the tea was brought in two young men and two girls came in bearing a birthday cake with a card and singing *Happy Birthday*. They brought Mike a gift – a model of the hotel – and took a Polaroid photo of the three of us with the cake. Even though I had ordered a cake, the hotel apparently scan all passports of visitors when they arrive and note any person who will have a birthday while staying at the hotel. For dinner Mike and Tim wore their blazers which they had taken out for the occasion, and we started the meal with a 'Singapore Sling'!

The following morning we were up at half past six as we were taking the train to Kuala Lumpur. It was a very pleasant journey and I was sorry when it came time to leave the train. We found a good hotel with our room looking straight out at the famous Petronas Towers. Next morning Tim and I went out to look at the shops, and, in particular, Mydin, a large wholesale store, leaving Mike in the hotel reading a book. As we walked around we noticed an overhead monorail, and after lunch we three went out for a ride on the monorail.

Next day we flew down to Brisbane and, after retrieving our luggage, found the car provided by our airline Emirates to take us down to Surfers Paradise on the Gold Coast. It was here that I met my second cousin, Desiree van Riemsdijk, Tim having met her earlier at Coffs Harbour. Reuter's daughter, Mattie, had married Johan van Riemsdijk, known as 'Peppie', and they had three sons, one of whom was the father of Desiree.

Back in Brisbane, and not feeling well, I went to see a doctor who gave me some medication and told me to rest. Mike and Tim said they would go down by train to Sherwood to see where Dad had lived when he first went out to Brisbane to join his father and stepmother. As Dad had left a sketch of the house in his journals they knew it would be quite easy to find alongside the station. On arrival, there was no house; it had been demolished when the railway was enlarged to four tracks.

The next Sunday was Anzac Day (Australia and New Zealand Army Corps), which we spent at Ipswich Railway Museum, where there was a huge model railway something Mike and Tim were keen to see. I must say it was a very impressive layout; some of the engines had cameras on the front and the scenes could be viewed on a screen over the track.

While in Brisbane we met Wally, the son of Dad's half-brother Walter. He was feeling somewhat lonely as his wife, Joyce, and their two children were in the United States. Then it was time to move on to Coffs Harbour, which we did by train. We spent a couple of nights here before flying on to Sydney. To get around we hired a car, and one of the first places we visited was the Parramatta Convent where Dad had lived when his father returned to London to qualify as a doctor before he was taken to England by Reuter and his wife.

We spent a weekend with Barrie Reynolds and his wife, Ena, at their home in the Blue Mountains where they took us around to see surrounding countryside. Barrie is an English Professor teaching at a Queensland University who was researching and writing a biography of my grandfather, Dr Walter Roth. Back in Sydney, we went to the Rookwood Cemetery to try and find the graves of Dad's mother and his baby sister, Eva Vincent. In fact, we had to make two visits but we eventually found what we were looking for.

Our next port of call was the Sydney Museum to look at my grandfather's collection of Aboriginal artefacts. Here we were met by Kate Khan, with whom we had communicated for the past forty years! She invited us to a meeting the following day where we met Iain Davidson for the first time, as well as Russell McDougall and several others.

In the afternoon, we took a ferry to Rose Bay where we were met by Louise Minutillo, another second cousin. Louise had married Michael Minutillo and they had two children, a boy and a girl, but sadly Michael died at the early age of forty-six. At her home we met her mother, known as 'Tweetie', and her brother Frederick. In the evening, we took Louise out to dinner at a restaurant by the harbour, during which she produced a signet ring with the Roth crest on it that Dauna, another second cousin, had given her, saying a male member of the family should wear it, Dauna not having any children.

We then flew back to Brisbane where I was laid up in a hospital in Sydney after not feeling well and having been to see the local doctor again, who said I should be admitted for observation. Tim and Mike used this time to visit the Brisbane Grammar School, which Dad had attended and where my grandfather had taught for a while. They also managed to visit the John Oxley Library where they found copies of letters my grandfather had written to a friend in Brisbane when he was living in British Guiana, and were able to get copies to take back home.

On our way home, we broke our journey at Dubai as Tim wanted to see the famous hotel, Burj al-Arab. When we arrived outside, Tim got out to take a photograph of the place and when he came back to the car he said we would not be having lunch in the coffee bar as to get in one needed to have a reservation and pay an entrance fee of US $100 per head!

So ended a wonderful trip, and it was thanks to Tim's organising skills that it was all so enjoyable.

Dinah had established her home at Durham with Natalie, while she was working at Durham University Business School. While there she developed an initiative supporting women who were trying to set up and grow their own businesses. This was known as Women Into the Network (WIN). It became very successful and each year an award ceremony was held, usually at the Hilton Hotel, to which Mike and I were invited. The years of hard work put in by Dinah was rewarded in 2005 when she was awarded the Queen's Award for Enterprise Promotion. When Dinah and her sponsor, Lynn, were invited to Buckingham Palace to collect the award, we were also invited. It was indeed a wonderful occasion. There were about twelve people in the room (which overlooked the gardens at the back of the palace), standing in a semicircle. As the Queen spoke to Dinah, Prince Philip asked Mike if we had any more like her. Mike told him we had two more who were doing quite nicely but he was not sure if they would make it to the palace.

After the ceremony, Tim took us all to the Hilton Hotel on Park

Lane to celebrate the occasion. A year or so later Dinah was back at the palace to receive her OBE from the Princess Royal. This time she was accompanied by her sister, brother and daughter.

In 2008, we set off to visit Kosice in the Slovak Republic to see where my great-grandfather and his three brothers had been born. For the past few years Mike had been researching the Roth family history and Tim was amazed at the material that was coming up. Mike had been in touch with the Jewish Record Centre in Vienna to find out about the family of Felix Roth, elder brother of Mathias, my great-grandfather. Tim suggested we should go to Kosice and see what we could find there, calling in at Vienna on the way.

We went up to St. Pancras International Station where we took the Eurostar train to Brussels, going through the Channel Tunnel for the first time. On arrival, we had about an hour to wait for our next train, which took us to Cologne. Having deposited our cases in a left-luggage locker we went outside to have a coffee in the shadow of the famous cathedral and then moved to a riverside restaurant for our evening meal before catching the night sleeper to Vienna. Our cabin was en suite and quite comfy, and we had a good night's rest, arriving at Vienna in the early morning.

We found a small hotel which was quite close to the Jewish Record Centre which we visited as soon as we had seen our cases taken up to our room. We stayed several days in the city as Mike and Tim wanted to see the Bourse (stock exchange) where Felix worked, and look up an address where one of his sons had an apartment. We also enjoyed a bus trip around the city where all the landmarks were pointed out to us, and a visit to the Schönbrunn Palace which Tim had not seen before.

Then it was time to take the train to Budapest where we hired a car and drove to Kosice, calling in on the way to see Debrecen where my great-grandfather had volunteered to go to London to seek help for Kossuth, who had set up a provisional government there to break away from the Austrians.

We drove on to Kosice where we found a very pleasant hotel near the city centre. The old part of the city was closed to traffic, which made getting about so much easier. Our first port of call was the library, where we made enquires as to where we might find some information about my family. After several false starts we found an office where they were very helpful, producing a book of prominent citizens including the Roth family; the only problem was that the book was in the Slovak language! We took a copy all the same. They even produced an old map of the city, which Mike was keen to have.

After a general look round Mike and I returned to the hotel, Tim saying he would follow on as he wanted to buy some postcards. When he returned, he had a smile on his face, saying, 'I've found it.'

'What have you found, Tim?' I asked.

'The kosher restaurant of Anna Roth, and if we hurry we can have lunch there.' This we did, and after the meal we had a quick word with the Rabbi who was passing through. He told us to come to the synagogue, which was across the courtyard from the restaurant, at seven o'clock and he would be able to talk to us then.

We were the first to arrive and then some men turned up who gave us rather a strange look as they entered the building. A young woman, Sonia, came along and I got into conversation with her, explaining why we were there.

She said, 'If you sit at the back with me and the other women I will be able to explain what is happening.'

When the Rabbi arrived, he asked Mike and Tim if they had Jewish skullcaps, which of course they had not, so he produced two for them to wear. He then led us into the building and showed us where to sit. The ceremony got underway in what we understood to be Yiddish. After a while the men at the front turned around to look in our direction.

The Rabbi said in English, 'I'm telling them who you are and how I never imagined that one day I would meet descendants of Anna Roth, the founder of the kosher restaurant.'

When we came to leave several of the men went over to Tim and Mike and wished them 'Shabbat Shalom'. The Rabbi met us at the door as he had said he would take us to his rooms and see if he had records of the family. As we walked along he asked us if we were Orthodox or Ultra-Orthodox. I said I was a Catholic and Mike said he was Anglican, and the Rabbi looked a little puzzled but said nothing more. He could find no mention of the family in his records. He told us that Anna Roth was said to have given food to all young children regardless of their background. Mike asked him about the Jewish cemetery but was told it had been badly desecrated over the years and part of it was now a school. We did pay it a visit all the same. After a few more days we drove back to Budapest from where we flew home after a very interesting tour.

The year after we came back from Kosice I was trawling the internet when I saw the name of Mojdeh Morakabati, one of our old Iranian friends. I got in touch with her and she immediately got on to her parents, who, since arriving in America, had wondered whether it would be possible to ever make contact with us again. Apparently, her mother, Giti, was overwhelmed on hearing the news. All three of their children had married and had families of their own. Shohleh and her husband Fred came over to spend a few days with us. Through them I managed to make contact in Tehran with my beloved friend, Nina, and her husband Behrooz. Their son, Sina, was married and living in Canada and doing very well for himself, and had recently had a baby daughter. His younger sister, Maryam, and her husband are also living in Canada and hoping that their parents might join them one day. Nina and Behrooz were not well; Nina had a stroke and while she was in hospital, Behrooz was admitted too, where he sadly passed away.

On another occasion, I came across a message from Clive Wilson saying he wished to contact the Bennett family to thank them for looking after him when he was a young boy. We spoke several times on the phone; he told me he was living in New York with his family. Mike and I were very happy to hear from him.

Although Mike had retired we kept in touch with the many friends we had met over the years. The Uzmay family came over from Turkey and we took them to see the local sights as well as the ones in London. Selmin and Selen Soylemez came to see us twice when they were over here to attend conferences. They insisted that I let them help with the cooking!

Derya, from Düzce, has been to see us several times since she came over here to work, and even attended Fiona's wedding.

Louise Minutillo, my newfound second cousin, also dropped in to stay for a few days before going on to see Dinah in Durham. In 2015, she was planning to attend the annual ceremony at Fromelles to commemorate the Battle of Fromelles in July at which our great-uncle, Dr Reuter Roth, was in charge of all the field hospitals in the area. He suffered from ill health for the rest of his life. The ANZAC forces suffered their worst losses here, more than in any other field of conflict they have ever served in. Sadly, Louise died of cancer a month before the event. Mike and Tim attended together with another cousin, Patrice van Riemsdijk, from Holland. Tim and Mike took the opportunity to visit the grave of Mike's uncle, Arthur Gilpin, another victim of the Great War.

In November 2008, Fiona married Richard. Normally the venue would be at the bride's church but Richard's father was not at all well and could not travel, so it was decided that it would be held at Great Shefford, Berkshire, instead. Mike and I went over to meet the family and see the church and the place chosen for the reception afterwards.

One thing that made the wedding for me was the presence of a bagpiper in full dress! I have always loved the sound of bagpipes. Dinah managed to hire one for the day and I asked him to stand outside the church looking down the long path, to the public road, lined on either side by a row of mature trees.

When Fiona and Mike arrived, and started to walk up to the church Fiona said to Mike, 'Am I really seeing what I think I am seeing?'

'Yes, you are.' He replied

'Only Mum could have thought of that,' said Fiona.

It was a lovely service; Dinah gave a reading, as did two of Richard's nieces, and it all felt very homely as it was quite a small church.

The reception was held at an old mansion used during the week as a school for deaf children, but at weekends was hired out for functions such as ours. It was said that General Eisenhower used it as a base during the war, and scars could still be seen on the main staircase where he had driven up in his jeep! We all stayed the night at the Hilton Hotel in Newbury before returning to our various homes.

Professor Barrie Reynolds, researching material for his book on my grandfather, Walter Roth, went to Scotland to find out more about Eva Grant, Dad's mother. There he met Derick Grant, the family historian, and said we might like to make contact. We did. Derick sent us many details about the family and a year or so ago we were invited to a family reunion at Stirling, Scotland. I was unable to go so Mike and Tim went instead. With Derick, we arranged for plaques to be placed over the two graves at Rookwood Cemetery.

As we age, getting about is becoming more difficult so we welcome visits from the family. We love to see our four grandchildren, Natalie, who is currently working in Beijing, Octavia (known as Tavi), Milo and Adelaide, and friends who are still with us. Mike and I are trying to grow old gracefully and enjoy life to the full. Our wider, international family also keep in touch. Giti Morakabati and I speak on the phone at least once a month as she asks about our wellbeing. I also speak to Nehal Uzmay, although not quite as regularly. Her son, Evrim, always asks after 'Uncle Mike'. Contacting my dear friend, Nina in Tehran, is a little difficult due to the time difference and she has not really recovered from the death of Behrooz.

Selmin and Selen from Turkey phone us regularly. They are due to visit us again soon.

Derya Kap phones regularly as she considers us part of her family – and she, ours. She came to Fiona's wedding and Tavi's christening. She comes to see us at least once a year bringing a relative who may be over here from Turkey. She is now planning to retire, sell her house in Watford and move to the south of Turkey.

The whole family has been privileged to live in different countries and learn about different cultures and religions. From our travels, we have made close friends of all ethnicities and religions. The world today feels so unsettled in so many respects and I feel lack of education, in understanding others and tolerance, has played a large part. All we wish for is peace and harmony on this planet.

We are often asked what the children are doing now. Immediately after graduating, Dinah, worked in Sudan and then moved to the Royal Courts of Justice in London as a Chancery Associate. She then joined Durham University, where she spent twenty years, before starting her own business.

She works internationally, supporting small business development. Her daughter Natalie studied at the Mackintosh School of Architecture in Glasgow, Qualifying as a Chartered Architect. She has been living and working in Beijing for the last six years.

After University, Tim went into stockbroking as an investment analyst. Eventually, his lifelong interest in aircraft came to the fore in his professional life, becoming head of aerospace research at Morgan Stanley. He now lives in London and Cognac with his son Milo, who is almost 4 years old.

Fiona, completed her Masters at Durham University and then worked in enterprise education at two universities. She lives with her family in Berkshire, England and is a full-time mother to Tavi (Octavia) seven, Adelaide three and half, and Maude her ageing Labrador.